CENSORSHIP
AND THE PUBLIC LIBRARY
WITH OTHER PAPERS

CENSORSHIP
AND THE PUBLIC LIBRARY
WITH OTHER PAPERS

George F. Bowerman

Librarian, Public Library of the District of Columbia

Essay Index Reprint Series

BOOKS FOR LIBRARIES PRESS, INC.
FREEPORT, NEW YORK

First Published 1931
Reprinted 1967

LIBRARY OF CONGRESS CATALOG CARD NUMBER:
67-30199

PRINTED IN THE UNITED STATES OF AMERICA

TO
SALLY
MY BEST CRITIC

PREFACE

A librarian, more than almost any one else, knows that too many books are published. Why then, add to that number one consisting for the most part of reprinted papers?

These twenty essays are collected primarily for my own convenience. However, many of those previously published have been quoted or cited in bibliographies. One essay is reported to be required reading for the students of a large library school. It is my hope, therefore, that in this convenient form these papers, including the four not heretofore published, may have a wider reading by members of the library profession and especially by its younger recruits, and that they may not altogether lack readers among non-librarians.

It is thirty-seven years since I entered the library profession thru the door of the New York State Library School. In my excursion of nearly three years into the newspaper and encyclopedic editorial field, though I did not cease to be a librarian, I was compelled to write. That I brought back to library work proper the habit of writing is, perhaps, the cause of the existence of these twenty papers, the thirty listed but not reprinted and the many others not even listed.

In these thirty-seven years I have seen great changes in library development and practice. I have seen a more general recognition of the public library as an essential factor in public education; that recognition is gradually expressing itself in constantly increasing support from the public treasury. I have seen a fuller recognition of librarianship as a profession, with advancing standards of education, training and personal qualifications. I have seen library salaries increased from meager pittances to salaries that in certain cases are on a par with those paid to other professional workers. Library work for children was all but unknown thirty-seven years ago. Now it is fast coming to be recognized as one of the most important fields of library work, requiring special personal gifts and training, and meriting proper recognition in salaries and professional standing. Adult education was a term practically unused thirty-seven years ago, perhaps because it was then thought that adults needed no further education. Some librarians, perhaps considered visionary by others of their colleagues, long since saw the opportunity and looked forward to its realization. Now, a strong world-wide adult education movement is well under way, and in America at least the library is generally recognized as a large and indispensable factor in it. The writer desires to record his satisfaction at having a part in this forward movement in librarianship, his joy in the work of being a librarian.

These essays express some of the special interests, preoccupations and endeavors of the writer—to emphasize the literary and sociological aspects of library work, to multiply the cooperative relations of the library with other and allied agencies, to raise the standards of librarianship, to increase library salaries, and to secure professional recognition for librarians. That the usefulness of these papers to these ends may be increased by their publication in book form is also the hope of the writer.

G. F. B.

The Public Library
Washington, D. C.
December 1, 1930

CONTENTS

CENSORSHIP AND THE PUBLIC LIBRARY 13

Read before the Washington Literary Society and other organizations in January 1930. (*Libraries*. 35:127-35, 182-6. 1930)

THE SELECTION OF BOOKS FOR PUBLIC LIBRARIES 43

First read before the Washington Literary Society in 1908; often revised and given before many other organizations.

THE NEW BIOGRAPHY 71

Read before the Washington Literary Society in December, 1928; the Columbian Library Association in January, 1929, and several other organizations. (Published as a pamphlet by District of Columbia Library Association, 1929; also in *Wilson Bulletin*. 4:107-11, 153-9. 1929)

THE CHOICE OF RELIGIOUS AND THEOLOGICAL BOOKS FOR PUBLIC LIBRARIES 95

Read before the Library Department of Religious Education Association, Boston, February 15, 1905. (*Library Journal*. 30:137-40. 1905)

SOME ASPECTS OF BOOK REVIEWING 105

Read before the Washington Literary Society January 26, 1924.

COOPERATION BETWEEN THE LIBRARY AND THE
     BOOKSTORE 119
     Read before the American Booksellers Asso-
     ciation, New York, May 15, 1913. (*Library
     Journal*. 38:324-31. 1913; reprinted in *Pub-
     lishers' Weekly*; in *Bookseller, Newsdealer
     and Stationer*; and in *Library Miscellany*,
     Baroda, India)

THE FREE PUBLIC LIBRARY: ITS POSSIBILITIES AS A
     PUBLIC SERVICE AGENCY 137
     (*American Federationist*. May 1926. p. 578-
     84)

THE PUBLIC LIBRARY AS A FACTOR IN EDUCATION 149
     (*Current History*. 27:516-19. 1928)

THE PUBLIC LIBRARY AND WORKERS' EDUCATION 159
     Remarks at Workers Education Bureau con-
     vention, Washington, April 5, 1929. (*Ameri-
     can Federationist*. July 1929. p. 846-9)

SOME LIBRARY PERSONNEL PROBLEMS 163
     (Essays offered to Herbert Putnam; edited
     by W. W. Bishop and Andrew Keogh. Yale
     University Press. 1929. p. 103-12)

A CHIEF LIBRARIAN LOOKS AT WORK WITH
     CHILDREN; PITTSBURGH'S CONTRIBUTION
     THERETO 175
     Commencement address, Carnegie Library
     School, Pittsburgh, June 7, 1930. Published
     as a pamphlet by the school.

THE PUBLIC LIBRARY AN INVESTMENT—NOT AN
    EXPENSE 195

Address before a luncheon meeting of the
Richmond, Va. Education Association, January 28, 1913. (*Public Libraries*. 18:182-6.
1913; reprinted in *North Carolina Library
Bulletin*. June 1913)

LIBRARY ADVERTISING 205

Read before Massachusetts Library Club,
Boston, February 16, 1905, and later before
the District of Columbia Library Association.
(*Public Libraries*. 10:335-9. 1905)

A SENSE OF FRIENDLINESS IN THE LIBRARY 215

(*Christian Science Monitor*. January 23,
1924)

PSYCHOLOGICAL HANDICAPS AND POSSIBLE REMEDIES IN INCREASING PUBLIC LIBRARY APPROPRIATIONS 221

Read at meeting of Librarians of Large Public Libraries, Chicago, December 28, 1922.
(*Wilson Bulletin*. 2:227-9. 1924)

THE PUBLIC LIBRARY IN SMALL AND MEDIUM
    SIZED TOWNS 229

Read before North Carolina Library Association, Salisbury, N. C. April 24, 1917.

MUNICIPAL POPULAR LIBRARIES OF PARIS 245

Read before District of Columbia Library Association, October 23, 1907. (*Library Journal*.
33:9-13. 1908)

12 CONTENTS

HOW TO STRENGTHEN THE SUNDAY SCHOOL LI-
    BRARY 257

Read at Sunday School Institute, Church of
the Epiphany, Washington, February 16,
1909. (*Sunday School Commission Bulletin.*
June 1909)

ON BOOKS AND READING 267

A talk given to several Washington high
schools in 1906.

LONGFELLOW AS A CLASSIC 279

Read at centennial celebration of birth of the
poet, at All Souls Unitarian Church, Washington, February 24, 1907. (*Washington
Evening Star.* March 2, 1907)

PARTIAL LIST OF OTHER PUBLISHED WRITINGS BY
    THE AUTHOR 289

INDEX 293

CENSORSHIP AND THE PUBLIC LIBRARY [1]

Within recent years there has been a marked recrudescence of the spirit of censorship, character- ized by attempts to censor not only many phases of our conduct but also much of our thinking. The eighteenth amendment with its attendant legislation is perhaps the most notable example. The wide- spread movement for 100 per cent Americanism and the crusades against the various grades of redness in politics and economics, against modernism in re- ligion, against evolution in science, are but a few of the many manifestations of this spirit. This tend- ency may be accounted for in part by two facts: that during the war there was a combination of a crowd psychology, compelling a certain rigidity and uni- formity of speech and thought, with a greater laxity of conduct; and that since the war there has been a release of thought and speech, which have tended to run wild. Set free, youth of all ages, the liberals, the radicals, have been receptive to new ideas. They explore and discover and experiment. They have broken away from the old folkways. The older gen- eration, again of all mental and spiritual ages, the conservatives, are attempting to keep life, conduct, and thought in the old channels, that is, to maintain the old folkways. The newer generation looks toward the future unafraid, is interested and curious, desires to discover whether the new may not have more of meaning, truth and beauty—at least more of excitement—than the old. The older generation is dazed and alarmed at the new, does not want to recognize its existence, strives to ignore it. Because it is new it is suspect, probably bad, and so must not be permitted to exist. It must be censored, that is, either destroyed or robbed of the newness that makes it different, be made to conform to the old and familiar.

A discussion of censorship as applied to public libraries will be helped by a brief outline of the history of censorship in general, for the compilation of which I have drawn freely on the article on censorship in the new edition of the *Encyclopaedia Britannica,* on the recent speech of Senator Bronson Cutting of New Mexico in the United States Senate on pertinent clauses in the tariff bill,[2] on an article[3] in the January *Atlantic Monthly,* and other sources.

The Origin of Censorship

Censorship originated in ancient Rome, where it had to do with the registration of individual citizens to determine their duties to the community, and was a manifestation of the state control of conduct.

It next appears in the Roman Catholic Church. By papal authority the first *Index Librorum Expurgandorum* (or *Prohibitorum*) was published in 1564, a catalog of printed publications prohibited to professing Christians whether on doctrinal or moral grounds. The *Index* lists books absolutely condemned or those prohibited until they have been "corrected." The latest edition has been published within the last few months. By the way, it is reported to be the first book to issue from the new state printing house of the Vatican. The list still

---

[2] *Congressional Record.* p. 4650-82. October 11, 1929.
[3] *The Practice of Censorship,* by Edward Weeks. *Atlantic Monthly.* p. 17-25. January, 1930.

contains Gibbon's *Rome,* certain novels of Victor Hugo and Balzac, and all the works of Maeterlinck.

Modern censorship of printed publications has been almost universal thruout the continent of Europe. Its purpose has been to control opinion. Books have been suppressed, their authors fined and imprisoned and newspapers and periodicals subjected to censorship, always political and military and often religious and moral.

In Great Britain John Milton's protest against the tyrannous censorship of Parliament, in the *Areopagitica, a Speech . . . for the Liberty of Unlicensed Printing,* had no effect at the time (1644) but did produce results after the English Revolution. Since 1695 there has been almost complete freedom of the press, except that publishers of criminal and injurious matter are answerable to the laws of libel and blasphemy. Curiously Great Britain has maintained down to our own day a dramatic censorship exercised by a licenser of plays whose office goes back to 1737. In spite of repeated protests from dramatic authors, there seems no disposition to abolish this censorship.

Censorship in England

Such censorship of books as exists in England results from court proceedings under Lord Campbell's act, passed in 1857, "for more effectively preventing the sale of obscene books, pictures, prints and other articles." As originally enacted this measure was intended, according to its introducer, "to apply exclusively to works written for the single purpose of corrupting the morals of youth and of a nature calculated to shock the common feelings of decency in any well-regulated mind." Thru later court construction by Lord Chief Justice Cockburn it was decided that "the test of obscenity is this, whether the tendency of the matter charged as obscenity is to deprave and corrupt those whose minds are open to such immoral influences." This test, by the way, is the one which has been generally followed in the American courts. In actual practice the operation of the law has not proved oppressive, because of the conscientiousness and learning usually characteristic of English justices under whom such proceedings are taken. It should be noted, however, that within a year two recent novels were suppressed in England, both of which are now freely circulated in the United States. One, Hall's *The Well of Loneliness,* was denied admission by our customs censorship, but was later released by a court decision. The other, *The Sleeveless Errand,* by Norah James, seemed to attract little adverse comment here.

The new Irish Free State has established official censorship of films and books. A recent number of the *Irish Statesman* [4] has an amusing article on booklegging, in which it is stated that as a result of the law Irish people who had hardly ever opened a book before are now trying to acquire libraries of their own.

AMERICAN CENSORSHIP

In the United States, since the adoption of the first amendment to the Constitution in 1791 declaring that "Congress shall make no law . . . abridging the freedom of speech or of the press," there has been no official prepublication censorship, except in war time. Generally speaking, freedom of communication has been limited by the police power, acting

[4] *Irish Statesman.* p. 157. November 2, 1929.

after publication, to protect the state, public morals, or public peace. Such police interference has been called punitive censorship, since the fear of punishment often acts as a deterrent to publication.

The United States Post Office exercises censorship thru the denial of second-class mailing privileges to publications containing matter forbidden by certain Federal statutes, especially the so-called Comstock law enacted in 1873, which makes unmailable obscene printed matter. The postal authorities act at their own discretion, and it is extremely difficult to secure any judicial review of such action. At various times certain numbers of such periodicals as *Life, Hearst's Magazine* and the *American Mercury* have been excluded from the mails. A copy of Ovid's *Metamorphoses* addressed to a Johns Hopkins University professor was barred by one postmaster. Another held up a publisher's catalog because it advertised an edition of the *Decameron,* and still another because it listed *Elmer Gantry.* Books by Tolstoi and by Swedenborg, probably in every public library, have been barred from the mails; and the 1911 official report of the Vice Commission of the city of Chicago was excluded from the mails.

SENATOR CUTTING'S FIGHT

The United States Bureau of Customs, under the tariff act, also exercises censorship in forbidding entry into the country of obscene books, pamphlets, etc. In the pending tariff act, as passed by the House, it is proposed to extend its provisions so as to prohibit the importation of books, etc., "containing any matter advocating or urging treason, insurrection, or forcible resistance to any law of the United States, or containing any threat to take the life of or inflict bodily harm upon the President of the United States." Senator Cutting is making a vigorous fight to eliminate the provision altogether or at least to carry it back to the 1842 form which excluded only indecent pictures. As that section of the bill first passed the Senate (it may be changed in the final enactment[5]), he did succeed in having eliminated the provision forbidding entry of obscene publications and also secured the modification of the clause relating to sedition so that it now prohibits matter "urging forcible resistance to any law of the United States or containing any threat to take the life of or inflict bodily harm upon any person in the United States." By the way, librarians, who favor neither obscenity nor revolution, are earnestly supporting Senator Cutting's efforts. The Committee on Bookbuying of the American Library Association in a resolution gives its reasons for its support "on the grounds that this clause creates an effective censorship over foreign literature; will ban many of the classics of modern economics; will keep out material relating to revolutions in foreign countries; will indirectly stop the reprinting of such books by our own publishers; and is a reflection upon the intelligence of the American people by implying that they are so stupid and so untrustworthy that they cannot read about revolutions without immediately becoming traitors and revolutionaries themselves; and because the decision of questions of social policy is withdrawn from the ordinary courts and placed in the hands of officials primarily chosen for their special qualifications in dealing with the administrative details of tariff laws."

[5] It was changed before final enactment, so that questions of book censorship must be adjudicated by the United States District Courts.

A Federal Black List

Senator Cutting in his address in the Senate reported that the differences of opinion between the postal and customs authorities as to what books should be admitted to the country and what might be sent thru the mails within the country proved so numerous as finally to result in a conference between the experts in indecent literature in the two departments. Out of that conference a black list was prepared in October 1928; a supplement is dated April 1929. This list, a copy of which I have in my possession, contains 739 titles; of these 379 or more than half are in Spanish; 231 or more than a third are in French; five are in Italian; 10 are in German; 114 of these immoral books, barred by the censor, are in English. The absurdity of this curious list, and some of the vagaries and inconsistencies of attempts at censorship become evident when certain features are pointed out. Gautier's *Mademoiselle de Maupin* may be imported in the original French or in an English translation, but entry of a Spanish translation is forbidden. The *Memoirs* of Brantôme is likewise deemed entirely proper in its original French; likewise in English; but a translation in Spanish is taboo. The writings of Pietro Aretino, sixteenth century Italian humanist, may be imported, provided they are translated into Spanish, but are forbidden entry in the original or in English translation. Even more curious, the *Arabian Nights* is not barred in the translation by Payne or even the franker one by Burton, but a French translation by Mordrus is interdicted. A translation of the *Lysistrata* of Aristophanes, Rousseau's *Confessions,* Boccaccio's *Decameron,* and certain works of Balzac are also excluded. In February 1929 a Boston customs official confiscated thirteen copies of Voltaire's *Candide* intended for a Harvard classroom and did not release them till August when the class was no longer in session and so could not be harmed by this classic of irony. Finally, Mr. A. Edward Newton, a well known book collector with a notable private library about which he has written several interesting books, had confiscated by the customs authorities a certain edition of Rabelais, which he wished to add to the first and others which he already had. In the debate in the Senate it was brought out that the English translation of *All Quiet on the Western Front,* by Remarque, considered by some to be an exceptionally true picture of modern warfare as it concerns the individual soldier, was forbidden entry by the customs officers. The American edition is much expurgated. Senator Tydings, who had read the English edition, said of it in the Senate debate: "There is nothing immoral in the book . . . It simply tells what a soldier does, and it tells the truth." It is "a much better book for peace than the American edition." He said the "difference between the two books is due to the fact that we are looked upon as in the kindergarten class."

POLICE CENSORSHIP

Censoring of books has, aside from the enforcement of the postal and customs laws referred to, been done by the police in enforcing Federal acts applying to the District of Columbia or state laws, many of which are like the Federal "Comstock" law, some milder and some more rigorous. The New York Society for the Suppression of Vice has been active as prosecuting agent under both Federal and state laws in New York, the largest publishing center, and has secured convictions on the ground of pornography and the withdrawal of books considered by most critics of undoubted literary value. Many of the books so withdrawn as the result of conviction by a jury in the trial courts have later been restored by reversals in appellate courts. For example, Cabell's *Jurgen* was adjudged an obscene book in January 1920, but in October 1922 it became a work of art on the dismissal of the case. In certain cases publishers have fought back with suits for malicious prosecution. As a result there are now in New York relatively fewer prosecutions. In New York also the courts in interpreting the law take account of the intent of the book as a whole, whereas the Massachusetts law makes a book vulnerable if it is adjudged to contain a single phrase of "obscene, indecent, or impure language or manifestly tending to corrupt the morals of youth." As I write, word comes that a citizens' committee is attempting to secure an amendment of the Massachusetts law that will omit the words "impure language" and insert the words "which, considered as a whole" to the end that in the Massachusetts courts a suspected book shall be judged as a whole and not on isolated passages, as at present. Some results of the present law are as follows.

BOSTON'S EXPERIMENTS

In Boston, another important publishing center, the New England Watch and Ward Society by official agreement with the prosecutor's office, acts as unofficial censor in enforcing the law. It has listed for the booksellers the books that might be prosecuted. As a result not less than sixty-eight books, sold freely elsewhere in the United States, have in the last two years been suppressed and are not on sale, at least openly, in Boston. Only two of the number, Dreiser's *The American Tragedy* and Upton Sinclair's *Oil*, were brought to trial. The other sixty-six were withdrawn as the result of complaints and the fear of conviction, which no doubt could have been secured under the strict letter of the law. Some of the other titles on the list are Sinclair Lewis' *Elmer Gantry*, Percy Marks' *Plastic Age*, Deeping's *Doomsday*, Julia Peterkin's *Black April* and Bertrand Russell's *What I Believe*. Mention should here be made of the fact that one number of *Scribner's Magazine* containing an instalment of Ernest Hemingway's *Farewell to Arms* was suppressed in Boston, tho the novel when published entire was not molested; also the fact that the playing of Eugene O'Neill's *The Strange Interlude* was forbidden in Boston, tho the sale of the book was not interfered with.

But, why the need for considering censorship with respect to the public library? Do not public libraries leave questions of actual censorship of printed publications to the police, the courts, the United States postal and customs officers or other public authorities who are charged with the enforcement of the national and state laws and local ordinances? Is it not broadly true that the public library concerns itself with making a selection from the printed matter which has not been censored, that is, whose publication is not interdicted by public authority?

LIBRARIANS AS CENSORS

Yes, but librarians are often charged with exercising censorship because they refuse to supply a given book or because they withdraw altogether or restrict the use of other books already purchased. Perhaps as often they are also charged by others of their public with not exercising enough censorship, with placing on their shelves or refusing to withdraw books which give offense to some. In view of the situation created by such divergent opinions, or perhaps feelings—since in such matters people often feel more strongly than they think—is it possible for a librarian to discover principles and to chart a practice that will prove reasonably satisfactory to his democratic constituency made up of people with varying standards, literary and ethical?

Shall the librarian buy a given book promptly on publication, relying on his own judgment, reinforced by the opinion of critics in whom he has confidence? Or shall he await the influence of time, which will either bury it as inconsequential or by the change of public opinion render it innocuous and unobjectionable? Another administrative question involves the handling of the book when a decision to purchase it has been reached. Shall it be made accessible to all, including adolescents, even to the point of placing it on exhibition shelves and advertising it in printed bulletins? Or should steps be taken to confine its use to adults perhaps even limiting its readers to those considered sufficiently sophisticated? When the book has been added to the library, shall the librarian stand firm and defend his decision, retaining the book after it has been found offensive to some of his constituency or shall he yield to those who would remove it? In the case of an adverse decision, shall the librarian again stand firm against the jeers and railings of those who label him "prude," "Puritan," or, worst of all, "Victorian"?

THE STIFLING OF BOOKS

The public librarian has, also, more than simply an administrative interest in the question of censorship. He is interested in the publication of works of genius or of talent, in their importation, and in their free purchase, not only by the library, but by individuals. If such books are to be stifled before publication, for fear of various censorships, or are to be published only in emasculated form, the library is decidedly interested. The library also takes note of the greater freedom accorded to newspapers, many of which publish all sorts of filth, especially in connection with divorce and murder cases, and seem to undergo almost no censorship, except self-censorship, when libel suits and punitive damages are feared. Also the public library is interested in the apparent lack of any attempt at a censorship of the sex-saturated magazines, which never get into libraries, but which are estimated to circulate to the extent of more than 55,000,000 copies annually[6] among the young and others who ought instead to be reading the more wholesome books and magazines they could get from public libraries.

Another difficulty faced by the librarian is the prevailing inconsistency in the matter of censorship among different localities and among different censoring authorities. For example, such books as the *Decameron,* Rousseau's *Confessions,* and the works of Rabelais may be denied entry by the Customs Bureau for a private individual and admitted for a library; their sale may be freely permitted in New York but not in Boston; well edited and well printed editions may be denied the mails, at the same time that cheap, poor editions are easily obtainable from booksellers. This situation is confusing. No library wants to appear to be a law breaker, a booklegger,

[6] Ernst and Seagle. *To the Pure.* p. 35.

but the present chaotic situation involves dangers in that direction.

RESPONSIBILITY FOR CENSORSHIP

In most libraries the librarian makes the selection of books for purchase, or at least approves such selection, and must take the primary responsibility. But the ultimate authority rests with the board of library trustees, functioning perhaps thru a book committee. Such committee and board usually rely on the librarian, if they have confidence in his judgment. But in effect the board, representing the public, public opinion, the *mores* of the community served by the library, is the censoring body. The librarian in making his selections must make them such that they will meet the approval of his board, which theoretically at least, represents the average opinion of the community.

CENSORSHIP REPUGNANT TO LIBRARIANS

The idea of exercising censorship is one that is repugnant to any liberal public librarian. If exercised at all, it is done under protest and its operation is reduced to the lowest terms. The scope and purpose of the public library imply the widest possible freedom and tolerance; it is only the character of its constituency that suggests the little censorship that is found expedient. The public library as now conceived is the universal democratic continuation school for adult education. It does and should conserve the literature and teaching of the past. It is not a static or backward looking institution, but is rather dynamic and forward looking. It is not an institution for the inculcation of standardized ideas, and it is not afraid of new ideas, new art forms, new literature.

It stands for free opinion and to that end it supplies
material on both or all sides of every controverted
question of human interest. It takes no sides, plays
no favorites, but counts itself fortunate if it can induce its constituency to read widely and make up its
own mind to the end of developing an enlightened
public opinion. The library's constituency consists
of rich and poor, cultured and uncultured, enlightened and ignorant, those with high I. Q.'s and those
with low, strong and weak, old and young. As I see
it, such little censorship as the public library exercises comes about, in part at least, because of its desire not so greatly to offend as to alienate some members of its constituency. But the librarian must also
be on his guard not to make the library appear a
weakling so that others of the community will lose
respect for it and come to regard it as an institution
intended primarily for morons.

POVERTY NOT SUFFICIENT REASON

The chronic poverty of the book fund of most libraries enforces a rigid selection of books. It is almost always such a pressing problem to find the absolutely necessary funds to buy the books which will
best meet the broad purposes of popular education as
to leave little room for the consideration of questioned
books. Under such circumstances it is easy to pass
over the doubtful books and to make "lack of funds"
a sufficient excuse to oneself and to the public. From
the point of view of comparative values, this is probably a legitimate position for an institution expending
public funds and intent on getting the largest return
in public service. But when the public library, a
democratic institution, gives a standing invitation to
the public to make recommendations of books to be

purchased, the question must be definitely faced. The decision may even then be that the requested book is too weak, poor, or trivial, so lacking in literary value that its purchase, cataloging, storage and handling cannot be justified as an educational service. Since a better book in substitution may be offered, here is no real censorship. But censorship does arise when a requested book, let us say by an author of previously high repute, is found on examination so offensive in certain particulars as to cause its rejection by the library. It is clear that here censorship is exercised by the library.

SOME EXAMPLES

Some instances of library censorship, or attempts at censorship, are interesting.

The threat of the Mayor of Chicago to have a bonfire of books of history found in the Chicago Public Library which did not uphold the traditional anti-British prejudices is recent enough to be recalled by all. Tho this was perhaps a gesture for political effect, yet it did probably represent the feeling of a portion of the community that books which are likely to upset well-settled ideas of history (and other subjects, for that matter) are anathema.

FLORIDA AND PITTSBURGH CASES

Maynard Shipley, President of the Science League of America, reports that "last year the State University of Florida and the State Women's College . . . had their libraries ransacked by a committee of ten (clergymen) authorized by the State Senate to ferret out heretical books on history and psychology—more especially on psychoanalysis." [7] It appears that a list of the demoralizing books found

[7] *New York Times Book Review.* p. 38. December 8, 1929.

by this committee contained such titles as Wells'
Outline of History; Westermarck's *Origin and Development of Moral Ideas;* Shaw's *Man and Super-
man;* E. A. Ross' *Principles of Sociology;* Kroeber's
Anthropology and Allport's *Social Psychology.*[8] Mr.
Shipley, in a personal letter, also informs me that
when his book *The War on Modern Science* was published in 1927 it was impossible to induce public
libraries in some of the smaller cities to purchase
it or even to accept copies purchased for them. This
book, the subtitle of which is *A Short History of the
Fundamentalist Attacks on Evolution and Modernism,* is a well documented work, treating, perhaps a
little too militantly, a subject that needed attention.

The most recent example of an attempt to induce
a public library to exercise censorship is in connection with the Carnegie Library of Pittsburgh. It is
authoritatively reported that on the appearance of
Edwin F. Dakin's *Mrs. Eddy; the Biography of a
Virginal Mind,* a committee from "the Christian Science church called at the Carnegie Library with a
request that it be excluded from the collection." The
director "decided that, while consenting to keep the
book out of the *Monthly Notes* published by the library and off the shelves that are open to visitors, his
duty to the people of Pittsburgh obliged him to carry
it in his circulation department, and since that time
it has been one of the most sought for of all present-
day publications."[9] The publishers of the book,
Charles Scribner's Sons, write me that the librarian
of a public library in another large city was "under
pressure . . . but responded by putting the book into

[8] *Current History.* p. 803. March 1928.
[9] *Carnegie Magazine.* p. 181. November 1929.

full circulation." I should suppose the same would be true in most other large cities, but in view of what is happening in the case of some booksellers, who are being influenced not to stock this book, or in some cases not to display it, I am wondering what is happening in the smaller public libraries. For years most public libraries of the country have accepted and made available to their publics large numbers of copies of *Science and Health* and other Christian Science publications. The present case is simply one of affording the public the opportunity to hear the other side thru a temperate, well-documented book.

RELIGIOUS CENSORSHIP OF LIBRARIES

When the matter of religious censorship of books is discussed, the question is often raised as to the present-day attitude of the Roman Catholic Church toward the presence in public libraries of books attacking the position of that church. I have heard that in the case of some libraries attempts have been made by Catholic interests to keep out books of scholarship at variance with the Catholic position, but I have never been able to verify them. In my own fairly long experience, not a single suggestion of the exclusion of any such book has come to me from Catholic members of my board or the public. Once, a number of years ago, a Catholic University professor found on a display case a copy of Rénan's *Life of Jesus*. He brought it to my office with the remark that of course the library should have it but that he thought it ought not to be included among books especially recommended. To this I readily agreed. Note the mildness of the request and the reasonableness of the attitude.

WASHINGTON'S EXPERIENCE

One aspect of what might be termed censorship affects juvenile Catholic readers. For years the Washington Public Library has sent out to public school classrooms hampers of books from a special graded collection, now consisting of about 37,000 volumes but of less than 1700 titles. In order to induce parochial schools to avail themselves of this service, a plan was devised by which a committee was organized by the Catholic Women's Literary Guild, who read the books in this collection for the purpose of indicating any not considered by them acceptable for use in Catholic schools. The library omits to send any of about sixty titles on the confidential list. As a result the parochial schools find this service very acceptable and make large use of it.

The Washington Public Library was a few months ago accused of censorship because it did not have the books for young folks written by Father Finn. The editor of the *Baltimore Catholic Review,* an official weekly of the arch-diocese, on finding by inquiry that certain of Father Finn's books were in the public libraries of several other large cities and that it had been decided no longer to stock them here, attacked the Washington Library for having reached this decision. Unfortunately the library was never afforded adequate opportunity to state its reasons, which were that these books had been outmoded, that their literary quality left much to be desired, and that they brought in doctrinal matters too frequently. On somewhat similar grounds, the once widely popular *Elsie Dinsmore* books, of the type generally known as Sunday-school books, are likewise not in the library. It is gratifying to record that in this controversy the library was defended by certain parish priests of Washington and by a Catholic University professor who in a letter to the same journal wrote as follows: "At a time when so much bigotry is rampant it seems rather stupid, as well as unjust, to waste your ammunition on an institution which has always been so conspicuously fair and generous towards Catholics."

INCONSISTENCIES OF CENSORSHIP

I have mentioned a few actual instances of library censorship, or attempted censorship. Probably most cases of doubtful books fall in the field of belles lettres. Every library has constantly to decide whether a given book, a candidate for admission to the library, should be excluded because it is too indecent, obscene or pornographic.

The inconsistency of almost all censorship, whether by other authorities or by the public library, is shown when we consider the attitude toward the Bible, Shakespeare, and other so-called classic literature. With them the usual attitude is "hands off." Of course the Bible has many indecent passages; a list of one hundred fifty such passages was once compiled as part of an argument in a censorship case. In another case an eighty-page pamphlet of obscene extracts from the English classics was compiled and printed. Different editions, such as the Loeb Classical Library, the Everyman's series, the Oxford editions, multiply such classics and it is now rare that the heavy hand of the censor is laid upon one of them. If it is, as in the recent case of *Candide*, already referred to, ridicule usually saves the day.

WHAT AND WHEN IS A CLASSIC?

But what and still more when is a classic? Literary history is strewn with examples of the most radical change of opinion concerning many books now accepted as classics or near classics. Some of them have passed thru all the stages from suppression or violent condemnation to the beatification implied from being made required reading in high school and college. Charlotte Brontë's *Jane Eyre*, when published, "was pronounced too immoral to be ranked as decent literature;" [10] George Eliot's *Adam Bede* was characterized as "the vile outpouring of a lewd woman's mind" [10] and Mrs. Browning's *Aurora Leigh* was described as "the hysterical indecencies of an erotic mind." [10] Hawthorne's *Scarlet Letter*, when it was published, was condemned in a long review by the Reverend (afterwards Bishop) A. C. Coxe, who protested "against any toleration to a popular and gifted writer, when he perpetrates bad morals. Let this brokerage of lust be put down at the very beginning." [11] Recall the furor raised by Hardy's *Tess of the D'Urbervilles* and still more by *Jude the Obscure*. Remember that DuMaurier's *Trilby* was threatened with suppression and that Walt Whitman lost his position in the Interior Department because of *Leaves of Grass*, the first edition of which was withdrawn in Boston, but republished in Philadelphia. Hamlin Garland's *Rose of Dutcher's Coolly*, when first published, was asked for at the public library in a large college town in western New York by a student who was told that the library did not have it, as it was a bad book. Now it would be incapable of shocking anyone, but, ironically, its distinguished author, considered a radical in his youth, today inveighs against the indecencies of modern fiction.

[10] Thompson. *Philosophy of Fiction.* p. 191.
[11] Review in full in Mordell's *Notorious Literary Attacks.* p. 122-37.

To these examples I may add experiences of my own with two novels which were violently discussed when they were published, Wells' *Ann Veronica* and Dreiser's *Jennie Gerhardt*. The former of these I at first found altogether too strong, but long since it has been quietly admitted to the library. The latter was even taken out after purchase, but later restored.

Such examples and experiences as these should make us cautious in condemning today what may, thru the change of public opinion, tomorrow be found acceptable and even come to be called classics.

Would that we librarians might have sufficient prophetic vision to pick the books destined to become classics or near classics; to discern the trend of public opinion, what the public of today and of the on-rushing tomorrow will approve!

THE YOUNG RADICALS

The young experimentalists, naturalists, realists and expressionists among the writers of today think they know what the public wants, and the young radicals among the critics insist that the public shall accept and find good whatever is thus produced. For example, just now the touchstone with them seems to be the acceptance of D. H. Lawrence and James Joyce. Writers of genius they may possibly be, but their indecencies do impose a severe strain, however desirous one may be to extend the hand of fellowship to genius and however much one may wish to refrain from exercising any censorship.

THE CASE OF LAWRENCE

Take Lawrence. Dr. Henry Seidel Canby, editor of the *Saturday Review of Literature* and one of the most influential of present day critics, writes: "Signs are not wanting, indeed they are abundant, that the most prepotent novelist of our day in the eyes of the younger writers of advanced fiction is D. H. Lawrence." But Dr. Canby further writes: "He is obsessed by sex. . . With rare exceptions Lawrence's characterizations turn upon the possession, or the lack, or the perversion of the sex instinct." [12] Another critic, who is also a distinguished neurologist, Dr. Joseph Collins, recognizes the genius of Lawrence but also says of one of his works: "A large portion of the book is, in my judgment, obscene, deliberately, studiously, incessantly obscene." And again: "He libels and he bears false witness against men. There are persons in the world such as Mr. Lawrence describes. So are there lepers and lunatics. We do not talk of them as if the whole world were made up of them." [13] Recently, however, at the trial in Cambridge, Massachusetts, where one of Lawrence's novels not published in this country was adjudged an obscene book, it is reported that a Harvard professor of English testified that current English literature cannot be taught without taking account of D. H. Lawrence, about whom countless articles and at least one book have been published. When asked in court, however, whether the particular book concerning which the proceedings were taken was actually used in the instruction at Harvard, the professor replied that he would never think of making any mention of it in his classroom. How far then should a public library go in refusing to supply such of Lawrence's books as are not suppressed by the courts?

[12] Canby. *Definitions* (2d ser.) p. 113-14.
[13] Collins. *The Doctor Looks at Literature.* p. 278, 286.

AND JAMES JOYCE

Then there is James Joyce with his *Ulysses,* a work of more than 700 pages "taken up with thoughts of two men during twelve hours of sobriety and six of drunkenness." [14] In it, according to Dr. Canby, the author "demonstrates his genius in brilliant narrative passages of a candid realism almost unequaled in English." But, Canby continues, it is "often incoherent, ordinarily extravagant, and sometimes vicious. Its indecency would have appalled Rabelais and frightened and disgusted Chaucer" and further "Such a book is valuable in a world trying to be sane, trying to save itself by humor or insight from the perversion of honest instincts and from mental confusion, only because of its new and brilliant technique, and its passages of undoubted genius." [15] And Dr. Collins in a long chapter, in which he too recognizes the genius of the author, says: "The author is a psychologist, and I find his empiric knowledge supplements mine, acquired by prolonged and substantial effort. . . Mental hygiene takes on a deeper significance to one who succeeds in reading *Ulysses* and psychology has a larger ceincture." Again: "Mr. Joyce has made a contribution to the science of psychology. . . He has shown us the process of the transmitting of thought to words. It isn't epoch making like 'relativity' but it will give him notoriety, possibly immortality." [16] Some of Joyce's critics, however, have no doubt about his immortality. Edmund Wilson devotes a ten-page article in the *New Republic* for December 18, 1929, to an analysis of *Ulysses* and Joyce's next work soon to appear; and

[14] Ibid. p. 50.
[15] Canby. *Definitions* (2d ser.) p. 110-11.
[16] Collins. *The Doctor Looks at Literature.* p. 58-60.

says that an entire critical book on *Ulysses* is in preparation. *Ulysses,* by the way, tho on the customs list of forbidden books, seems to have been acquired by many individuals in America, in spite of its high price, and is in some libraries. It is probably only a question of time before its publication in this country will not be illegal and it will then be a candidate to be considered by public librarians. What shall we do about it?

SAFE BOOKS FOR CHILDREN

Everybody will agree that it is desirable to protect from injurious books the young and immature, who are highly impressionable and whose self-control is still undeveloped. That responsibility rests primarily on parents, who share it with, to a large extent shift it to, teachers and librarians. If one could be sure that the reading of the young were confined to the books in the children's departments of public libraries, then parents might feel very secure. Where libraries have separate rooms for children the dangers of securing undesirable books from adult shelves is minimized. However, parents often send their children to get some of these very doubtful books or at least do not cooperate with librarians to keep their children from them. Then there are always the gutter magazines, to which reference has already been made, easily accessible on payment of a few cents.

In the case of adolescents who are beyond the control of parents and teachers and who insist on being grown-ups in the library, the situation is more difficult. Here the prohibition of books, whether to be found in the public library or for sale or rent at commercial libraries, seems but to stimulate the desire of headstrong youth to have such forbidden books at all hazards. Moreover, as is pointed out by President W. A. Neilson of Smith College:

The attempt to save our children from what we regard as dangerous knowledge is likely, in our times, to be a locking of the stable door after the steed is stolen. It is my impression that most freshmen (of both sexes) come to college today already familiar to the point of losing interest with many of the facts and ideas which anxious parents are terror-stricken lest they acquire. And not only are they familiar with them, but they seem to have acquired a kind of immunity which leaves them quite as fresh and unspoiled as their ignorantly innocent parents were at their age.[17]

PRINCIPLES GOVERNING CENSORSHIP

Granting some responsibility to make the library useful and not harmful to children, tho at the same time recognizing the difficulty of making effective the steps it may take to that end, it is, I suppose, not claimed that the library as a whole should be so keyed as to make it all safe for children and adolescents. What principles and standards should we adopt for the inclusion or exclusion of books for this democratic institution which, in America at least, ministers to the strongest as well as the weakest members of the community? How much and what kind of censorship should the public library exercise?

As has already been indicated, the least possible censorship should be the public library desideratum. If the official censoring bodies, the Post Office, the Customs Bureau, and the courts did their duty soundly and sanely there would be little for the library to do. They should, of course, protect the youth, especially, from printed matter intentionally and actually pornographic. But in excluding works whose sole intent and purpose is to be obscene, they should not lay violent hands on works of genius because they may offend by running counter to con-

17 *The Theory of Censorship. Atlantic Monthly.* p. 14. January 1930.

ventional ideas. If that counsel of perfection could be achieved, then every book not unlawful might be a proper candidate for public library choice. Then, assuming adequate funds, it would be largely a question, within the field of belles-lettres, of selecting for the library such books as achieve certain standards of literary value.

Is there then to be no censorship exercised by the public library? Yes, there are limits beyond which a public librarian who is liberal-minded but not weak-minded will not go. When books are notoriously, consistently, and deliberately obscene—sometimes so admitted by critics very sympathetic with the younger generation—or when they show evidences of a pathological mind in the author, the purchase and free circulation by the public library of such books can hardly be justified. But the exclusion of the extreme books of an author should not mean that his reasonably acceptable books may not be admitted.

The Time Factor in Books

Sound policy dictates that the public librarian shall, in the case of the definitely objectionable books, wait; that is, for the time being decide in the negative. The influence of time will result either in the submergence of such books, so that the question will settle itself, since they will be so dead as no longer to be sought after; or in their permanence thru their transcendent vitality, by the presence in them of such qualities of greatness as exist in the *Decameron* and the *Gargantua,* so that they deserve to live from generation to generation, in spite of their indecency. When these affirmative qualities become apparent, then it is always possible to change a negative decision into a positive one and to admit them to the library. Is the author really a genius and his book a masterpiece? "Genius" is an easy word to say, but hard to prove. Time only can tell.

BOOKS ON PROBATION

Some books, together with positive qualities, have objectionable features, perhaps not sufficient to exclude them. Such doubtful books may be admitted on sufferance or probation. If they die in a year or two, as is frequently the case, it is not necessary to replace them when they wear out.

Almost every book published has a place in some library; some are perhaps more suitable for a specialized library than for a public library. For example, Joyce's *Ulysses* seems more appropriate to a medical library or a library of abnormal psychology. Some might possibly be admitted to a public library, to be kept in locked cases, sometimes called the "inferno" and to be made available only to special students. This plan would be applicable to some of the extreme books on psychoanalysis, Havelock Ellis' *Studies in the Psychology of Sex,* Krafft-Ebing's *Psychopathia Sexualis,* and books on specialized medical subjects. This is a plan, followed in many libraries, in order to make such books available to those who have a legitimate need for them and at the same time to withhold them from those to whom they might be harmful or whose principal interest in them would be pornographic. Administratively, this plan has its disadvantages. The pushing reader, who can give a plausible reason, is likely to gain his end, while the less persistent student with a better case might be unsuccessful. Then, too, the segregation of books calls attention to them and the prohibition on their general use often makes them especially sought after. The same books, if standing in their regular places in the classification, might often be entirely disregarded.

PUBLICITY UNDESIRABLE

When a librarian is led to make a negative decision, he should do it as quietly as possible. Some books are complete failures unless they can succeed in being censored and having the fact blazoned abroad in the newspapers. That will sometimes galvanize a weakling book into some sort of life and save it from being a commercial failure. A negative decision by the library will sometimes bring embarrassing commendation as well as condemnation Those who commend will suggest the removal of other books, equally offensive to them, and those who condemn will seek to prove illiberality on the part of the library by requesting the purchase of other doubtful books. Since the librarian cannot meet the demands of both, he will in the end gain the condemnation of reformers and the opprobrium of radicals.

I have asked a number of questions. I am not going to attempt to give categorical answers to them, but in part to consider them rhetorical and in part to let the answers be drawn from my general arguments. In fact these are questions to which there are no straightforward, undeviating answers. Not only does each book present a separate problem, but times and circumstances change, so that often a decision, especially if negative, may require reversal. In this whole matter there is need for opportunism and compromises.

ENLIGHTENED PUBLIC OPINION

The librarian as censor must try to represent the best and most enlightened public opinion. He should perhaps be a little in advance of his public, as an educational leader, but not so much in advance that it will lose confidence in his judgment and discretion. Certainly he should not be less enlightened than the average of the public which he serves.

The disquieting thing about this whole matter is not that the librarian must at times act as censor, but that there are so many books published of such a character as to be candidates for censorship. This is so true as to suggest the question whether the people of this day and generation are not better than the books offered to them. For, after all, human beings are essentially decent. Signs are not wanting that there is a reaction against certain of the excesses of this age. This more hopeful note is expressed in an exceedingly thoughtful and constructive article on *The Crisis in Morals,* by Professor Gilbert Murray, in the January *Harper's* (1930), from which I quote a few sentences by way of conclusion:

THE INTERNAL CENSOR

"The new psychologists talk much of the Internal Censor and delight to show us the unpleasant objects which he has attempted to hide. . . The point is that man, who has risen from the ape, has apparently done so by the help and guidance of this inward spirit which rejects filth and denies it. It is not Victorian prudery, it is not Christian asceticism, it is not even the Hellenic tradition, which dislikes uncleanness, physical and moral; it is something that springs eternal in the nature of man." Of this Internal Censor he writes further: "It is an instinct both moral and aesthetic, which rejects things both because they are bad and because they are ugly and pursues things both because they are good and because they are beautiful." And again: "Though not

infallible, this moral or aesthetic instinct is a true
fact. I believe it to be generally very strong in young
people, at any rate in those who have real life in
them, and, though often misdirected while they make
their usual experiments, it has a way of correcting
its own errors and ultimately finding its right
course." And finally: "I refuse to be frightened...
I trust to the general maintenance and gradual raising of the moral standard in a society such as ours
. . . Most of all to this Inward Censor . . . by which
men have from the very beginning of civilization
rejected and denied what they feel to be vile within
them, sought what they love and imitated what they
admire."

THE SELECTION OF BOOKS FOR PUBLIC LIBRARIES [1]

A paper on principles and practice in the selection of books for a public library may at first seem to have too much the flavor of the shop. The subject is, however, a literary one and readily appears to be appropriate to the Literary Society. Many of the papers presented at our meetings deal critically with the works of some writer or group of writers, with the purpose of appreciation and interpretation. This paper is designed to deal with criticism applied practically to the constructive purpose of securing the maximum of efficiency in the literary equipment of an agent for popular education. The members of the Literary Society are actual or potential users of the local public library and hence are presumably more or less interested in this question as it affects conditions here. It presents itself to the librarian as but one phase of library administration. To the reading public, or at least the library using public, diverse in its tastes and interests, it is, assumed liberal support and sympathetic and skillful administration, the supreme question, for on it depends the adequacy of the book stock to meet legitimate demands.

SIZE OF THE PROBLEM

With fairly liberal funds for book purchases, perhaps some one may say that a library for a large city should be not so much a selection as a collection —that the function of the library is to gather widely

[1] First read before the Washington Literary Society in 1908; often revised and given before many other organizations.

and let the users of the library select from the ample
stores so collected. Consider for a moment what
this would mean. Estimates of the number of printed
books since the invention of printing make the huge
total of more than 25,000,000 separate works and the
annual book publications of the world approximate
160,000. Of these the books published in the United
States (in 1929) numbered 10,187—all but 1845 of
them new publications. Great Britain published
10,347; Russia, 36,680; Germany 27,794; France,
11,548; Italy, 6533; Japan, 19,967 and other countries smaller numbers. A mere statement of these
figures, without reference to qualitative values, shows
the present futility of any attempt at universality,
even for the great national libraries, much less for
municipal libraries. But even if our municipal library had the money, the staff, the buildings, and
could otherwise cope with the mere physical problems
involved in developing a library which should be an
omnium gatherum, the purpose of the library would
make such a course undesirable. I am convinced
that even with the most ample funds for book purchases a municipal library with a carefully selected,
organic collection of from 300,000 to say 500,000
volumes (depending on the population), closely
adapted to local needs, is much to be preferred to
one possessing from 800,000 to 1,000,000 volumes.
These figures would vary according to the need of
multiplication of duplicates for branches. In building up the larger collection, efficiency and quality
are likely to be sacrificed to numbers and quantity;
collections of doubtful utility are accepted or purchased *en bloc;* the hobby of the librarian or some
trustee or a donor is ridden hard to the neglect of
some more vital subjects of practical interest, with
the result that the library becomes a more or less

heterogeneous congeries of books, by no means organic, and poorly adapted to the needs of its natural public.

The idea of selecting, in the interest of efficiency, from a constant stream of new books also involves its correlative of the constant elimination of antiquated, worn out books. Much of such elimination takes place in a public library whose books are in active use, thru the replacement, when a given book wears out, by a later edition or an entirely new work. In the interest of efficiency, however, forcible decapitation is not only justifiable, but desirable, in order that undiscriminating readers shall not get misinformation from out-of-date books. In these times books are no longer the sacred, rare and unusual things they once were. Now they get easily written and are published all too easily. With increasing ease also they are being revised, rewritten or superseded, to conform to changing conditions. In many fields of knowledge it might be well to adopt, could we have the cooperation of the publishers, the plan suggested by H. G. Wells, who proposed (in *Mankind in the Making,* 1903) that there be prepared for every important field of knowledge a text book, comprehensive in scope, simple in treatment and issued in a very large edition at a very small price (25 to 50 cents) and that such books be frequently revised, with the idea of completely replacing the earlier editions.

FUNCTIONS OF THE LIBRARY

As the function of the library determines the character of the book collection, some definition of the scope and purpose of the public library will be helpful in arriving at the principles which should govern its choice of books. The public library is essentially an educational institution. Our thought of education, of course, conceives of it as lasting thruout the life of man, and by no means confines it to the instruction afforded by the schools, which simply gives the individual a start so that he may later become educated. Our system of public schools has taught practically all citizens to read and has thus made them potential library users. In so far as they use a public library suited to their needs they may become educated. The education afforded by the schools consists partly of studies severely practical, designated to aid in gaining a livelihood, and partly of humanistic studies, designed to increase intelligence, develop enlightened citizenship and cultivate the spirit. Both of these parts of the education of its citizens the public library should carry on. For strategic reasons it makes its first appeal to children—partly to help them in their school work, but even more to capture them early in the hope of making them lifelong library users. Next it appeals to teachers, clergymen, editors and other leaders of the people—to help them and indirectly to serve the whole people. But its proper clientèle is nothing less than the entire body of citizens; cultivated and uncultivated, rich and poor, young and old, enlightened and bigoted. With such a constituency in mind, it strives to meet the widest possible legitimate needs and to stimulate new and diverse demands, in order to touch the intellectual life at as many points as possible. The problem then is how to secure and maintain the interest of a constantly enlarging circle of readers who look to the public library for their intellectual food.

In an attempt to realize this very broad and comprehensive but reasonable program for public library service, other elements besides a properly selected collection of books are of course necessary; but book selection is vital. No haphazard, uncoordinated collection would be at all adequate, even with administration otherwise expert. Since the public library is not conceived of simply as a miscellaneous collection of books, either for harmless self-culture and innocent amusement or as a literary bar-room, but as a highly efficient machine for producing very definite and practical results, it follows that its collections must be carefully adjusted to accomplish its work, that is, they must be composed of books that will minister to humanism and to utility, and in such proportions and with such content as will best meet local conditions.

ADAPTATION TO POPULATION

In establishing a new library, in choosing the collection for a new branch, or for the most effective development of the collection of an old library, the librarian should make a careful study of the population to be served to learn the grades and degrees of culture, the foreign population, the professions, trades, and industries represented, the avocations, interests, tastes and prejudices, etc.; that is, he should make an intellectual survey of his constituency and adapt his selections accordingly. With recognition of the two-fold function of the library to furnish cultural and utilitarian literature, it is desirable to make some apportionment of book funds between these two broad classes, and then a further subdivision of funds within the classes, based in an established library somewhat on demands as shown by home circulation figures. It is partly a mathematical question, but more a question of proper correlation and adaptation.

The selection of books implies some person or

group of persons to make the selection. On whom should this responsibility rest? By all means fundamentally on the librarian and not in any real sense on a book committee of the library trustees and not on any committee of citizens. Book orders are properly submitted for the approval of the book committee but the original work of selection must be done by the librarian. The librarian may also be glad to avail himself of the occasional or regular advice of experts or of cultivated readers in whose judgment he has confidence. On the librarian, reinforced by the advice of his principal assistants, most of whom are in more direct contact with the public and hence know more definitely the needs, and in certain cases possess more expert knowledge of specific classes of literature than does he, should rest the selection of books for purchase. For the proper exercise of this function he should have the broadest possible sympathies and interests, tempered with discrimination and judgment as to comparative values. His knowledge of books should be broad, for in the face of the overpowering number of subjects his library will need to cover, it cannot well be deep. In few cases will he be the "walking encyclopedia" once considered the standard type of librarian. He will naturally be a person of diverse reading; but most of the knowledge specifically needed in making his selections must perforce be acquired at second-hand, thru the general guides and subject bibliographies in the case of non-current literature, and thru trade bibliographies, selected lists of new books, like the American Library Association *Book List,* and book reviews, especially the *Book Review Digest,* for current publications.

Mention of the book review tempts one to comment at length on the inutility of much of present day book reviewing. Many reviews, perhaps most of them, are next to useless for the purposes of the librarian who needs to decide, often without seeing the book, whether he should buy it or not. The monthly and annual *Book Review Digest,* published for the last twenty-five years, separates the wheat from the chaff of such reviews and presents a composite and consensus of critical judgments. The *Book List* of the American Library Association in its monthly issues gives the cooperative judgments of contributing librarians on the current publications considered to be most needed in public libraries, with brief notes of description and evaluation. This publication supplements the *A. L. A. Catalog* of the 10,000 volumes considered to be best (in 1926) to form the basis for an American public library.

Good Print and Paper

In the practical problem of choosing books for public libraries certain physical considerations must take precedence of questions more purely literary. From the point of view of utility it is essential that a public library book be accurately printed from good clear type on good paper. Good printing is not so difficult to get as good paper; on this vexed question much might be said. Even if it is not considered a calamity from the point of view of the public library that most book paper now in use will not last more than fifty years, it is at least important that the eyes of readers should not be injured by highly glazed surfaces and that the paper be sufficiently durable to make rebinding practicable. Not a few books, perhaps otherwise desirable, are properly denied admission to public libraries because they are crudely and tastelessly printed on thick, clay-loaded paper, flimsily bound and garishly illustrated. Sometimes, however, the particular subject about which literature is needed is covered only by a book that offends in some or all of these particulars and it is a case of that or nothing.

Even with the fairly liberal funds which we assumed for the purchase of books for our library, the element of cost is an important factor and one that may not be disregarded by the librarian in the expenditure of public money. Should he decide that a given book is physically fit and worthy in the character of its contents, he may find that it is to be obtained only at an unreasonable price. The book may, for example, be one of a limited edition, held at such a price that the library must definitely decide to get along without it unless it is later reprinted in an ordinary edition. Or it may be a work sold at first only by subscription, at a price which includes large selling costs. In such cases the librarian may decide to wait; he therefore simply approves the book for purchase, makes a record of that fact, and then in perhaps 75 per cent of such cases buys it a little later at second-hand or from a remainder sale at a fraction of the original price.

In a review of the various classes of literature, let us lay down certain broad principles of selection, in part derived from what has already been said and in part to be further worked out in this discussion. For this purpose the motto of the American Library Association, summing up as it tries to do the whole purpose of the modern library movement, serves as the most terse and the most comprehensive statement of principles governing book purchases for public libraries: "The best books for the largest number at the least cost." Expanded, this means the books judged to be best according to more or less absolute standards of accuracy, and of artistic and moral excellence and according to relative standards of suitability to the needs of the entire reading population, within the limits of available funds.

In the selection of books, we are dealing with the works of the human mind, with artistic creations, the products of varying degrees and proportions of imagination, skill and industry. Each book is an individual thing and every selection worthy of the name must particularize. Our problem first involves three elements: whether particular books are true— true as to fact or true as to purpose; whether they measure up to appropriate artistic standards—one standard for a treatise on engineering and another for a novel; whether their moral purpose and probable moral effect are such that a public institution can justify itself in possessing and in circulating them. The task is not, however, complete without the application of the important fourth element: whether the particular book found to be worthy in itself is requisite to the given library. In the practical application of these principles, the fourth element, the need of the library for literature on particular subjects, will bulk so large as in practice (given limited funds) often to put it first and practically to preclude the present consideration of the worthiness or unworthiness of many new publications.

APPLICATION OF PRINCIPLES

In the application of these principles, it is desirable to divide literature for the purposes of selection for public libraries into four somewhat rough and overlapping classes, as follows:

1. Books of information or fact; comprising science, technology, fine arts, history, biography, economics, sociology, psychology, education, phil-

ology and encyclopedias and other reference books generally.

2. Books of opinion or speculation; including most of theology and religion, much of philosophy and some of sociology.

3. Books of imagination or creative literature; including poetry, fiction, drama, and belles lettres generally.

4. Children's literature, a parallel and overlapping, rather than a coordinate class.

In choosing books for our first class, information or fact books, our first concern, in deciding whether particular books are worthy, is to determine their truth as to fact or as to intent: is the author capable, honest and reasonably free from bias—not a colorless analyst, but not a partisan; or if a partisan, an honest partisan? In the case of controverted questions, such as the tariff, the World War, peace versus war, the literature of both sides should be represented by its most capable and fair minded advocates. The library should also encourage a broad and liberal spirit of free inquiry; its purpose is not to restrain but to foster comprehensive curiosity. New or present-day subjects, such as prohibition, eugenics, birth control, companionate marriage, international relations, behaviorism, socialism, anarchism, etc., should be represented, with entire impartiality so far as possible, by advocates and opponents. The library as an institution is impersonal and has no ax to grind. It seeks only the complete enlightenment of public opinion by affording all readers the opportunity to read all sides of every question. Other things being equal, the most comprehensive, the most clearly and simply written and the most readable books in this class are the most desirable.

Books much in demand and often bought by public libraries because they fall into the highly esteemed classes of history and biography are court memoirs, biographies of royal mistresses and similar books whose success rests on the scandals retailed therein. The expenditure of public funds for such literature is surely not very defensible.

Speaking generally, the library should furnish the most ample stock of books in the class of informational literature. The chief reason for the exclusion of any candidate for purchase within this field is likely to be some glaring misstatement of facts, some distinctly immoral tendency, or offensiveness in matter or manner of treatment.

RIGID SCRUTINY NEEDED

In the actual choice of books for our first class, the first question should not be: Is this a book worthy of a place in my library? or even the more searching one: Does the library need the particular book offered? but rather: Are the library's resources on the subject covered by this book already adequate? If answered in the negative the next question is: Is this the best book to meet our needs or is there another book not now owned by us that would prove a better investment? These questions are all highly important and are becoming more so with the multiplication of authors and publishers and the increasing flood of books published. It is more and more happening that different publishers are issuing almost simultaneously books which largely duplicate each other. The publication of a book which proves highly successful is very likely to induce other publishers to issue rival works. Because published later, these may be considered to contain more recent information and therefore to be preferable. The author of a later work may have profited by the criticism called out by the earlier book and his work may represent a distinct advance. It may, on the other hand, be but a weak imitation, hastily put together in the hope of catching part of the market discovered by the earlier work. Again there are certain fields of knowledge, including especially those occupied by the Bible dictionaries, cyclopedias of religious knowledge and dictionaries of recent and contemporary biography that are becoming very much overworked. Often a mere glance at rival books, with comparison of prices, typography, arrangement, presence or absence of a satisfactory index, will dictate a decision. A knowledge of the comparative standing of authors and publishers is a help. Reviews, particularly in professional and technical journals, are usually trustworthy, as to the accuracy and standing of the book covered.

Having decided that a given book is in itself an able and honest piece of work, and the most authoritative work on its subject, there may still be questions to settle before it is decided to buy it for our library. Perhaps it is not sufficiently popular in treatment. Perhaps, after all, the somewhat less excellent book, judged by the standards of the specialist, is better suited to our needs, because from it the complex mathematical formulae not understood by most of our readers have been eliminated. Possibly we should, instead of buying any of the new books, devote the available funds to buying several duplicate copies of the very popular work on the subject we already have, the demand for which we have never been able to satisfy.

Lest I should be understood as thinking that the public library should satisfy the popular demand only, I hasten to say that in my opinion it should satisfy that demand first, but also if possible it should, so far as supply and demand warrant, aim to have under each subject an assortment of books graduated to meet the needs of varying grades of culture: primers of knowledge for the boy and for the man whose early education has been neglected and whose understanding is simple, and thorogoing treatises for the most advanced students. According to these principles it could never be said that the ten best books on any given subject—supposing it were possible for anybody in authority to pronounce an infallible judgment upon them—would necessarily be the best ten books on that subject for the library.

BOOKS TO MEET DEMANDS

In this group of subjects it is important to have adequate books to meet demands; the calls, especially from the uninstructed reader, are for books on a given subject rather than for specific books, and such readers docilely take what is given to them, thereby enforcing the responsibility for choosing wisely. In the case of the more sophisticated reader who knows what he wants, the calls are for specific books. With such readers it is sometimes not so easy to apply the foregoing principles consistently, for in the face of their requests the library may be impelled to reverse its decision not to buy a given book which contains no new contribution to the subject in question. One may surmise that the reader wishes to examine it for the purpose of eliminating it from further consideration. It may seem a pity to spend public money for such a purpose, and if the book has no other real value for the library, one should decline to purchase. But this reader may never before have visited the library and the expense involved may not be sufficient to outweigh the opportunity of winning him.

In the more literary and humanistic sections of this group, such as history, biography and the fine arts, the calls to purchase specific works as opposed to books on certain subjects will be proportionately larger. Certain books of history, biography and art history approach more closely to being works of pure literature and hence are in request for their own sakes and a larger proportion of readers know exactly what they want. As these subjects are less matters of exact knowledge than of interpretation and give freer range for imagination and opinion, so it is not easily possible to subject their literature to any acid test of truth to fact. In the choice of such books the emphasis will be thrown as much on their artistic excellence as on their truth.

BOOKS OF OPINION

In defining the principles governing the choice of books for our second class, those of opinion and speculation, including theology, religion, certain portions of philosophy and partisan politics, it is desirable to call attention to the fact that the viewpoint of the public library in judging of any books, whether theological, religious, political, etc., is not primarily religious or political, but literary and educational. Its standards are those arising from educational aims. The library is not irreligious or even non-religious, not political and certainly not partisan, but simple lacking in religious or political color or bias. It is properly interested in religion, in philosophy, in politics, for these are great facts in human life. In some form or other they appear to be necessities to mankind and are practically universal, and calls for books on these subjects are deserving of consideration. In addition to the broad field of religious, philosophical and political literature, de-

void of sectarian or partisan bias, the literature
representing many different and often antagonistic
beliefs should be supplied, according to the demands
of readers. The public library will therefore have
a representative collection of books on all shades of
opinion: idealism and materialism; monism and dual-
ism; orthodoxy and heterodoxy; Protestantism and
Catholicism; Mormonism, Christian science; Socialism, anarchism and all the other isms of political
theory. The library does not of course hold itself
responsible for the opinions expressed in the books
on its shelves. As long as it supplies, so far as possible, books on both sides of a controverted question,
such for example as those of Henry Charles Lea and
of Abbé Vacandard on the Inquisition, Irving
Fisher's *Prohibition at its Worst* (1926) and Fabian
Franklin's *A B C of Prohibition* (1927), it will keep
itself free from a charge of partisanship and afford
the public the means for forming independent judgments. Frequently in the case of doctrinal or controversial books, it is a question of the acceptance
of gifts. In such cases they should be accepted, even
tho the purpose of the donor is propagandism, provided they do not violate all the canons of good taste
and are not in thought indecent or subversive of
morals. Books which are illiterate or vulgar in expression, coarse or immoral in thought, according to
generally accepted standards of morality, and cheap
and tasteless in printing and binding should be
declined— but never on account of disagreement on
the part of the librarian with the opinions expressed
in them. (See the fuller statement in paper on
"Choice of Religious and Theological Books for Public Libraries.")

The principles laid down as applicable to the
choice of books of opinion are designed to be espe-

cially supplemental to and not in contravention of our general principles or of those governing books for our first class or books of information.

I suppose that thus far there has been little in the principles or practice outlined to which my readers are disposed to take exception. In the search for principles for the choice of books in the field of pure literature, including fiction, the drama and poetry, as well as much of history, biography, travel and the fine arts, a few words in further definition of the functions of the public library may prove helpful.

CREATIVE LITERATURE

On this, the esthetic side, the library is an agent for the cultivation of refined taste thru the instrumentality of literature considered as a fine art. Here the library influences both the readers who approach it with the definite purpose of using its facilities for the rounding out and the continuing of their education by wide and deep reading in the best literature of every age and language, and also those who simply seek books for recreational reading, to "kill time," to read themselves to sleep, or otherwise divert themselves. The latter class, as well as the former, tho no doubt to a less degree, are influencing their tastes, are using the library to pursue a course, however scattered and fragmentary, of reading in belles lettres.

What should be the library's principles and policy of inclusion and exclusion with reference to books in the broad field of belles lettres? Should it confine itself practically to books that may be regarded as classics? Should it decide not to buy any book until it is three years, or one year old, as has often been suggested? Should it on the other hand, since it is a public institution desirous of meeting public demands, procure any and every new book that succeeds in making a stir in the literary world? If not, should the line of exclusion be based upon lack of literary merit, or upon moral considerations, or both?

At once I answer that in my opinion the public library should first of all furnish an abundant stock of classic literature, but that it should also have a fairly ample and catholic selection of the best current literature, judged by a reasonably high standard of literary art.

It may be taken as a matter of course that the accepted classics of all the great world literatures should be found in the public library in the originals, if a fairly large number of readers can read them in that form, and in all the best English translations in a sufficient number of copies to meet demands. I am very glad to say, and I know that the statement will be welcomed by my readers, that such demands form a large, perhaps the largest part, of the library's work in the field of pure literature. Outside the library the "hot from the press" best seller makes the most noise. Persons who seek such literature exclusively and who never willingly or knowingly read a book more than six months old even invade the public library and sometimes unblushingly sneer at the classics, calling them "poky old things" or saying "everybody has read them long ago" or "they are already in private libraries." I venture the assertion that comparatively few even cultivated persons have read more than a fair proportion of the world's books best worth reading. The growth of apartment house life has reduced the storage capacity of many homes, so that in spite of the publication of cheap, compact editions of the classics, with increase in the efficiency of the public library, there is a distinct tendency on the part of cultivated readers to rely on it to supply them with the books they read, including classics for first reading or rereading. The universality of popular education is training a constantly enlarging body of readers, many of whom, partly by the direction of teachers, and partly by the suggestion of librarians, are discovering the classics and are reading them with avidity. By classics, I of course do not mean simply the Greek and Latin classics, but the whole body of the world's literature that has survived from generation to generation because of real vitality. Such world classics are not simply possessed by the public library, embalmed in well-printed editions, properly labelled but seldom disturbed; they are living pieces of literature, because, in spite of the attractions of current literature, they are being read by a constantly increasing body of eager readers, whose taste they undoubtedly influence. To supply multiple copies, which constantly wear out and need replacement, of the most sought of such classics, such as *The Merchant of Venice, Nicholas Nickleby, Ivanhoe, Vanity Fair, Les Miserables, The Idylls of the King* and hundreds of other titles, is no small item of expense. Undoubtedly the library should be very sure to have an adequate stock of such books, before it should listen to calls for lesser books. If it is objected that the provision of such books is not really book selection, but simply the collection of books already selected, the answer is that when book money is spent for a classic or a near classic, it cannot also be spent for some inferior book.

Contemporary Literature

In order not to allow the question to be closed too soon by being crowded into the *cul de sac* of "no funds," we assumed that our library should have fairly ample appropriations for book purchases and general administration. But even then there is the question of the wise use of the public funds committed to our care to devote to public education. I believe that a public library to be fully responsive to the intellectual and esthetic needs of its community should also furnish a generous supply of the best contemporary literature, judged by liberal standards of inclusion. Altho we may have no Tennyson or Browning, no Thackeray or Dickens or Scott or other transcendent literary genius writing today, yet we do have John Galsworthy, Arnold Bennett, Hugh Walpole, Virginia Woolf, Shaw, Joseph Hergesheimer, Edith Wharton, Willa Cather, Thomas Mann, Knut Hamsun, Johan Bojer, Sigrid Undset, and many others, some of whom may be esteemed as classics when we get a little further away from them. In spite of much in current literature that is machine-made, scamped, false, pernicious and meretricious, it is still true, I believe, that the average will be found to equal if not exceed that of any earlier generation, particularly if one considers the vast proportionate increase in the reading population and in the writers of books. Each generation must for the most part write its own books, sing its own songs, make its own dramas. The real tragedies, comedies, problems, struggles, with nature and of the souls, of today are being incorporated into present day literature; and when the tale, the song or the drama of the present is truthfully conceived and executed with insight, with imagination, with power, and with art, it should be promptly admitted to the republic of letters and recognized as a part of the public possession. A city like Washington contains a large number of cultivated readers who properly expect the public library to enable them to read the best of contemporary literature. Keeping in mind the needs of this class, no doubt above the average of its readers, but fairly typical and a good touch-stone, the library's obligation would seem to be both inclusive and exclusive; that is, it should aim to stock anything that possesses sufficient positive literary merit so that such readers might properly desire it and to exclude all the many weak and colorless books, the reading of which from the point of view of the reasonably cultivated reader would be a waste of time and the purchase of which would therefore be, from the point of view of the library, a waste of money. Objection may be raised to making the taste of the cultivated reader the standard for a democratic institution, but were we to have municipal theaters and opera houses, we should scarcely expect them to include ragtime music or melodrama in their reper-toires, tho such programs would undoubtedly be pop-ular. We should, however, expect to have presented in them not simply the classic drama and opera, but the best of contemporary productions.

CRITICAL EXAMINATION NECESSARY

If the problem were merely one of furnishing all current books of pure literature that appeal to cul-tivated readers, tho it would be a portentous one, due to the number of books to be considered and the number of copies of approved books that must be sup-plied to meet demands, it would be a fairly simple one in practice. Every book, or at least every novel and drama, not vouched for by unimpeachable testi-mony, including the new books of well-established authors, should be read entire or examined with care by the librarian, or some person or persons in whose literary judgment he has confidence. With the exer-

cise of care and patience this important and delicate
task may be accomplished to his own satisfaction
and to the reasonable satisfaction of the public. I
use the expression "reasonable satisfaction" advised-
ly. In fiction, now the dominant form of literary expression and the most sought of all literature, the
great majority of books selected pass without comment. Against a certain number of those included,
objections are raised, ranging all the way from those
that do not end happily, the presence of which in the
library is a grievance to some delicate souls, to those
against which real objection may properly be raised
—which may perhaps have slipped into the library
thru some oversight or thru error of judgment on the
part of the fallible librarian or his proxy.

With regard to children's books, the strongest emphasis should be laid on the responsibility of the library for their choice. To a large degree parents
have shifted the responsibility for the choice of books
for their children to the public library which they
consider to be expert in that field. Since this is the
attitude of parents, the library is trying to measure
up to the task. I mention this matter here, for it
seems to me that many adult readers are similarly
holding the library responsible for the books on its
shelves. To them the presence of the public library
book plate in a book is taken as a kind of guarantee
of pure intellectual food, composed of wholesome in-
gredients, and free from adulterants and preserva-
tives, because needing none. Who will say that this
is not a fairly reasonable demand to make of the library? The establishment of standards and the application of them is perhaps beset with more difficulties than are experienced in determining the purity
of food for the human body, for the tests of literature
are chiefly those of taste and are not resolvable into

exact physical and chemical formulae. Moreover, in
literature, every layman regards himself as good a
judge as the official expert, and he no doubt sometimes
is. Nevertheless, the responsibility rests upon the librarian to make the decisions, and even tho he knows
he will make mistakes, he must not shirk. In other
words, the librarian is forced to exercise a certain degree of what may by some be regarded as censorship.
But this does not mean that with the establishment
on firm foundations of our system of free public libraries we are creating a general literary censorship.
That authority, so far as exercised at all, is exercised
by the police and the post office when they suppress
or deny admission to the mails of books that exceed
the limits prescribed by law. It does mean that there
are certain books readily obtainable in the shops or
thru the commercial circulating libraries that are not
considered necessary or appropriate to the educational work of the public library, supported by public
funds.

Exclusion by Deficiencies

Most books of literature that are denied admission
to the public library are excluded thru deficiency in
qualities. They are simply not worth while and exclude themselves by their dullness, their unnatural-
ness, their crudeness, their cheap clap-trap, their sen-
sationalism, their poor English, and similar negative
qualities. Books written with insight, with power
and with art, that would otherwise be cordially welcomed to the public library, should, I believe, be excluded whenever the sum of their offending is sufficient in one or both of two principal ways: if they
have a distinctly immoral tendency or if they offend
too greatly against the decencies, they either have no
place in the library, or in the rare cases when they

are admitted, it should be for other very special reasons and their use should be restricted.

The public library should strive in its necessary censorship to be fully abreast of or a little in advance of the thought of the age and be prepared to face the criticism that such a position is sure to entail rather than to content itself with smug, self-complacent innocuousness. Its standards should be fresh, robust, out-of-doors standards, rather than sickly, anemic, hot-house standards. The public librarian would much prefer never to feel obliged to exercise any censorship; but when he has taken his stand on the most advanced and liberal ground of inclusion, there are still books whose presence in the public library cannot well be defended. If a book, especially a novel, makes evil appear good, by glorifying dishonest acts and principles, if it makes treachery and rascality appear as cleverness or upholds fundamentally wrong ideals, it has no proper place in a public circulating library whose privileges are fully open to young and old. Typical of this class are the "Raffles" books, absorbingly interesting as they are. Books of another class, the largest group of all, are objectionable because they unduly glorify the animal, the passionate side of man's nature, usually regarded as his less admirable side, and often by contrast hold up to contempt and ridicule his intellectual and spiritual qualities, prudence, self-control and other homely virtues. Altho such books are often filled with unpleasant details, our real objection is not on the score of indecency but rather on their perversion of the moral sense, their exaltation of the physical with a corresponding subordination of those qualities which make man human and differentiate him from the rest of the animal kingdom. With some writers sex seems to have become an obsession, to have become so nearly the whole of life as to subordinate all else to it. Their books are surely false to nature, or if not, one cannot but have pity for authors whose acquaintances or at least the creations of whose minds are such uniformly sorry creatures. (See also the fuller statement in the paper, "Censorship and the Public Library.")

RESPONSIBILITY FOR CHILDREN'S BOOKS

I have already indicated my belief that the public library must accept complete responsibility in the choice of books for children. By this I mean that there is no room for compromise or for shifting of responsibility to the individual reader. Altho we might wish that parents generally would supervise the reading done by their children, yet evidences that in most cases they do not are too plentiful to admit of much doubt in the matter. Since this is to a large degree true, so that many children read without hindrance the colored, so-called comic, supplements of the Sunday newspapers, and the often sickly and unwholesome books secured from the Sunday school libraries, as well as more or less innocuous nickel novels, together with nameless horrors from the news-stands, it behooves the public library to supply such books as will successfully compete in interest with the inferior material they aim to supplant. But the library must give to children only such literature as will stimulate curiosity and naturally and wholesomely interest, inform and develop taste to aid in the formal education of the child as well as to secure his enrollment in a life-long course of education thru the means of the library. Since children seldom read book reviews but may generally be led to read the book placed in their hands, provided only it interests them, it has been agreed by children's librarians, who form a specialized group in the library, that it is better to provide an ample stock of thoroly or reasonably satisfactory books, rather than to endeavor to multiply titles to include second and third rate books, except for special reasons.

I have been able only to touch lightly, by no means to exhaust, all the various and many-sided aspects of this large subject. In many specific instances the librarian will find that, whichever way he has decided, he wishes he had decided the other way. Here are some of the special perils into which he may fall and some precautionary suggestions. In the choice of books for public libraries beware:

Perils to Avoid

1. Beware of the faddist, the hobby rider who would have you buy everything published on a subject such as socialism, or the Shakespeare-Bacon controversy. If we could be alive one hundred years hence these people would still be digging in the bottom of the Wye or delving in the Public Record office for ciphers. The library can take no stand for or against such controverted questions; but it cannot dissipate its funds in purchasing, cataloging and storing all the masses of material published. It can at most make a selection, perhaps of typical or representative books or better of comprehensive statements of the arguments in these controverted fields.

2. Beware of his near kin the propagandist, who seeks to use the machinery of the public library, expensive for the public to maintain, but cheap for his use, for the exploitation of his peculiar religious or medical theories. There is a difference between being hospitable to all shades of opinion to the extent of having a reasonable representation of the literature of the subject on the library shelves, and a condition

in which the library is "worked" to circulate political, religious and medical tracts. For example, there is a question in the minds of some librarians of the advisability of accepting the large number of copies of Mrs. Eddy's *Science and Health,* willingly presented by the Christian Science Literature Distribution Committees for circulation by the public library. On the other hand the persons not connected with the Christian Science Church who wish to investigate the subject appear to be so numerous that the library may regard itself as performing a public service in furnishing literature to answer such inquiries, tho even so there are times when we are not quite easy in our minds about the matter.

Beware the Booster

3. Beware of the "booster." He may come to the library in large numbers asking why the library has not a dozen or more copies of Jones's new novel. Now Jones, not finding a publisher who would take the risk, may have published the book at his own expense, and still have money left to employ a claque. Or perhaps Jones's novel may be indecent and he may prefer that the public library should refuse to stock it. If he can entrap the librarian into giving, over his own signature, his real reasons for excluding it, or if his friend the reporter can secure an interview from the librarian denouncing the book, which can be published with scare heads, he thinks its success will be assured.

4. "Beware of the Greeks bearing gifts." Such gift may be either a volume of modest but weakling poems (published at the expense of the author) or it may be a fifty volume quarto subscription set containing the garnered wisdom of the world that a modern four-room apartment can no longer accommodate.

Or it may be what the young newspaper reporter would describe as "a rare and valuable private library," but which examination proves to be a lot of school and college text books published before 1860, some volumes of antique theology, an out-of-date encyclopedia and other similar household impedimenta, with perhaps a dozen or fifty volumes which the public library is glad to get, if it can select them and not feel obliged to take the whole mass, certainly not if obliged to keep the books together and label them the "Blank Memorial Collection."

BEWARE THE BOOK AGENT

5. Beware of the smooth tongued and persuasive subscription book agent. Examine his book carefully —provided you can get him to leave it behind so that you can do so at your leisure and out of the sound of his caressing voice. If you find his book a good one, purchase it, tho not from him, but from the second-hand dealer to whom some private purchaser will soon sell it and thus save your library half or more.

6. Beware of building up a well-rounded collection or of owning every book that no "gentleman's library should lack." Get instead the books you find the people really need, without too much regard for the symmetry of your collection.

7. Beware of the spirit of dogmatism, narrow-mindedness and finality in your choice of books. If you find that you have bought a book whose presence in the library you cannot defend, do not hesitate to reverse yourself and take it out, or to stock a book, previously rejected, if you are convinced of error. Because of this liability of error and the fickleness of taste in readers, some librarians admit most new fiction to their libraries only to a sort of probationary

standing, giving full fellowship only if the demand still continues one, two or three years after publication.

The choice of books by public libraries is of interest and importance not only to the individual users of the libraries concerned, but has large economic and educational bearings. According to the most recent figures (1927) American public libraries in cities of over 50,000 population spend annually for books more than $7,000,000. Undoubtedly the financial success or failure of many a book depends directly on the extent to which it is selected by libraries. Moreover, both librarians and booksellers know that the presence of a book in a public library, with the official approval this fact carries, more and more influences purchases for private libraries.

THE NEW BIOGRAPHY[1]

The novel is the form of literature that at present appeals to the widest circle of readers. Biography comes next and seems to be gaining on the novel. Is there any connection between these facts? Perhaps some answer to this question may appear from this paper.

A SCHOOL OF BIOGRAPHERS

A school of biographers has grown up, almost entirely since the great war, called by others and often by its members the "new biographers" or the "modern biographers." The protagonists and practitioners of the "new biography" profess to have developed a new literary *genre*. Six names stand out as leaders: three Englishmen, Lytton Strachey, Harold Nicolson and Philip Guedalla; one Frenchman, André Maurois; one German, Emil Ludwig; and one American, Gamaliel Bradford. Other lesser names might be mentioned, but these have been chosen partly because of their outsanding achievements in producing notable examples of the "new biography" and partly because each, to a greater or lesser degree, has given his theories of biographical writing, his confession of faith of the why and the how of this so-called new and different form of biography.

It seems desirable first to give thru quotation and summary some of the ideas of these men as to what they are doing that is so different from what has gone before, the reasons for this revolt, their motives and their methods.

[1] Read before the Washington Literary Society in December 1928; before the Columbian Library Association in January 1929, and before several other organizations.

STRACHEY THE FATHER

By common agreement Lytton Strachey is considered the father of modern biography. Although he has not set forth his theories in any such systematic and elaborate way as has André Maurois, yet the three-page preface to his *Eminent Victorians,* published in 1918, does give his ideas. He says: "The art of biography seems to have fallen on evil times in England. We have had, it is true, a few masterpieces, but we have never had, like the French, a great biographical tradition. . . With us, the most delicate and humane of all the branches of the art of writing has been relegated to the journeymen of letters; we do not reflect that it is perhaps as difficult to write a good life as to live one. Those two fat volumes, with which it is our custom to commemorate the dead —who does not know them, with their ill-digested masses of material, their slipshod style, their tone of tedious panegyric, their lamentable lack of selection, of detachment, of design? They are as familiar as the *cortège* of the undertaker, and wear the same air of slow, funeral barbarism. One is tempted to suppose, of some of them, that they were composed by that functionary, as the final item of his job. The studies in this book are indebted, in more ways than one, to such works—works which certainly deserve the name of Standard Biographies. For they have provided me not only with much indispensable information, but with something even more precious—an example. How many lessons are to be learnt from them! But it is hardly necessary to particularise. To preserve, for instance, a becoming brevity—a brevity which excludes everything that is redundant and nothing that is significant—that, surely, is the first duty of the biographer. The second, no less surely, is to maintain his own freedom of spirit. It is not his business to be complimentary, it is his business to lay bare the facts of the case, as he understands them. That is what I have aimed at in this book—to lay bare the facts of some cases, as I understand them, dispassionately, impartially, and without ulterior intensions."

The Maurois Idea

We are indebted to André Maurois for the fullest exposition of the theory of the new biography. This is contained in a long article entitled "The Modern Biographer," published in the *Yale Review* for January, 1928. The author believes that the modern biography differs from the old biography both in motive and in method. The motives of the old biography were chiefly commemorative and didactic. These were sometimes combined with the motive that a biography was written to order for a publisher or thru appointment from the family or even from the subject in advance of his death. The latter plan worked out unhappily in the cases of Froude for Carlyle and of Moore for Byron, and happily in the case of Monypenny for Disraeli. Maurois grants that "A good deal could be said in favor of the old type of life and letters in three volumes, with notes and appendix. It was an invaluable mass of material where the modern biographer is glad to go and dig for precious metal. It is even sometimes," he goes on, "fine work of real literary value. Macaulay's *Life,* by Trevelyan, is a very readable book. The custom is to praise Lockhart's *Life of Scott* and Forster's *Life of Dickens;* these are useful books, full of interesting documents; but shall I confess that I do not admire them unreservedly? They are long and badly constructed. On the other hand, Dowden's *Life of Shelley* seems to be perfect."

No Hero Worshipper

Maurois criticises the Victorian biographer, who may be otherwise a good historian and a good writer, for "his attitude of hero worship"—because in the case of public men he describes the mask which the public knows or at least the man he would like the public to believe in, rather than the man as he is known to his friends and himself. He refuses to look behind the mask. In praising Lytton Strachey as the master of the school of modern biography, Maurois says that he "is no hero-worshipper. On the contrary, he is a hero-wrecker, an idol-breaker." He is also, Maurois says, "a very deep phychologist." This latter point he illustrates by quotations from Strachey's *Queen Victoria* concerning the pathetic figure of Albert, the Prince Consort. Maurois grants that if this new type of biography were "written for the pleasure of destroying heroes, it would be a rather despicable art" and admits that even Strachey himself has in some instances been "a shade nastier than is really fair"; for example when he makes Disraeli out "a courtier without scruples, who dominates through flattery a rather unintelligent old woman." Maurois goes on to show that some of Strachey's disciples "without imitating his deep insight, have only got hold of his familiar tricks," chiefly that of irony, and that the resulting books "make us regret the three-volume life and letters which, after all, was an historical and a scholarly work. We sometimes get tired," he says, of "the plucking of dead lions by the beard." But, the modern biographer "represents a reaction and a reaction always goes too far." Maurois goes on to analyze another motive of the modern biographer, that of self-expression, which he illustrates by his own books on Shelley and Disraeli and then sums up by saying that "modern biographers have one thing in common; that is their refusal to paint masks, their desire to get to the real man." He reinforces this point by saying that the "danger of the old type of biography is that nobody believes in it." As a contrast he claims, "In spite of his somewhat brutal sincerity, we must give credit to the modern biographer for his genuine respect for truth."

A WORK OF ART

The methods of the new biographer as outlined by Maurois are likewise interesting. "The essential point about him is that his aim is to build a work of art" with symmetry and form as in the case of the novel. To accomplish this in the case of a biography, the biographer must follow the method of the portrait-painter who is also obliged to deal with a given reality and yet build a harmony of colors and lines. "He selects; he leaves out a great many things . . . he builds by suppression, by concentrating the interest of the onlooker on the important features of the face. This is exactly what the biographer should do. He must not invent anything, but his art is to forget. If he has at his disposal 200 letters and a long diary, he must know how to extract the few sentences that will convey a genuine impression." Maurois makes much of harmony, rhythm and an impression of unity to be gained by repeating certain themes, as Wagner does in music. For example in his own *Ariel* (Shelley) the theme had to be water, since water played a great part in Shelley's life and he died by drowning. "This impression of impending fate" should be given. With *Disraeli* rain and peacocks were the themes by the careful handling of which the biographer was to achieve "some sort of musical composition." Maurois concludes with certain rules which include: (1) follow the chronological order of development; (2) avoid the pronouncing of moral judgments, but instead tell the story in objective and impartial style; (3) read every word and collect all available testimony in order to find the fact or anecdote that will suddenly reveal the character.

LUDWIG'S CONFITEOR

Emil Ludwig in the preface to his *Genius and Character* gives his confession of faith. He claims that the most modern of all portraitists is Plutarch, whom he seems to take as his model. But "perhaps the portraitist of today, who is first of all a psychologist, is much nearer to the biologist than to the historian . . . His problem remains a constant; it is the discovery of a human soul. Of course, the portraitist reworks the material supplied by the scientific biographer and is always indebted to him. With a kind of naïve cynicism, he appropriates the scientist's laboriously collated facts for purposes of his own . . . The portraitist begins with the concept of a character and searches in the archives for what is at bottom the corroboration of an intuition. But woe to him if he is tempted to improvise, to shift his dates ever so little, thereby encroaching on the novelist. . . The biographer cannot obtain adequate results unless he has a picture of his subject to work from. . . Anecdotes were" (that is in the older biography) "recorded skeptically, shamefacedly, as though by a lowering of professional dignity. Yet for us, the most trivial habit will often suggest the interpretation of some major trait of character, and the accredited anecdote becomes an epigram."

Ludwig criticises the older biographies which, he claims, "occasionally close with a chapter designed to show the hero 'as a man'—which is put in as a kind of insert . . . But how," he asks, "is the portraitist to represent his subject except as a man? And what else must he do but trace this man's every thought and act, every motive and impulse, back to the indivisible elements of his personality? For this purpose . . . he must be versed in the study of man, must be a psychologist and an analyist. He must be skilled, through both intuition and training, in interpreting a character by the symptoms of its behavior. . . Yet a knowledge of genius is demanded also. . . When writing of genius one must draw upon resources in himself which are akin to its dominant characteristics." That is, he must be a genius too.

A DIDACTIC PURPOSE

Ludwig differs from Maurois in that he claims an ethical, a didactic purpose in biography. He says: "Our educational intent is to show all readers, and especially youth, that great men are not gods, that they have been gripped by the same all-too-human passions, repressions, and encumbrances as affect every other mortal, and that they have fought through, regardless, to their goals. In this way one is incited to minimize all shortcomings and to exact of himself the fullest utilization of his powers." And again: "Why write of characters at all, unless an example, or perhaps even a warning, can result from the process!" And finally his idea of symbolism: "If we are to make copies of men, we must see ourselves mirrored in mankind. It is not until our own life appears to us as symbolic that we are prepared to discern the symbolism behind the lives of others."

BRADFORD THE PSYCHOGRAPHER

Emil Ludwig thinks of himself as a portraitist. Gamaliel Bradford thinks that term inadequate to describe himself. Instead of a biographer he calls himself a psychographer. In describing psychography, a word which he has borrowed from Sainte-Beuve, he says, in his *A Naturalist of Souls*: "As a portrait-painter I could present a man at only one moment of his career, and depict his character in only one phase, one situation, one set of conditions and circumstances. Now the aim of psychography is precisely the opposite to this. Out of the perpetual flux of actions and circumstances that constitutes a man's whole life, it seeks to extract what is essential, what is permanent and so vitally characteristic. . . From the vast and necessary material of biography, psychography selects only that which is indispensable for its particular purpose, and as the accumulation of books becomes yearly greater and greater, it seems as if this principle of condensation must become more and more pressing in its appeal. . . Psychography . . . is the attempt to portray character. . . Character . . . is the sum of qualities or generalized habits of action. Psychography is the condensed, essential, artistic presentation of character . . . It must be admitted that psychography is always in danger of degenerating into gossip . . . Psychography picks, chooses, and rejects; in a bushel of chaff finds only a grain or two of wheat, but treasures that wheat as precious and invaluable." It will be noted that Bradford's method involves a complete disregard of chronology, thus differing from the methods of the other new biographers.

NICOLSON ON TASTE IN BIOGRAPHY

Harold Nicolson has recently published an entire volume on *The Development of English Biography*. In his chapter on the present age he says that "the development of biography is primarily the development of the taste for biography." Changes in taste in biography, he thinks, are "governed by the ebb and flow of religious belief. In periods when the reading public believe in God and in the life after death . . . biography becomes deductive, ethical, didactic, or merely superficial. In periods . . . of speculation, doubt or scepticism, the reading public becomes predominantly interested in behaviour, and biography . . . becomes inductive, critical, detached and realistic . . . The less people believe in theology the more do they believe in human experience. And it is to biography that they go for this experience . . . The intelligent reader also demands literary form . . . He asks for more and more . . . details: and yet he insists that the mass of material be presented in a readable form." The biographer must therefore "accumulate a vast amount of authentic material" and then "produce it in synthetic form. A synthesis . . . requires a thesis, a motive, or . . . a point of view." The biographer's problem is to combine the maximum of scientific material with the perfection of literary form. . . The public now demand that the vast and various sea of human experience be put before them in a portable form."

The single point that I glean from Philip Guedalla, from his just published *Gladstone and Palmerston,* (the first instalment of the Palmerston papers) is one in which he stresses the need, especially in the case of statesmen, of publishing letters and documents separately from the biography. "Half the weakness of 'full-length biography'," he says, "comes, I believe, from the misguided effort to incorporate a vast legacy of documents in the *Life.* For it is the attempt to give us a '*Life and Letters*' that is generally responsible for the submergence of the *Life.*" This "method followed with Disraeli gave us his tragic funeral procession of six lumbering pantechnicons, barely re-

deemed from undeserved oblivion by the incongruous
spectacle of a sprightly Frenchman bringing up the
rear in a neat gig . . . A single volume provides the
ideal form of record . . . It is conceded that biography
must be a distillation, but we are all entitled to a
sight of the materials from which the essence is distilled. . . . Having recorded his hero in a single
volume, let his biographer put out his papers *in
extenso.*"

Altho these somewhat extended quotations and
summaries do not cover all the points that all the
modern biographers think important, yet the principal tenets of the new biographical faith have been included.

STRACHEY'S BIOGRAPHIES

I now turn to a consideration of the biographical
works by these six writers or at least to typical examples of them.

Lytton Strachey should come first. Certainly he
measures up to high standards of long research and
few and brief books. Except for a single volume of
reprinted essays, *Books and Characters,* originally
written in an earlier period, and one very slight volume on Alexander Pope, Mr. Strachey has in 10 years
published but three books, *Eminent Victorians*
(1918), *Queen Victoria* (1921) and *Elizabeth and
Essex* (1928)—all outstanding examples of the new
biography.

The characters portrayed in the first of them, Cardinal Manning, General Gordon, Thomas Arnold and
Florence Nightingale were certainly Victorian and
all eminent; but when we see mercilessly exposed "the
worldliness of Manning, the harsh muddleheadedness
of Arnold, the ill temper of Florence Nightingale and
the eccentricity of Gordon," possibly we will conclude
that he intended his title to be somewhat ironical.

For example, Strachey tells us that Cardinal Manning notes in his diary that, having determined to mortify himself, he decided during Lent "to use no pleasant bread (except on Sundays and feasts) such as cake and sweetmeat." "But," says Strachey, "he added the proviso 'I do not include plain biscuits.'" No comment from Strachey, but his intent is clear.

HIS QUEEN VICTORIA

Strachey's *Queen Victoria* is not a history. It is not a political portrait, but is a personal, a psychological portrait. It is also a brilliant and fascinating achievement. The aim of the author was not the discovery of new knowledge, but a new interpretation of facts already known, a selection from many books, including the Queen's diary and a recombination of what would contribute to the portrait he desired to paint. His method was more that of the novelist than of a biographer. His book is dedicated to the novelist Virginia Woolf. Different readers will gain from this book different impressions. To some the facts and quotations here collected will chiefly "evoke the image of a fat and resolute little woman, full of pride, accessible to flattery, and at the same time touching and ridiculous." To others, including an English critic, "there is not a sentence which the most fastidious reader could wish to alter." Another English critic praised Strachey's intimate and conspicuously sympathetic comprehension of the woman whose life is the subject of his analysis, and a third (an American critic of standing) praises him for ignoring "a thousand opportunities for ridicule . . . He displays Victoria with completeness, but without cruelty. He is benignly caustic, bountiful and exact, profoundly humorous and inclusive, infinitely exhilarating. He discerns the nature of the underlying element which in Victoria's personality really counted: 'It was a peculiar sincerity'."

ELIZABETH AND ESSEX

Strachey's latest book, *Elizabeth and Essex, a Tragic History,* is but newly published and as I write this paper I am glowing with the pure joy of its reading. It is an extraordinarily brilliant piece of work. It is not only fine as literary craftsmanship, but it has commended itself to the historians who thus far have been able to pick very few flaws in it. In the seven years since the publication of his *Queen Victoria* he has examined mountains of material and has produced a book short of three hundred pages, each sentence of which is well chosen to give the exact shade of meaning intended. Nowhere is there superficiality or slovenliness, but everywhere the swift, concise, exact, revealing characterization which gives us pictures that are vivid and delightful. It is a thrillingly interesting story of the meteoric rise and fall of the last and perhaps the most illustrious of the Queen's favorites, Robert Devereux, Earl of Essex, from the time when, less than twenty, he became the intimate of Elizabeth, who was fifty-three, until he was beheaded for high treason at the age of thirty-three. The personal side of their relations is always in the foreground, but interwoven at every point into a background made up of the issues of peace and war, the clash of creeds and economic interests, the rivalries, jealousies, and sycophancies of the great Lord Burghley, of his son, Sir Robert Cecil, and especially of Sir Francis Bacon.

ILLUSTRATIVE EXTRACTS

Some idea of the quality of the book may be gained from extracts. These are no purple patches, but typical of the entire book.

Soon there was no occasion for pushing Essex forward. It was plain to all—the handsome, charming youth, with his open manner, his boyish spirits, his words and looks of adoration, and his tall figure, and his exquisite hands, and the auburn hair on his head, that bent so gently downwards, had fascinated Elizabeth. The new star, rising with extraordinary swiftness, was suddenly seen to be shining alone in the firmament. The Queen and the Earl were never apart.

It was the age of *baroque*. . . Certainly no more *baroque* figure ever trod this earth than the supreme phenomenon of Elizabethanism—Elizabeth herself. . . Under the serried complexities of her raiment—the huge hoop, the stiff ruff, the swollen sleeves, the powdered pearls, the spreading, gilded gauzes—the form of the woman vanished, and men saw instead an image—magnificent, portentous, self-created an image of regality, which yet, by a miracle, was actually alive. . . Nor was it only her intellect that served her; it was her temperament as well. That, too—in its mixture of the masculine and femine, of vigor and sinuosity, of pertinacity and vacillation—was precisely what her case required. A deep instinct made it impossible for her to come to a fixed determination upon any subject whatever. Or, if she did, she immediately proceeded to contradict her resolution with the utmost violence, and, after that, to contradict her contradiction more violently still. . . Undoubtedly there was a touch of the sinister about her. One saw it in the movements of her extraordinarily long hands. . . Though she was infinitely subtle, she was not cruel; she was almost humane for her times; and her occasional bursts of savagery were the results of fear or temper.

I regret that space and the lack of single short passages prevent my quoting anything depicting Francis Bacon, whom Strachey represents as the villain of the tragedy, or Robert Cecil, Elizabeth's deformed Secretary, who "could but labor, and watch and wait." But I must quote the sentences describing the death of King Philip of Spain:

One thought alone troubled him: had he been remiss in the burning of heretics? He had burnt many, no doubt; but he might have burnt more. Was it because of this, perhaps, that he had not been quite as successful as he might have wished? . . . He could dictate no more, and sank into a tortured stupor. When he awoke, it was night and there was singing at the altar below him; a sacred candle was lighted and put into his hand, the flame, as he clutched it closer and closer, casting lurid shadows upon his face; and so, in ecstacy and in torment, in absurdity and in greatness, happy, miserable, horrible, and holy, King Philip went off, to meet the Trinity.

NICOLSON'S TENNYSON AND BYRON

Harold Nicolson has published a number of biographical works, but only two of them are well defined examples of the new biography. In his *Tennyson; Aspects of his Life, Character and Poetry,* published in 1923, he has made an important and fascinating contribution to the new style of interpretive biography, joining in the modern revolt against the Victorian idolatry of Tennyson. According to Nicolson's theory, "the essential inspiration of Tennyson was the inspiration of fear." "He was afraid of death, and sex, and God. And in all these matters he endeavored instinctively to sublimate his terrors by enunciating the beliefs which he would desire to feel, by dwelling upon the solutions by which he would like to be convinced." Altho Nicolson disavows the Freudian terminology, this case of wish fulfillment is a good example of the Freudianism which is so much in evidence in the new biography.

The other Nicolson book to be mentioned is his *Byron: the Last Journey,* published in 1924. This is a good example, so common in the new biography, of one in which a single brief phase of a man's life is so treated as to give a strong impression of his character. The book is based on newly discovered documents, which are quoted, and gives a brilliant, entertaining and amazingly vivid picture of Byron in the final Greek adventure. This book also illustrates another characteristic often found in the new biography. I refer to the use of the mental monologue or stream of consciousness, so often used in some modern novels, best exemplified in those of James Joyce. Strachey uses this device and Nicolson, probably Strachey's aptest pupil, uses it again and again. A good example of this is Nicolson's interpretation of Byron's

thoughts when the family of Leigh Hunt invades his
house at Genoa:

Leigh Hunt was Shelley's fault entirely: Shelley was like
that, he let one in for things. One would just mention an idea,
and expand it a little, and before one knew what had happened,
Shelley had shrilled off into another of his enthusiasms. That was
the worst of Shelley; he could never see the difference between
an idea and a proposal; obviously there was a very great difference.
Byron that hot night at Ravenna when they had sat up together
drinking gin and water, had merely suggested that, in certain
circumstances, it would be great fun if he and Shelley and Leigh
Hunt were all to edit a radical newspaper together from Italy,
which could be published by John Hunt in London. Shelley had
called it a "generous proposal"; it wasn't a proposal, it was only
an idea; on second thought it was a devilish bad idea. And there
was Shelley writing to him from Pisa saying "Poor Hunt is de-
lighted with your noble offer." Had Byron ever made an offer?
He certainly never intended to: at least not exactly an offer, only
an idea. And then before he could explain it away, there was
the Hunt family already embarked and well on their way to Italy.

Philip Guedalla is included because he, too, is a
voluminous practitioner of the new biography. His
earlier volumes, such as *Masters and Men* and *Supers
and Supermen* are lively studies of some great and
little figures, whom he uses as targets for his epi-
grams. They are highly spiced and abound in parody.
More serious are his *The Second Empire,* of France,
and *Fathers of the Revolution,* the latter including
French, English and American fathers. This book,
therefore, contains some "eminent Americans" to
match the "eminent Victorians" of Strachey and the
comparison is not unfavorable to the pupil. He has
also recently published *Bonnet and Shawl,* which he
calls "an album" in which he gives some sketch portraits of Jane Welsh Carlyle, Catherine Gladstone,
Mary Arnold, Mary Anne Disraeli, Emily Tennyson,
and Emily Palmerston and three ideal portraits of
the imaginary wives of Henry James, Swinburne and
the Goncourt brothers, that is, one for both of them.
The book on which his principal claim for considera
tion is based is his *Palmerston,* published in 1927.

This book is the result of prodigious research including the study of much unpublished material. It will be recalled that the documents have been or are to be published separately, so they do not encumber this single sprightly volume which gives no impression of the immense labor and research underlying it. The book is written with the charm, the wit, the satire and the irony that characterize the best of this school of writing. The personal interest, the human details, the vivid setting and the absence of moral, fascinate the reader and carry him from page to page.

MAUROIS THE BRILLIANT

I have already quoted the confession of faith of André Maurois as a modern biographer. His own two brilliant contributions to the new biography merit fuller attention than I can give them.

Ariel, the Life of Shelley (1924) is in form almost a novel, and reads as easily and as amusingly as a novel; but the facts, the words put in Shelley's mouth are true. The title expresses the author's conception of Shelley as more of an engaging sprite than a responsible human being; his absurdities, extravagances and complete impracticability are revealed with an irony that is sometimes cruel. There is little about his poetry, but much about his amours. Of Shelley's friends who figure in the narrative, Byron as Don Juan fares badly.

Disraeli; a Picture of the Victorian Age (1928) has been written with considerable artistry. It is a sympathetic view of Disraeli, who is interpreted as a sentimentalist and a romantic with an immense relish of life and a "long youthfulness of heart." Disraeli is so entertainingly and lightly portrayed as to make this one of the most readable if not one of the best biographies of the decade. Maurois has been

attacked as a plagiarist because of it, but he has
proved that he has made very wide study of many
books from which he has distilled this brief, vivid
portrait.

LUDWIG'S CONTRIBUTIONS

Emil Ludwig is an important member of the school
of new biographers. Of the six leaders included in
this paper he seems to be the most strongly influenced
by the Freudian psychology.

His last book to be published in English (other
than his *Son of Man,* a life of Jesus, which I shall
consider as falling outside the scope of this paper) is
his *Goethe: the History of a Man* (1928). This is,
however, one of his earlier books, first published in
1920 and but recently translated into English and
reduced to about one-half its original length. That
Freudianism dominates his conception of Goethe is
evident from his introduction in which he announces
that, "Here you will be a spectator of the sixty-yeared
battle which his Genius fought with his Daemon, and
from which he finally wrested a kind of tragic vic-
tory." The reader is never allowed to forget this Daemon thruout the course of the book. The Daemon
seems to be Goethe's emotional temperament, whereas
his Genius is his intellect. Ludwig is too much a
propagandist for his Daemon, dual personality theory
to be a scientific biographer.

Surely his rhapsodizing fancy outstrips even that
of Goethe himself, when he thus interprets him:

His existence was one long self-contradiction. He was sensual
and transcendental, amoral and Spinozaistic, all egotism and all
self-surrender, now delighting in companionship, now imperious
in his demand for solitude; today religiously, tomorrow cynically,
inclined; misanthropic, philanthropic, arrogant and kindly, patient
and impatient, sentimental and pornographic, absorbed in form or
intent on act, untamed and pedantic, a far-reaching thinker but
an instinctive doer, coldly objective yet essentially and passionate-

ly erratic, entirely masculine yet very feminine—a dual being, if
ever there was one; and so unlimited in scope that circumstance
would have its way with him whose avid thirst for all experience,
intent though it was on form and measure, found satisfaction in
one faith alone, and that faith he now shaped into verse:

"Call it Joy! Heart! Love! God!
For me there is no naming
Of this. We can but feel it."

His Bismarck

The central idea of Ludwig's *Bismarck, the Story
of a Fighter* (1927) is that Bismarck, the autocrat,
to the extent that he failed, did so because he failed to
keep in touch with his time and people thru current
literature and thru human contacts. He preferred to
think things out for himself and by himself and to
launch his decisions from the Olympian heights of
his master mind. He was petty and revengeful, did
not know how to convert enemies into friends, but always punished his enemies, thereby always gaining
greater enmity.

The *Wilhelm Hohenzollern* (1927) that Ludwig
portrays is not the redoubtable war lord, but a cow-
ardly neurotic, with an inferiority complex due to
his withered arm. All of his braggadocio and self
display were part of a protective mechanism arising
from his inferiority complex. Ludwig makes him out
a rather despicable figure.

Napoleon's Pride of Family

Ludwig's *Napoleon* (1926) is not the world conqueror, but Napoleon the Bonaparte, interested fundamentally in the aggrandizement of his family. His
heredity is stressed in that he derived his strength
from his redoubtable mother, Letizia, who outlived
him many years and for whom he had the greatest rev-
erence. Ludwig features up the family councils he
held on many affairs. His pride of family was further

shown by his consuming ambition for a legitimate
son who should succeed him and establish a dynasty.
The book contains so few facts of public historical
importance that the reader needs at hand for reference a history of the Napoleonic era. So far as Ludwig's book is concerned, the reader would gain almost no idea of Napoleon the great conqueror, the
maker and unmaker of states, the creator of a code
of laws. He emphasizes Napoleon's belief in his own
destiny as a favorite of fortune.

BRADFORD'S PORTRAITS

The last of the half-dozen leading biographers to
be considered in this paper is our own Gamaliel Bradford, who calls himself a psychographer and who has
produced no less than thirteen volumes of biography
that are properly classifiable in this literary *genre*.
Indeed, H. L. Mencken claims that Bradford "in-
vented the formula" long before it was followed by
Lytton Strachey, tho he does not accuse the latter
"of lifting the scheme from Bradford." Another
critic writing in the *Virginia Quarterly Review* hotly
contests Mencken's attempt "to group Bradford and
Strachey together," claiming for Bradford difference
in method, particularly stressing his "entire disregard of chronology" as followed by the other members of the school. In his own critical writings,
however, Bradford seems to group himself with this
school by his appreciative reviews or other favorable
mentions of Strachey and Maurois.

The body of Bradford's biographical writing is
large and excellent enough to justify an entire separate paper. I can do scarcely more than mention
titles. In the case of most of his books each consists
of seven or eight short biographies, and his scheme
of psychographic portraiture seems better adapted to

small than to large canvasses. His volumes devoted to groups are entitled *Confederate Portraits* (1918); *Union Portraits* (1916); *Portraits of Women* (1916); *A Naturalist of Souls* (1917); *American Portraits, 1875-1900* (1921); *Damaged Souls* (1923); *Bare Souls* (1924), and *Wives* (1925). The volumes which he has devoted to single characters are entitled, *Lee, the American* (1912); *The Soul of Samuel Pepys* (1924); *Darwin* (1926); *D. L. Moody, a Worker in Souls* (1927). Altho Bradford's psychographic method is always the same, each portrait is an individual creation. His portraits are in the highest degree analytical of the inner motives and characters of his subjects. He has a real passion for distilling the final essence of the man or woman, writer, or artist, or statesman. Each sketch leaves with the reader a distinct picture of a real and interesting personality.

Is the New Biography New?

We have now considered the theories of these six leading new biographers in justification of their method of biographical writing and something also of their work. We have seen that somewhat generally they consciously hold the theory that only in their time and by them has the true art of biographical portraiture been discovered.

Is it true that this method is new or that the older biographers ignored "the man" or were so oblivious to personality? Is the so-called new method sound and is it likely in the long run to produce good results when followed by the rank and file of biographical writers?

Is the new biography really new? The authors of the *Book of Job* and of the *Book of Esther* were psychological biographers, as were Plutarch, Mon-

taigne, Voltaire and Sainte-Beuve. Macaulay sometimes employed this method, likewise Lord Charnwood in his *Life of Lincoln.* Tho the method is different, who will say that "the man" in all of his greatness and pettiness does not emerge from Boswell's
Johnson or Lockhart's *Scott* or Moore's *Byron* or
George Henry Lewes' *Goethe,* or even from Monypenny and Buckle's *Disraeli,* with its six fat volumes?

The sound biographer must always combine the
functions of chronicler and interpreter. The real
difference between the so-called new and the old rests
largely in the placing of emphasis on one or the other
of these two functions. The older style biographer
largely contents himself with setting forth a chronicle, not simply of external facts, but also of moods,
impulses, motives and spiritual struggles, but leaves
to the reader the cooperative exercise of his own
mind in drawing the conclusions implied by what is
set forth. Or he may make interpretation his chief
concern, offering a minimum of chronicle and setting
forth his subject in the colors that his own special
scrutiny of the facts justifies. If we have confidence
in the insight and the spirit of the biographer, his
work will approve itself to us. These depend on the
keenness of his perceptions and the manner of their
employment. If he is kindly and genial one kind of
biography results; if cynical or malicious another
emerges.

Special Thesis Biographers

In the cases under review the results have been
varied; many of them highly satisfactory. But it
will have been noted that these new biographers are
special thesis biographers. They make full use of the
full length biographies—without them they would be
lost. But having laid down their thesis, they have

an inevitable tendency or temptation to pick and choose what will best fit into their preconceived ideas, suppressing a little here, heightening effects there and always choosing the telling, the brilliant, the piquant. It is, therefore, charged that biographers of this school are more eager to find a formula than they are to find the facts.

The danger, therefore, is that less capable and less conscientious men who observe the popularity, the color, the readability of this style of biography, who note also the external technique, will use it to the debasing of biography. In their hands it becomes a vehicle for the so-called "debunking" of the great, for the cheap rewriting, the popularization and the jazzing up of biography. One critic, in commenting on a horde of recent biographies, all written in this new style or at least according to the superficial aspects of this formula, says that they are not true biographies at all, but are the work of second rate novelists or first rate journalists, who have simply rewritten earlier biographies to make them picturized and readable. Some members of this school specialize in pulling down idols from their pedestals, while others dramatically serve up the scandalous and the unsavory. In doing so they make use of the jargon of psychoanalysis in their reading of character.

FICTIONIZED BIOGRAPHY

Another tendency in such biographical writing is its drift toward the novel. The new order of biography too often involves such a romanticizing of biographical materials as to bring it perilously near to fiction. It is only a step from Maurois's *Ariel*, which claims to be a biography of Shelley, to E. Barrington's *Glorious Apollo* (Byron) or to her *The Divine Lady* (Emma, Lady Hamilton) or to C. E.

Bechofer-Roberts' *This Side Idolatry* (Dickens). The author of the last wanted to write a professed biography, but was prevented from publishing the documents and so put forth his book as a novel, with the purpose of pulling Dickens down from his pedestal. As a result we have a sort of bastard biography that is a blend of fact, comment and criticism dressed up with conversation that makes it in form fiction, if intended as biography. Too often such books of fiction, which contain at least a modicum of fact, are accepted as veritable biography.

In order not to close on too pessimistic a note, I wish to point out that at least these new, brief, vivid, readable biographies get read in much greater numbers than do the full length biographies, and by readers who would be repelled at the inordinate length of the two- or three-volume and especially of the six-volume biographies. Not infrequently also these same readers end by turning to the great, full-length, indispensable biographies that most of us prize so highly.

THE CHOICE OF RELIGIOUS AND THEOLOGICAL BOOKS FOR PUBLIC LIBRARIES [1]

(Altho the examples given in this paper have to a considerable extent been superseded in the lapse of 25 years, yet the principles stated hold good today.)

In the 1893 edition of the *A. L. A. Cataloy* 220 out of 5230 titles fell under the group of Religion and Theology, or 4 per cent of the whole number; in the 1904 edition 319 out of 7520 titles, or 4.2 per cent were included in this group.[2] Taking into consideration the great variety of subjects upon which books are written and the enormous yearly output of books in the classes of such popular interest as fiction, biography, travel, history, fine arts, useful arts, and general literature, this 4 per cent is perhaps a fair conservative estimate of what is due religious literature. It would seem, however, that public interest in religious and theological subjects might easily justify a larger percentage, even allowing for the fact that with so many persons the spoken sermon seems almost entirely to preclude the necessity of the religious book. If and when such is the case, the public library should allow a more liberal proportion to religious works than is represented by these figures. Broadly speaking, the department of religion and theology in a public library should be as well equipped as any other department, and only the reasons which operate to restrict the collections in other departments should be valid in the religious

[1] Read before the Library Department of the Religious Education Association, Boston, February 15, 1905.

[2] In the 1926 edition of the *A.L.A. Catalog*, out of 10,295 titles, 340 or 3.3 per cent were in this group.

department, namely paucity of funds and in some cases lack of use.

With the adoption of a principle of proportion, the question of choice of books arises. In general it may be said that the same rules of choice should be adopted that apply to books in other classes, and thus in theory the question raised by the title of this paper is disposed of. But in practice difficulties often arise in choosing for purchase religious, and especially theological books, or in deciding concerning their acceptance as gifts, difficulties which do not arise in connection with books of other classes. In my own case I have often found it necessary to give the matter some thought because of objections which were raised by prominent and educated users of the library, and in several cases by trustees, to the presence of certain books in the library, and more rarely, to the absence of others from its shelves. Numbers of individual cases which have come up for decision have led to the adoption of a rather general policy governing the subject. In the first place, the standpoint of the public library in judging of any books, even religious books, is not primarily religious but literary and educational. Its standards are those arising from educational aims, or should more or less closely approximate such standards. The public library is not irreligious or even non-religious, as I said before this department last year, but it is simply lacking in religious color. This does not mean that as an institution it is not interested in religion. Religion is one of the great facts of human life. Its forms of expression are varied, extending all the way from totemism to a purely ethical religion. But in some form it seems a necessity to mankind, and is practically universal. Examined extensively, therefore, as one of the important facts of humanity, it is entitled to respect and consideration. Also, religion is one form of education, education of the spiritual side of man, and the history of religion has in some ages seemed to be inseparable from the history of education. The library therefore is rightly interested in religion and calls upon it for religious books are just as deserving of consideration as calls for poetry, for fiction, for philosophy, for fine arts.

NEVER PARTISAN

But, tho recognizing this almost universal religious need and aiming as fully as possible to aid in its satisfaction, the library can in no way be a partisan. Since religion today is not a unit, but is manifested under various forms, the library cannot cooperate with the adherents of one form while discriminating against those of another. Its shelves must fairly represent, in addition to the broad field of religious literature devoid of sectarian bias, many different and often antagonistic beliefs, according to the demand of readers. If some one asks why a certain volume of an anti-Catholic tone is allowed in the library, the answer must be that the library collection is not one-sided, that it represents many differing views. Or if some opponent of Christian Science objects to the presence in the library of Christian Science magazines and books, the obvious reply is that Christian Scientists are part of the community to which the library ministers and so must justly be considered.

In the selection of reference works, a broadly inclusive policy should be followed. All the leading works on religion and religions should be purchased, from those on the earliest pagan religions to those on the leading Christian and non-Christian religions of the present day. Encyclopedias, dictionaries, com-

mentaries, concordances, and bibliographies, those of
earlier publication so far as they are still of value,
and those of recent date, the most conservative and
the most liberal, should all find a place in the public
library. Such works may well be included as M'Clin-
tock and Strong's *Cyclopaedia of Religious Literature;* the series of dictionaries by the late William
Smith and his associates; Hastings' *Dictionary of
the Bible,* based on recent conservative criticism; and
the *Encyclopaedia Biblica,* setting forth the most
advanced criticism of today; Lange's commentaries,
representing the old, and the new *International Critical Commentary,* representing the latest biblical criticism; Cruden's, Strong's, and Young's concordances;
the new edition of Bliss's *Cyclopaedia of Missions,*
Julian's *Dictionary of Hymnology,* Brewer's *Dictionary of Miracles,* Schaff's *Creeds of Christendom,* and
Brewster's new work on the *Saints and Festivals* of
the *Christian Church,* as well as the *Jewish Encyclopaedia* and Hughes' *Dictionary of Islam.* A liberal
selection from the various sectarian encyclopedias
and the religious year books, almanacs, and director-
ies published by various denominations should also
be purchased, even those of denominations having
few adherents, if there is any demand for them. The
purchase of all such purely sectarian works will, of
course, be regulated by the demand and by available
funds. In addition to these, the more important
Sunday-school lesson helps, which are almost always
much used, should form a part of the reference collection. The Bible, in the King James and revised
versions, the Douay Bible, and a polyglot edition
should also find a place in the reference department.

Pursuing the same general policy with regard to
periodicals, the public library may properly be a
subscriber to a leading journal of each denomination

which possesses any considerable number of adherents in the community. Many denominations are glad to present to the library their leading periodical. Of course this is done in the spirit of propaganda and the magazine may then be considered a tract, which some libraries are unwilling to accept. For the sake of consistency they are therefore inclined to refuse admittance to all such denominational periodicals. If church journals are used and enjoyed by readers, however, as they undoubtedly are, there seems to be as good reason for supplying them as for supplying the various technical and trade journals.

Lives of Christ

Of religious histories and biographies the public library should of course have a liberal supply. All the standard lives of Christ should be included, regardless of their doctrinal point of view, and new works as they appear should be purchased on their merits. The best works on the various ethnic religions would also form part of a well-rounded collection.

There is a large number of books which are thoroly religious in character, without being doctrinal or controversial, such as works on practical Christianity and general religious thought and life, as well as books of devotion, meditation, and some volumes of sermons. Concerning such books there is usually little difficulty in deciding. They should be purchased with discrimination, according to the demand for them, and according to their general literary excellence and the value of their thought.

Religious books of a decidedly doctrinal and controversial nature form the class regarding which there are likely to be differences of opinion. Many such books are offered to the library as gifts, just as denominational magazines are offered, by persons who wish to propagate certain doctrines. In general I should say that all such doctrinal books which come to the library as gifts should be accepted, provided they do not violate all the canons of good taste and are not in thought indecent or subversive of morals. Of course, any book which is illiterate or vulgar in expression, coarse or immoral in thought, according to generally accepted standards of morality, and cheap and tasteless in printing, binding, etc., should be politely declined, always with the true reason, tactfully and perhaps not always fully explained. But a book should not be declined simply because the librarian or some of his associates or the trustees of the library do not agree with the opinions expressed in it; and in declining a gift for any of the reasons already mentioned, the librarian should be careful to make clear to the donor that it is not declined because of its doctrines. It is hardly necessary to say that to insure fairness this policy of acceptance of gifts must be carried out in all cases. A book advocating the doctrine of eternal punishment must not be accepted today, and one on universal salvation be refused tomorrow. Someone may object that even if this policy is consistently carried out still unfairness arises, because the gifts to a library will undoubtedly not include books on all doctrines. There will be a larger representation of the works of the denominations in which the spirit of propaganda is strongest. But a reply to such an objection is that any member of the community who wishes to insure the presence in the library of a book supporting his especial belief may present such a book to the library, or, if he does not wish to present it, he may request its purchase. The privileges of

presenting books to the library and of requesting
the purchase of books are, or should be, open to all.
The plan of putting a book-plate with the name of
the donor in each book given to the library is a good
one.   This will often explain its presence in the library.   The library, however, does not, either in the
case of gifts or of purchases, assume the responsibility for all opinions expressed in its volumes.   Its
office is not to direct the thought of its patrons, but
to supply the means for the forming of independent
thought.   As a matter of policy, in order to assure
every citizen of the absolute impartiality of the library, it is well to secure for the library a representative collection of the literature, especially on
its historical side, of each denomination having a
number of adherents in the community.

CONTROVERSIAL BOOKS

The selection of doctrinal and controversial books
for purchase should be guided by the same standards
of taste that prevail in the case of gifts, that is, by
demand and by the condition of the book fund.   A
library would hardly buy an expensive work on the
creed of some small and obscure sect, represented
perhaps by only three or four persons in the community.   Nor would it perhaps be able to purchase
many works of such detailed and scholarly criticism
as would be of use to only a few theological scholars,
tho where the fund is sufficient, even such scholarly
works may very properly be purchased.

The question of what to purchase and what not
to purchase in the class of so-called religious fiction
is one that arises almost every week.   Here it is best
if possible to eliminate the religious question altogether and to judge each novel as if it had no religious motive.   If it is absolute trash of course it

will be rejected; if it has some literary merit it may
be accepted. Decisions in individual cases will depend entirely on the attitude of the library toward
the fiction question in general, on whether its policy
is to exclude all but the best, or to purchase rather
liberally from the ever-ready supply of new novels.
But whatever the policy, a novel should not be either
accepted or rejected solely because its theme is a
certain religious doctrine.

Religious historical fiction of a fairly high liter-
ary standard is always a valuable part of the library.
Such books as Wallace's *Ben Hur,* E. E. Hale's *In
His name,* Mrs. Charles' *Chronicles of the Schönberg-
Cotta Family,* and *The Early Dawn,* and Amelia
Barr's *Friend Olivia* are distinctly educational.
Books, too, with a general religious motive, such as
Bullen's *Apostles of the Southeast,* Gordon's *Black
Rock* and *Sky Pilot,* and most of George Macdonald's
books find many readers and should have their place
in the library. And in the realm of doctrinal fiction
such books as *Robert Elsmere* and *Helbeck of Ban-
nisdale, John Ward, Preacher, John Inglesant, Yeast*
and *Paris, Rome,* and *Lourdes* will establish themselves entirely apart from their religious themes,
whereas there will always be grave doubts in the
minds of many about the literary value of Marie
Corelli's *Sorrows of Satan,* Voynich's *Gadfly,* and
John Chester's *Ruth the Christian Scientist,* tho
their religious or anti-religious doctrines should not
cause their exclusion.

The selection of all religious books, especially of
all doctrinal and controversial books, if not made
by the librarian himself, should of course be en-
trusted to a person who is sufficiently broadminded
so that his literary judgment will not be affected by
his own religious bias.

In the children's department of a library it seems to me that a somewhat different policy should be pursued with regard to religious books. Adults either have already formed their religious opinions when they come to the library and know what they wish to read, or they are of sufficient maturity to be entitled to a free selection of material to aid in forming their opinions. It is different with children. They have undeveloped but impressionable minds and tho the public library very appropriately aims to form in them good literary taste, it has nothing to do with forming a religious bias. It is perhaps also unfair to parents to furnish their children with material for forming religious beliefs contrary to what they wish, tho it may justly be said that parents should themselves supervise the reading of their children. Many parents do not do this, however. Therefore it seems to me that the children's room of a public library is no place for religious literature of a doctrinal or controversial character.

BOOKS FOR CHILDREN

The religious books that may properly be found in the children's room of the public library are those of a very general religious character, such as Bible stories told in a simple way, lives of Christ arranged for children, and that great favorite of nearly all children—*Pilgrim's Progress*. The list of books for boys and girls prepared by the Brooklyn Public Library contains only fourteen titles under Ethics and Religion. That prepared for the Iowa Library Commission by Miss Moore, children's librarian of the Pratt Institute Free Library, contains only eleven under that heading. Both lists include Foster's *Story of the Bible,* Eva March Tappan's *The Christ Story,* the *Bible for Children* arranged from the King

James version, with an introduction by Bishop Potter, and *Pilgrim's Progress*. The Iowa Library Commission list also includes the Old and New Testament stories in the *Modern Reader's Bible*. Such books as Coffin's *Story of Liberty*, which, aside from its historically inaccurate statements and "snap" judgments, is venomous against the Catholic Church, might fairly be excluded from the children's department of a public library. There are many other children's books of this class, as well as the enormously large group which may be termed "namby-pamby," all of which are better excluded. A small number of titles of well-selected books, and those often duplicated, forms a better religious collection for a children's room than a more extensive list.

The views expressed in this paper are of course the individual opinions of the writer. If the Library Department of the Religious Education Association has adequate reasons for its existence, and I believe it has, one of those reasons I conceive to be that by associated effort it may improve the religious and theological departments of libraries, especially of public libraries. To accomplish that end I believe it is of the first importance to discover the principles of selection of books in this field, and I therefore offer this tentative contribution.

SOME ASPECTS OF BOOK REVIEWING [1]

The members of the Literary Society are interested in and probably habitually read many book reviewing journals. The authors among us probably watch to see whether their books have intelligent and adequate treatment at the hands of the critics. Most of our members have, no doubt, done some reviewing. As readers, all of us follow some one or several literary journals, pages or columns, for their news, their comment, their interpretation and their criticism of the new books. What do we, whether as authors or as readers look for in such reviews? What do we, when called on to write, try to put into such reviews? Do we find what we look for? What is lacking? What way lies improvement? It is the aim of this paper to offer some comments on the art of book reviewing, particularly on the contemporary practice of that art, in the hope of indicating some sound principles, and also in the further hope of arousing some discussion.

The subject may perhaps be best approached by making a somewhat cursory survey of current book reviewing, chiefly in America, with some glances toward the past.

There has been a notable increase in the attention paid to books in the press. There is hardly a daily paper in the country that does not treat of books, either in a Sunday supplement or special feature or in a column once or twice or several times a week on its editorial page. Among the best examples are the *Book Review* of the Sunday *New York Times* and *Books* of the Sunday *New York Herald-Tribune*.

[1] Read before the Washington Literary Society, January 26, 1924.

Three of the great monthly magazines have within recent years added book departments, including the delightful *As I Like It* of William Lyon Phelps in *Scribner's,* Harry Hansen's *Among the New Books* in *Harper's* (from which consideration of Harper publications is excluded) and the *Bookshelf* of the *Atlantic.* Then there are the old time *Nation,* with viewpoint changed to radicalism in recent years; *The New Republic,* able and liberal; *The Bookman,* no longer very effective or interesting (at least to me); *The Saturday Review of Literature,* progressive and devoted exclusively to books; and the *American Mercury.* There must have been a demand for these new features and these new publications or they would not have been produced. It is gratifying to observe these new evidences of a widening interest in books, particularly at a time when it is popularly supposed that automobiling, the movies, the radio, and other non-literary interests have absorbed all the remaining leisure in our speeded-up lives and have left no time for reading. A reading of the book news and reviews implies a reading of the books mentioned in them.

NEWSPAPER BOOK COLUMNS

Such reviews or comments are of varying types which fall into several overlapping and not very well defined classes.

The simplest form of book review, not necessarily the poorest or least effective in its influence in affording guidance for readers toward good reading tastes, is the newspaper column of book news, chat or gossip. Since it is a part of a daily newspaper it goes into most homes of the community and so is presumably read by large numbers of persons who would never think of getting a distinctively literary journal, largely devoted to book reviews. Such a feature may be written by a reporter at odd moments between assignments to fires, crimes or deaths (this perhaps in a country newspaper), or may be prepared by a competent editor having ripe literary culture. It may consist of verbatim reprints of publishers' puffing notes and "blurbs"; or it may be written as the result of definite critical examination of the books, and sometimes perhaps it may grow out of an editor's regular leisurely reading of current literature. It may cover the books that accident or predigested notes bring to the office or it may result from careful winnowing of the best wheat from the superabundant chaff. In most cases, however, the work for such book features, when it is conscientiously and adequately performed, consists simply in giving the public the results of expert book tasting.

Much is often made of the well-known fact that reviewers do not always read, or at least read thoroly, all the books they review. On this point let Arnold Bennett be quoted. As is well known Mr. Bennett writes several novels, short stories, plays and essays every year. At odd moments he also writes many book reviews. He says:

> The sense of justice of the man in the street is revolted. "You do not read through all the books that you pretend to criticize?" he hints. I have never known a reviewer to answer this insinuation straight-forwardly in print; but I will answer it. "No, I do not." And the man in the street says, shocked: "You are unjust." And I reply: "Not at all. I am merely an expert . . ."

Mr. Bennett goes on to describe how he can taste and test a novel in five minutes, judging it from title-page, names of the author and publisher, etc. He continues:

> The very chapter headings deliver a message of style. The narrative everywhere discloses to me the merits and defects of the writer; no author ever lived who could write a page without giving himself away. The whole book, open it where I will, is

murmurous with indications for me. In nine cases out of ten, to read them through would be not a work of supererogation—it would be a sinful waste of time on the part of a professional reviewer. The majority of novels . . . holds no surprise for the professional reviewer . . . There remains the work of the true artist, the work that the reviewer himself admires and enjoys, say one book in fifty, or one in a hundred. The reviewer reads that through.

Before leaving this type of review I desire also to quote Theodore Roosevelt, the omnivorous reader, on current books and the reviewing of them:

"Each reader," he says, "must settle for himself . . . the dividing line between (1) not knowing anything about current books, and (2) swamping one's soul in the sea of vapidity which overwhelms him who reads *only* 'the last new book.'

ROOSEVELT ON NEW BOOKS

"To me the heading employed by some reviewers when they speak of 'books of the week' comprehensively damns both the books themselves and the reviewer who is willing to notice them. I would much rather see the heading 'books of the year before last.' A book of the year before last which is still worth noticing would probably be worth reading; but one only entitled to be called a book of the week had better be tossed into the waste basket at once. Still, there are plenty of new books which nevertheless are worth more or less careful reading; partly because it is well to know something of what especially interests the mass of our fellows, and partly because these books, although of ephemeral worth, may really set forth something genuine in fashion which for the moment stirs the hearts of all of us."

Altho Mr. Roosevelt started out with being hard on the reviewer who deals with the "books of the week," he after all found a place for him, which is to make tentative and preliminary selections, from the great mass of published books, of the few most promising candidates for present consideration and perhaps for continued life.

The type of review already mentioned, the crisp, pointed note, whatever its other qualities or defects, sticks close to its subject—the book under treatment. At the opposite extreme is, or rather was, for it is becoming obsolete, the elaborate review or essay which took a book for its text and then speedily forgot the book in a brand new treatment of the subject. Sometimes the book died and the essay lived on as literature. More often the book survived in spite of the weight of dullness of the ponderous essay which threatened to drag it down. The best and preeminently successful examples of such essay-reviews are Macaulay's *Essays,* most of which appeared originally as book reviews. Nowadays the essay-review is all but out of fashion; the essay stands by itself instead of basing its theme on recent publications. The type comes nearest to surviving in the *Edinburgh* and the *Quarterly Reviews,* in which most of the articles are based on groups of several recent books on a given subject.

Another somewhat similar type of review, now practically obsolete, was that represented by the exhaustive reviews appearing about twenty-five years ago every Sunday in the *New York Sun* over the initials of Mayo W. Hazeltine. These reviews fairly gutted the books under consideration, chiefly histories and biographies. Altho it used to be said that one of these reviews insured the sale of several hundred copies of the book, I could never understand why it should have that effect, since in most cases the summary was so complete as to make it unnecessary to read the book. Nowadays, such reviews, if they survive at all, are to be found only in the specialized journals.

The review by the superior person is likewise nearly obsolete. The best known examples were reviews that appeared in the *New York Evening Post* and its weekly edition, *The Nation*, in the days of Godkin and Garrison. They were elaborate and capable, but frequently the anonymous reviewers took no pains to conceal their convictions that they could write much better books on the subjects, if they but chose to do so, than the books they reviewed; that the present ones would perhaps answer as stop-gaps until such times as they saw fit to publish. Usually such a review closed with a rather formidable list of mistakes, both of statements in the book and of bad proofreading, misspelled proper names, wrongly placed accents and especially with a comment on the inadequacy of the index. If no index at all were supplied, Jovian wrath was expressed. Remarks on indexes appeared so consistently in such reviews, written by various authors, as to make it seem likely that they were all added by Wendell Phillips Garrison, the literary editor, since he long advocated a proposal that books of information lacking indexes should be denied the privilege of copyright.

Still another type of review, also largely obsolete, was the rather narrow-minded and prejudiced review, often venomous and frequently uncomprehending. Such were frequently found in the·early English reviews, the *Edinburgh*, the *Quarterly*, *Blackwood's*, and others. Witness the *Edinburgh* which pronounced Southey as "nothing less than a champion and apostle of a new sect of poets—all dissenters from the established system in poetry and criticism." The *Edinburgh* protested against the "representation of vulgar manners in vulgar language," preferring the

classical Milton. It was in the *Edinburgh* too that
Jeffrey reviewed Wordsworth's *Excursion,* beginning
with the words: "This will never do." And a little
later Croker wrote for the *Edinburgh* the article on
Keats that has popularly but erroneously been held
responsible for his death. Tennyson was likewise
ridiculed in the *Edinburgh.* It was in *Blackwood's*
that Lockhart published his virulent attack on Leigh
Hunt and the Cockney school of poetry, including the
"minor adherents" of the school, "the Shelleys,
the Keats's" and others. In this period it was not
uncommon to use such phrases as "contemptible
scribbling puppy" and "purveyor of sedition and
heresy." Of these reviews Andrew Lang has written:

MALEVOLENT CRITICS

There was a time when reviewers loved to trample on the
young—on Keats, or on Tennyson. Misdeeds of this kind . . . are
remembered, but it is forgotten that even these malevolent critics
often did hit the palpable blots of their victims, and that their
victims amended their ways. In the later editions of Tennyson . . .
the points which the reviewers most assailed were altered or
expunged. The critics had been right in detail, though grotesquely
wrong in tone and spirit.

It was in this same period that Walter Scott wrote
for the *Quarterly* his review of Jane Austen's *Emma*
which gave her encouragement to continue to write.
Scott also reviewed (anonymously) his own *Tales of
My Landlord* and commented dispassionately on certain of its defects.

But Andrew Lang points out that even at that
period "critics have helped to make or to accelerate
the making of the fortunes of authors much more frequently than they have crushed them," and that not
all writers feared adverse criticism. For example,
Dr. Johnson expected to be attacked for his *Lives of
the Poets.* "However," said he, "I would rather be

attacked than unnoticed; for the worst thing you can do to an author is to be silent as to his works."

Bernard Shaw satirized modern examples of prejudiced reviews in *Fanny's First Play*. Tho it is of a play that the view is given, the same attitude of mind sometimes holds in the case of views on books. It will be remembered that one of the critics who came to review the play asked:

> But is it a good play? That's a simple question.

To which this reply was given:

> Simple enough when you know. If it's by a good author, it's a good play, naturally. That stands to reason. Who is the author? Tell me that; and I'll place the play for you to a hair's breadth.

And again:

> But what merits can it have except the author's merits?

MALADROIT REVIEWS

While enumerating the undesirable types of reviews we should not forget the maladroit review, usually written by the amateur and most commonly to be found in the provincial paper. Such a review, if of a novel, is very thoro in its retailing of the story, giving away the plot so completely as effectively to kill all possible desire for reading the book.

Tho it does not form a coordinate type, some mention should be made of the signed review, which fortunately is much more in use in recent years. Formerly most book reviewing in newspapers and general critical journals was anonymous, but there is a growing tendency to have reviews signed by initials easily identified, or to publish reviews by literary critics and scholars with well established reputations. That is now the regular practice in the case of most of the longer reviews in such critical journals as the *Book*

Review of the *New York Times,* the *Nation,* the *New Republic* and the *Saturday Review of Literature.* Reverting to the quotation from Bernard Shaw, a good book review is not necessarily assured when you know the name of the reviewer. However, the chances of literary log-rolling are less than under the plan of anonymous reviewing. This plan promises the double guarantee of editorial responsibility for choosing a competent reviewer and of the reviewer's sense of responsibility to his own reputation, to the writer of the book, probably a colleague in his own science or craft, and to the readers of his review. If it is thought that writing over one's name is likely to prevent sufficiently drastic treatment in the case of a poor book, it may be replied that any reviewer may decline such an assignment. If all decline and the book is unnoticed, so much the better.

SIGNED REVIEWS

The signing of reviews, now a growing custom in general and non-technical journals, is almost universal in specialized publications, that is, those devoted to history, economics, sociology, science, pure and applied, business affairs, the fine arts and the professions. Scholars and specialists must of course follow reviews of books in their own fields and the general reader would do well to seek out the reviews in such journals when his own reading leads him into specialized fields. Such reviews are by specialists for specialists and so may sometimes be found tough reading. Now that these same specialists are being drawn on to write in general journals and therefore in untechnical language, the general reader is greatly the gainer. Incidentally, also, the reviewer and the reviewed are gainers by the process of bringing the specialized book to the attention of a wider and non-technical audience.

In the field of book reviewing, I venture to mention a publication, edited primarily for librarians, which has a growing use on the part of others and deserves still wider use. I refer to the *Book Review Digest*. Published monthly and cumulated into annual volumes, and issued for more than twenty-five years, this journal by summaries, digests and quotations regularly from the book reviews in more than sixty general and specialized publications, and occasionally from others, brings together in convenient form the most important reviews of current literature. By juxtaposition of favorable and unfavorable reviews, various and diverse opinions are correlated, so that the best available published judgments on any given book are brought together in usable form. This enables the reader to arrive at a consensus of the opinions of those best qualified to speak.

It is time to draw a distinction between book reviewing and literary criticism. This has perhaps best been done by Professor Brander Matthews who has worked to good purpose in both fields. He has often made the point that criticism devotes itself to the evaluation of the fixed stars of the past, whereas book reviewing concerns itself with the more or less nebulous or meteoric visitors of the present day. Employing another figure, he assigns to the book reviewer the task of dealing with diamonds in the rough, including those that are mere paste, and with gold bars, including those that are simply "gold bricks." He therefore concludes that "criticism ... is a department of literature, and book reviewing is (and must be) a department of journalism." "The great critics," he continues, "are so esteemed partly because they perceived this distinction, and the good book reviewers are good because they also perceive it. The task of the book reviewer, even if it is humble, is honorable; and it is his privilege to point out to the readers of the periodical to which he contributes what seem to him at the moment the merits and the demerits of such contemporary books as he may think important enough or significant enough to deserve careful consideration."

Granting this difference in function between the critic and the reviewer, in which the former attempts to fix the more or less final place in literature of the books of the past, whereas the latter tries to make tentative estimates of the literature of the present, none the less to do capable current book reviewing it seems to me necessary that the reviewer must have very much the same qualifications and equipment, educational and temperamental, as his elder brother the critic. He too must have a foundation of broad and deep culture, a ripe knowledge of the best standards, combined with a discerning open-mindedness for new forms of literary expression. Only so may we expect to have book reviewing that is worth paper and ink and the time of the reader.

What are some of the qualities and standards necessary alike to good criticism and good book reviewing? Inasmuch as this is a question of esthetics which has occupied the attention of philosophers and critics from Aristotle to the present, I can obviously only offer a very few of the opinions of those who have given attention to the subject and in doing so I shall draw chiefly from writers on what is called "the new criticism."

From Arnold Bennett, whom I have already quoted, I find this significant sentence:

Of late years I have come to the conclusion that the chief characteristic of all bad reviewing is the absence of genuine conviction, of a message, of a clear doctrine; the incompetent reviewer has to invent his opinions.

From Robert Morss Lovett, formerly professor in the University of Chicago, and now one of the editors of the *New Republic,* I cull these sentences and parts of sentences, found in his answer to the question: What is criticism?

WHAT IS CRITICISM?

It is a commonplace that a leading characteristic of the world today is the vast popularization of the arts of expression. To this democracy, literature has succumbed . . . No longer do writers form a caste apart, an institution devoted to the production of masterpieces . . . On the contrary in these days of popular education everyone writes or threatens to do so, and measures success . . . by the unfit and vast assembly of readers scattered over the whole world who for a week or a month may be held by the charm of a "best seller . . ." Everbody reads; and supplying reading matter to an immense and voracious public has become a business like supplying it with clothes and food. In these circumstances the function of criticism becomes one of immense importance . . . I believe the critic's chief occupation should be with himself. His first duty is to save his own soul. And this he will most surely accomplish by divesting himself of preoccupation and prejudices . . . He will aid the public not by imposing impressions of his own or theories of other men upon it, but by arousing it to reaction on its own account. For "The Aim of Criticism is to make every man his own critic."

Stressing the need for style, Professor William P. Trent, of Columbia, says:

There will always be persons who will care more for the subject-matter of a book than for the style in which it is written; yet we should none the less insist that it is the duty of every man to fit himself to tell a good style from a bad, to enjoy an excellent style, and to eschew, whenever it is possible, the books that are clumsily written.

The new criticism rejects alike the academic or objective method, the esthetic or dogmatic method, the impressionistic or subjective method, and substitutes for all these earlier methods that of interpretation. According to Edward Garnett, son of Dr. Richard Garnett, the well known English critic, the duty of the contemporary critic is described as follows:

He cannot hope to do more than fix a provisional value on the literature of his day. But his aim must surely be to discover in the great mass of literary "matter" the fresh creative spirits bringing new illuminations, new valuations into literature and life . . . He aims at justice, . . . and though he rarely attains it, perhaps his verdict on the newcomers, whom he greets, is about as useful as that pronounced by the academic critic upon the ages which have fled far from him."

Of what then does good book reviewing consist and what are some of the marks of a good book review? Before making direct answer to that question and closing my paper, I wish to give a few "Don'ts for reviewers" that occur to me:

DON'TS FOR REVIEWERS

1. Don't think it necessary to review all books that come to the editorial table. For great numbers of them mere listing, a sort of combination literary birth and death notice, is all that they deserve, or more.

2. Don't write reviews with an eye toward the publisher's advertising. Tho the immediate purpose of securing the advertisement may be accomplished, the confidence of readers is ultimately undermined and your reviews are discredited.

3. Don't withhold praise or blame from a book because a more highly placed critic writes counter to your convictions. You are just as likely to be right as he. But don't discover swans in all the geese that ride the stream.

4. Don't use such expressions as "undeniable charm of style," "notable contribution to contemporary thought," " there is not a dull page from cover to cover," "holds the reader's interest to the end." You may get away with such expressions once or twice, but your readers will soon learn that you have slight familiarity with the book and are using trite phrases to conceal your ignorance.

A good book review is an adequate review by a competent reviewer. As has been indicated, in the case of a poor book it may consist, if one may use the Hibernianism, of silence and plenty of it. A mere descriptive note, a slight expansion of the title, may be altogether adequate for some quite worthy books. In the case of many books and for many readers, the most effective review is the gossipy paragraph, which may with delicate touch strike a strong, individual note of recommendation, or may, by directing attention discriminatingly to some detail in the book, succeed in evoking the interest of the reader. In general the length of the review, aside from considerations of available space, is immaterial, so long as the task is well done and except that it should be kept short enough so that it will be read. Readability is an important consideration, for a dull review, if read at all, tends to damn a book that may deserve a better fate. The reviewer should analyze, explain and interpret, should commend or condemn the book. It should likewise discuss the book in its relation to literature in general and to the literary form to which it belongs, whether epic poetry, detective story, swash-buckling romance or tendency novel. And finally it must relate the book to the reader. The reviewer should remember that he will be read by all sorts of readers for all sorts of purposes. Some may read to observe, thru the eyes of the reviewer, the passing show of current letters; some to be told what to read and what not to read; some may wish to read the review instead of the book; some, having read the book and liked it, may wish to test their own judgments and, if possible, confirm them. Each case affords an opportunity, not simply for making a provisional estimate of a book, a candidate for literary immortality, but also the further opportunity for stimulating in the reader the comprehending, discriminating and critical attitude which will make him interested in the whole world of new books and lead him open-mindedly to seek for the best.

COOPERATION BETWEEN THE
LIBRARY AND THE
BOOKSTORE [1]

It is a rare privilege for a public librarian to address a national association of booksellers—altogether too rare for the sake of the most cordial relations between the two most important book distribution agencies of the country. In responding to your request to talk about cooperation between the book store and the library I propose to speak only of the free public library (that is, to exclude the commercial circulating library), and I address myself especially to the cooperation that is of most interest to you, namely, the cooperation on the part of the library that directly or indirectly helps the book store to increase book sales.

In order to pave the way for a brief description of the means and methods of such cooperation it seems desirable first to discuss briefly, tho by no means fully, the fundamental question whether the library is not, after all, an influence hostile to the book store, interfering with and reducing the total sales of books below the point that might be reached but for its maintenance in the community.

That this is still an open question instead of being long ago settled in the minds of booksellers that the library is a help to them rather than a hindrance, is suggested by the fact that in the able article, "Book Publishing and Its Present Tendencies," in the *Atlantic Monthly* for April, 1915 the distinguished

[1] Read before the American Booksellers Association, New York, May 15, 1913.

publisher George P. Brett, President of The Macmillan Company, in discussing and criticizing the effectiveness of the current agencies of book distribution, makes no mention of the public library. When in correspondence I asked him the reason for the omission he expressed the opinion that while libraries "are worthy of all encouragement" still they "are detrimental to the interests of publishers in that there can be no doubt that the purchase of books by individuals is curtailed by the increasing library facilities." If a leading publisher holds this opinion so strongly it is safe to say that some booksellers do also.

Influences Against Book Ownership

Mr. Brett claims that altho there has been an enormous increase in the number of titles published each year, there has not been a corresponding increase in the bulk of book sales. As no figures are produced, this may be regarded as an opinion to be offset by other competent opinions to the contrary. If for the sake of argument it is granted that there has not been an increase in book sales commensurate with the growth of population and the increase of popular education, there are other influences working so strongly in that direction as fully to explain the tendency without implicating the public library as a deterring factor. Some of these influences are the following:

In time past many families lived for several generations and died in spacious houses. Nowadays apartment house living and the frequent migration of families are not favorable to book owning. Motoring and world travel lure many of those whose economic condition and tastes formerly led them to remain at home and read the books they had bought. The swiftness of modern life and the multiplication of engagements, especially for those most interested in serious affairs, such as charities and reforms, require people to devote time once spent in their studies to attendance on committee meetings and in similar occupations. To meet the literary demands of such strenuous lives, there are excellent newspapers and magazines with summaries, instead of books. The appalling multiplication of books makes it less and less possible for any one individual even to know the titles of all the worth-while books, much less to buy and read them. When it is added that the prices of the better books have been advancing, whereas the tendency of the prices of magazines and newspapers has been downward, and that the cost of the necessities of life has been increasing, so that the ability of the public to buy books has been reduced, it would not be strange should the sales of books not have expanded in proportion to education and population, especially when it is remembered that much of our increase in population has been in the form of immigrants, most of whom have probably not become book purchasers. The ubiquity of the moving picture theater has undoubtedly been a strong factor in reducing the reading done by the young and by the comparatively uncultivated adults, and as a result has influenced their desire and ability to buy books. Here it should be noted that many of these influences which tend to reduce the reading of books and the purchasing of books similarly affect library use unfavorably.

Library a Conserving Force

Whether the sales of books have gone on increasing with the expansion of the country, as I believe and as I know many booksellers believe, or whether they have simply held their own, at any rate I am sure that the library, instead of being a hostile influence tending to reduce book sales, is, on the contrary, a conserving influence, counteracting those other tendencies by keeping alive and fanning the flame of interest in books, so that for every sale of books to an individual that has been lost to the bookseller by reason of the presence of the desired book in the library, probably at least two sales of books have been made by reason of the library's existence and influence.

LIBRARY AS CONTINUATION SCHOOL

The public library stands in the community as the great continuation school. One of its most important functions is to furnish expensive reference books and technical journals that individuals cannot often afford to buy. Thru the use of such material the earning capacity of large numbers of the community is being increased to such an extent as to lift them out of a state of economic dependence that precludes personal book ownership into one that makes book purchasing possible. The library also stands for good taste in literature. People without money cannot buy books. People without good taste do buy books, but I think it is safe to say that they cannot usually be depended upon to be steady and persistent readers and buyers. The public library also stands as the expert in the community for the choice of the best books, so that discriminating readers and buyers are coming more and more to depend for their own private purchases upon the selections made by the individual library or the organized choice of librarians as contained in the American Library Association *Booklist*. The public library is engaged in the business of converting as large a proportion of the community as its too meager support enables it to influence into the condition of being readers—not simply occasional readers, but habitual readers, not merely newspaper and magazine readers, but readers and lovers of books. It is also supplying effective help toward such economic independence as will enable its readers to own the books they most need as tools or most want as companions in their homes. The library, if well supported, reaches a far larger number than the book store can ever hope to have as customers. The library then sends on to the book store as customers as many as possible of the persons it has helped to bring up to an economic and esthetic state demanding private book ownership.

LIBRARY AN EXPERT ADVISER

To the person who is already economically and esthetically a possible book owner, the public library need not be, and usually is not, a deterrent to book buying, for then the library is approached for expert advice and as a laboratory for experiment in book values preceding book purchasing. When the discriminating reader finds that the library has purchased a certain book, this fact puts the seal of public approval on the book and sends him to the book store to buy it. Or, if he is still in doubt, he procures the library copy—gets it "on approval" from the library instead of from the book store—and if he finds it a necessary book for his private library proceeds to buy it from the bookseller. In this sense the public library is an institution for the display of sample copies of approved books—a sort of perpetual book advertising emporium, conducted at public expense.

But I think I hear some one object that at least the public library reduces the sum total of the sales of current fiction. This also we do not believe. The figures recently compiled by Fred E. Woodward show that fiction forms each year a smaller and smaller percentage of the total number of new publications. Of this progressively smaller number of books of fiction published, the leading public libraries (those whose example is being more and more followed) are approving for purchase as appropriate to an educational institution a smaller and smaller number of titles. And of the comparatively small number of titles so approved, its book funds, always severely limited and for the most part definitely required for other classes of literature, are only a drop in the bucket to supply the number of copies of current popular successes demanded by the seekers after the latest sensation. It is my experience also that many of the current novels most insistently demanded by the well to do and rich, who might buy, are in many cases the very books that do not measure up to the library's standards. Such readers are referred to the book stores or to the commercial circulating libraries. Unless it is claimed that the library's failure to approve for purchase most of the new novels has a damning effect on their popularity, it cannot successfully be shown that in this field the public library's existence has any serious depressing effect on book sales.

FEWER AND BETTER BOOKS

This very sifting process, whether applied to fiction or other classes of books, is one of the most important functions of the library. It means too much economically to the public—both as regards purchases of books from the public purse and in helping the individual to spend his own book money wisely—to be omitted. It ought to be done by libraries all over the country to the end of influencing the publication of a much smaller number of books that will better deserve being owned either by the public or by private individuals. In the interest of cooperation booksellers should, with a view to stable, remunerative business next year and every year, join in this movement for fewer and better books, instead of giving too much attention to present profits from weak books that ought never to have been published, and whose lives, if they can be said to be alive at all, are scarcely longer than that of yesterday's newspaper.

THE LIBRARY AND BOOK OWNERSHIP

When the bookseller claims that there is no use in his trying to seek the cooperation of the public librarian or to respond to the overtures of cooperation made by the librarian, for anyway the library is taking his business, the librarian is inclined to conclude that the real reason for this attitude is that the public library stands for the best books and for good editions, readable type, durable paper and binding and artistic illustrations, whereas the bookseller, tho he may appreciate these things, is ordinarily not averse to handling anything that is a book, and thinks he can make more money out of the sale of the poor and mediocre books rejected by the library than from those recommended by it. Very likely this attitude of mutual suspicion is unfair to both sides of this proposed cooperative alliance. Before there can be any successful cooperation such suspicion should be eliminated. Another stone of stumbling in the road toward cooperation that should be removed is the thought in either the mind of the librarian or the bookseller that the only interest the bookseller has in the library is to sell books to it. If there is any doubt in the mind of the bookseller that the librarian sincerely believes that there should be private book owning, that should be dissipated. If there is a public librarian who so unduly and mistakenly magnifies the functions of his library as to think that if it were properly supported there would be no room for personal book ownership, he should be put in a glass case and preserved as a curiosity.

I have thus far tried to show that the public library is not a menace to the existence of the book store, but is, on the contrary, from its very nature an influence conserving the interest in books and reading, including not simply the reading of publicly owned books, but also, wherever possible and economically justified, the reading of privately owned books. I also hold that the public librarian defeats his own ends who does not encourage private ownership of worthy books.

LIBRARY COOPERATION IN SALES

How can the librarian cooperate with the bookseller in the sale of books? What measures is he justified in taking as a professional man, employed by the public and serving only the public interest? At once I answer that whatever he may do as a private individual, in his public capacity he is justified in encouraging the private ownership of such books, and such only, as he has in his own library or would be willing to have there. In other words, the librarian, as librarian, is not justified in specifically cooperating in the encouragement of the sale of any but approved books. This means that altho the bookseller may continue to sell books which do not measure up to the library's standards, the librarian can participate by offering his official encouragement only in the sale of approved books or books worthy of his approval. If I am correctly informed, the experience of the ordinary book store is that upwards of 25 per cent only of its sales are of books specifically asked for; that is, by people who know exactly what they want when they enter the store; the remaining

75 per cent are from stock displayed or by the suggestions of salesmen. As a basis, therefore, of a cooperation in which the librarian would be willing to
participate without stultifying his professional standards, which demand the distribution of approved
books, there must be on the part of the bookseller a
reasonable regard for such standards, both in choosing
his stock and in pushing sales. By this I do not
mean that the bookseller should turn the business of
buying his stock over to the librarian, but I do mean
that a bookseller cannot long hope for enthusiastic
cooperation from the librarian if he persists in fill-
ing his most prominent tables with weak, trashy or
salacious novels or low-grade, badly printed, crudely
illustrated children's books. The librarian should be
reasonable and recognize that the book store is a
commercial enterprise conducted to make money; but
the bookseller should in turn recognize that the library is an educational institution and that the public librarian is an educational officer. If, therefore,
the bookseller thinks the library's cooperation is
worth having, he should recognize that it is reasonable to expect it only so far as the librarian is convinced that by such cooperation the general educational purpose of the library (the distribution of good
books in the community) may be forwarded. If the
bookseller recognizes that the librarian can cooperate
only on this basis and still wants the library cooperation badly enough to meet the conditions, then the
public librarian should by all means respond. The library profession is deeply interested in having strong
(and therefore profitable) book stores in all considerable towns in America to supplement the work of
the local public libraries. If the sale of good books
is made more profitable it is possible that fewer bad

books will be published and sold to undermine the work the public libraries are trying to accomplish.

LIBRARIAN'S FIRST DUTY

It must, of course, be clearly understood that any efforts put forth by the librarian in the direction of encouraging readers to procure books by purchase must be secondary and supplemental to his first work, which is to supply them free. In so far as his resources will permit, he is in duty bound to supply to all members of his constituency—the rich who are able to buy their own books, but whose taxes support the library, as well as the poor who cannot afford to buy—the books asked for, so far as they are approved and can be afforded. But those who want to buy books, or who could be induced to buy, form no small part of the community. It is to the library's advantage to increase this number, provided the buying is intelligent and discriminating. Such buyers, to be encouraged by the library, include those who believe in building up a well-rounded private library, to consist of the best reference books, the worthiest editions of the classics, ancient and modern, together with a discriminating choice of modern works as they appear; the collectors of specialties; those who need expensive books that the library cannot afford to buy; the readers who believe in owning all the books they read (no small number); persons of literary tastes but slender purses who need a few well chosen books as constant companions and tools; makers of gifts to literary friends, who are often not pleased with the results of well-meaning but misguided efforts; parents and teachers who wish to give Christmas and birthday gifts and who regard the reading of their children as a matter of serious importance or who may want to take no chance of possible germs in public library books; and the large class of mechanics, engineers, business men, clerks, housekeepers, professional men, etc., who having tested out many books drawn from the public library's rich stores have found a few books that they must buy in order to have them always at hand for use in their everyday affairs.

The foregoing questions are so fundamental to the cooperative relations possible between the library and the book store that I trust the discussion has proved helpful, even tho it has left less time than I should like for description of actual and possible cooperative enterprises. Taking my own library as somewhat typical, the following are some of the things that have been done:

CHRISTMAS BOOK EXHIBITS

Beginning in 1904, the Public Library in Washington has each year conducted in the weeks preceding Christmas an exhibition of books suitable for gifts. Some years the exhibition has been large and has included a selection from the best current and classic adult books, as well as children's books. In many cases new, clean copies have been bought especially for exhibition purposes. For two or three seasons a catalog of the exhibition was printed, with prices furnished by the leading local booksellers. At least once two local booksellers cooperated in the cost of the printed catalog, each of them distributing special imprint editions. The catalogs distributed by the library stated that the books could be bought at the book stores (without mentioning names); the catalog distributed by the stores stated that the books had been chosen by the library and could be seen there. In other years the library has cooperated with libraries in other cities, securing imprinted editions of catalogs (especially of children's Christmas gift books) compiled elsewhere.   Last Christmas the library did not issue a catalog, but did hold an exhibition of children's books.   On special days the public was invited to hear the children's librarian discuss the books exhibited and the principles of selecting books for children.   On other occasions the children's librarian and other representatives of the library have accepted invitations (sometimes seeking such invitations) to address women's clubs and parent-teacher associations on books for Christmas gifts. Often the books recommended have been sent by the library to the club meetings for examination.   Always, in connection with such exhibits at the library, publishers' Christmas and other book lists have been given away in large numbers in addition to the library's own list of recommended books.   Hundreds of copies of E. W. Mumford's pamphlet, *Choosing Books for Boys and Girls,* extracted from his address to this association a year ago, *Juvenile Readers as An Asset,* were given away to parents last Christmas. Samples of priced catalogs issued by typical public libraries are on exhibition on the platform.   I also have for distribution to all persons present copies of a list entitled *The Child's Books: a List Recommended for Owning and Reading,* just issued by my own library.   This list is based on a group of books collected as the result of years of experience.   The books are permanently on exhibition in the office of the head of our children's department.   Parents and teachers so constantly came to us for advice in the matter of the reading of children and to inquire what books to buy for them that this model collection of books desirable for the child to own has been gradually formed to answer their questions.   This list was not printed until it was learned that the local booksellers could actually secure the books and until the prices had been revised by two dealers.

Among the catalogs issued by libraries for the specific purpose of stimulating and influencing the purchase of books should be mentioned one entitled *The Child's Own Library*, issued by the Brooklyn Public Library, first in 1907 and reissued in 1911 and 1912. This list, issued in handsome form, is priced and annotated. The Rochester Public Library recently distributed 7,000 copies of its priced list, *Books for a Child's Library*, at the child welfare exhibit in that city. Of earlier editions of the same list the Rochester librarian, while librarian at Louisville, had distributed 10,000 copies. Nearly 30,000 of the list had also been used for distribution purposes by thirty other library and six state library commissions. Similar lists have for several years been issued by the St. Louis Public Library, by the Buffalo Public Library and by the Pratt Institute Free Library, Brooklyn. In fact the plan of holding such an exhibition was begun by Mary Wright Plummer at Pratt Institute in 1892.

LIBRARIES CREATE BUYERS

Not many public libraries are so fortunate as to have as their chief librarians former booksellers, tho there are several holding such positions. One of these, Walter L. Brown, librarian at Buffalo, reports that the booksellers of that city believe as he does, that libraries create readers and book buyers. His 1912 Christmas list and a recent list of books for Boy Scouts both give prices and suggestions as to purchasing books from dealers. The librarian at Kansas City reports that in 1908, while he was librarian at St. Joseph, Mo., he distributed 10,000 copies of a priced list of industrial arts books. Notwithstanding the fact that all the books were in the library, the local booksellers reported very heavy calls for titles under each of the occupations covered by the list. An example of cooperation on the part of a manufacturer of filing devices and bookcases is the issuing by the Globe-Wernicke Company of an attractive list, *The World's Best Books*. This list includes most of the famous lists of titles, such as those compiled by Sir John Lubbock, President Eliot, Colonel Roosevelt, etc. This firm reports that it has furnished over 750,000 copies of this pamphlet to more than 500 different libraries for distribution. The libraries distributing them have included those at Spokane, Minneapolis, Cleveland, Chicago, Newark, Jacksonville, Atlanta, Washington, Denver, Springfield, Mass., etc. Undoubtedly the distribution of this list has influenced not simply library reading, but also the sale of books.

LIBRARIES USE PUBLISHERS' LISTS

For years I have followed the plan, whenever a particularly attractive publisher's classified list of books came to my desk, of asking the publisher to furnish the library quantities of the list for distribution. If the library had, or could afford to buy all or nearly all the titles, the publisher was asked to supply an imprint edition, or the list was stamped "These books are in the Public Library," or "Most of these books are in the Public Library," as the case might be. Thousands of such advertising pamphlets have been distributed and as they are priced they are undoubtedly used as personal purchase lists.

PERSONAL INFLUENCE OF LIBRARIANS

For years also in my own library, in common with other public libraries, the personal influence of the librarian and his assistants has been exerted in communicating to readers the love of the books treasured by librarians (for some of us are book lovers and not simply library administrators and purveyors of books)

that leads to book purchasing. In our reference room
we keep a copy of the *United States Catalog* for the
principal purpose of helping readers to look up the
prices of books with a view to purchase. Librarians
are constantly giving personal advice, addressing
clubs and writing for newspapers on the subject of
book ownership. Witness a recent brief article on
the book review page of the *St. Louis Post-Dispatch*
by Dr. A. E. Bostwick, librarian of the St. Louis
Public Library, with the caption "A Man's Own Library." Just now the Cleveland Public Library, in an
effort to help poor people economize, is circulating
large numbers of Gibbs' *Economical Cooking*. In
each copy a slip is pasted saying that copies may be
bought from the principal booksellers at fifteen cents
each.

If I have made my points that the library does
want to encourage personal book ownership and is
somewhat widely employing methods that influence
such ownership, it remains for me only to make a few
suggestions in conclusion.

Whenever the bookseller is convinced that the library's help is worth having, is it unreasonable to expect that he, rather than the librarian, will make the
first move toward establishing cooperative relations?
Remember that librarians have their professional dig-
nities to uphold and that many of them do not often
care to risk rebuffs. Not unnaturally many librarians
would be quite willing to respond to suggestions for
specific cooperation in this field who would never
attempt to initiate it.

LEAGUES OF BOOKSELLERS AND LIBRARIANS

The first paper yesterday suggests one line of cooperation. It appears that some book stores are holding staff meetings for the discussion of books, just

as libraries are holding meetings of their staffs for the same purpose; also that you have a school for training salesmen and saleswomen, just as we have library training schools and apprentice classes. I suggest the formation of local leagues composed jointly of library and bookselling people for the interchange of ideas, especially to increase knowledge of books on the part of those participating, in order the better to increase the love of books in our common constituencies.

The bookseller should strive to hold the public library trade, as a matter of pride as an efficient bookman in the community, to help swell his total sales and thus to get better discounts, to keep in touch with the better grade of books such as the library is buying and in order to know what the public library has, in expectation that the presence of the book in the library will create other business. The bookseller should, if necessary to hold it, be prepared to do the library business at a smaller profit per volume, realizing that the library is a large buyer, that all library accounts are collectible, and that the library purchases first and last for replacements a lot of so-called "dead" stock,—stock that otherwise could not be sold. With a spirit that will make for closer cooperation between the two associations (the American Library Association and this association) it should not be difficult to persuade librarians to purchase from local dealers more generally than they do at present.

ISSUE COOPERATIVE LISTS

Booksellers should issue lists in cooperation with the library, sharing the cost, agreeing on the editions, not with reference to those the bookseller has in stock (unless they are acceptable to the librarian), but using the editions recommended by the librarian. The librarian should in turn be willing to agree to editions that are practicable, easily obtainable, and of which the sales will yield a profit. The bookseller should then stock the titles, or at least secure the books promptly on order, for only thus can he keep faith with library and customers.

Why should not booksellers generally subscribe for the monthly A. L. A. *Booklist,* which contains the books approved by the American Library Association for library purposes, use it for suggestions in buying stock, have copies for consultation by customers, and even secure imprint editions for distribution among the most discriminating of them? Why cannot the booksellers get publishers to print on the wrappers of new books the brief notices contained in the A. L. A. *Booklist* instead of some of the puffery now used?

Boy Scout Reprints

The management of the Boy Scouts of America has made arrangements with the largest reprint firm in the country to issue at low prices reprint editions of books found successful by libraries and selected and approved by a committee of professional librarians, to compete with and drive out the weak stuff now published as Boy Scout books. Will the booksellers cooperate by pushing these books?

Finally let me appeal to every bookseller as an influential member of his own community not to regard the public library as a hostile influence, something to be tolerated and to be supported only under protest, but to be an enthusiastic library supporter. Support the library because it deserves your support as a citizen; support it because it is making readers and probable book buyers; support it, if for no other reason, because the library needs in your town and everywhere far more books than it is ever able to buy and a far larger number of copies of books, replaced oftener with clean copies. The book purchases of the libraries of the country total no small figure; they should be many times larger and you should sell them the books.

THE FREE PUBLIC LIBRARY[1]

ITS POSSIBILITIES AS A PUBLIC SERVICE AGENCY

The invitation from the President of the American Federation of Labor to write on the possibilities of the public library as a public service agency is welcomed as an opportunity to set forth the scope and purpose of the public library, what it has to offer to all citizens, and to urge more general and fuller use of its resources and services.

What is the present general thought of the public library as an institution of society? Has it now come to be estimated as of vital and fundamental importance, indispensable to the welfare of society? Or is it not still too often considered, tho desirable, yet of rather negligible importance, perhaps the last institution to be added to a community's resources, to be normally maintained on a precarious basis, and the first to be subjected to show starvation in lean years?

LABOR'S ATTITUDE

A study of the official literature of the American Federation of Labor shows that from the outset organized labor in America strongly supported the public school, and thruout its history has championed every forward movement in the development of the instructional part of our system of public education. During all these years and until very recently this same official literature has practically ignored the existence of the public library. Recently, however, there have been frequent marks of recognition of the

[1] American Federationist. May, 1926.

public library in official addresses and resolutions, in which organized labor has been advised to urge better support for public libraries, to seek participation in their administration and to secure the co-operation of libraries in plans for workers' education and other parts of labor's educational program.

EDUCATION LIFELONG

This change in attitude has no doubt come about because of the more general recognition of the fact that education is not a process that is finished with the completion of the instructional period of school life, whether that be long or short, but that real education can and should extend over the whole of human life.   In this conception of education the instructional process furnishes the individual with the technical equipment, by the constant and unremitting use of which thuout life he may progressively become an educated man.   In school he has learned to read; at best he has acquired some store of knowledge, relatively meager to his life needs; he has not really acquired a completed education, but only the aptitude for education.   In this conception of education the public library assumes a necessary and vital place.   It enters into the educational scheme from the outset, since it helpfully supplements and vitalizes the often dry instructional process; still more important, it seeks the formation of the library using habit to the end that education shall be carried on indefinitely when school days are over. Thenceforward to the end of life the public library, if constantly and habitually used, may become the primary agency for unlimited educational development.

What is a public library? For whom is it maintained? What kinds of services does it render?

Perhaps it is unnecessary to state that public libraries are not highbrow institutions serving only or chiefly literary persons and scholars; or that they are not charitable institutions serving only those too poor to buy their own books; and that they are not literary soda fountains dispensing chiefly current novels or other soft-drink literature to idle persons thirsting for the best seller of the moment. Libraries are for all of us; for the young of all ages and those not so young; for the rich and the poor and all between; for the highly educated and for those of meager education, provided only they can read; for the native Americans and new Americans, who still prefer the foreign language which was their mother tongue; for persons with plenty of time and for busy men and women with little leisure. The public library is not an institution to which we turn only rarely in case of extreme need, but is, or should be, an institution which is a vital and intimate part of our daily lives.

INFORMATION SERVICE

The public library gives three principal kinds of service. It is a bureau of information furnishing up-to-date facts on all questions of human affairs; it is an educational agent supplementing school instruction; and it is a storehouse of cultural and recreational reading suited to all tastes and needs.

The information service of the public library has been described by one recent educational writer,[2] not a librarian, as "a community intelligence service" working thru centers "as familiar to every inhabitant as the local post office, and as inevitably patronized." Such an information bureau will be

[2] W. S. Learned. *The American Public Library and the Diffusion of Knowledge.* p. 12 1924.

equipped to meet the demands for information in every commercial and vocational field; questions of government and legislation, national, state and local; labor, every trade and industry; banking, insurance, taxation; prohibition, crime, capital punishment, immigration, World Court; engineering subjects, such as road building and airplanes; chicken raising, cake making; and thousands of other subjects, new and old. The printed matter to answer such questions may consist of books, or it may be found in magazines or pamphlets, including government documents, newspaper clippings, maps or pictures. To answer the myriad questions put by the walking interrogation points who flock to libraries it is necessary to have all, or at least the best possible, sources of information, to have them all classified, cataloged, indexed, and so filed that they can be quickly produced for Americans of all ages, who by nature are always in a hurry and impatient at any delay. The American public library does meet just these specifications.

EDUCATIONAL SERVICE

The public library in its educational service may properly be considered as a universal continuation school, with courses on every subject of human interest. It has advanced, intermediate, and elementary books in all fields of knowledge, suited to the scholar, the ordinary reader of moderate education, or the beginner, including the foreigner. In addition to its collections of printed matter, it has, or at least it should always have, what is perhaps even more important, an educated and trained staff, sympathetic and tactful, to guide and facilitate the reader thru the flood and maze of modern print.

No matter when one may have dropped out of

school, whether very early in life, or after the university, more education is always needed for the highest success and happiness in life and the library always stands ready to take up that education where the school left off. Indeed the library is so eager to help in further education and so anxious that education shall not end with the school, that it carries public library books and pictures into the schools, as samples or bait to lure the child to the library, and it maintains children's rooms in its own library buildings in the hope that thereby young folks will come to love books, reading and the library, and will stick by the library when school days are over.

WORK FOR CHILDREN AND PARENTS

Library work for children has become highly developed, with a personnel specially trained therefor. The books used are carefully chosen by these experts, with wide and intimate knowledge of children's literature; stories are told to interest the children in the classics which are the heritage of all young people. Advisory service in the choice of books and right reading habits is given to individual parents and teachers, and to the parent-teacher and similar organizations, and often classes in the use of books as tools are conducted, to the end that the children may learn to love and enjoy books and use them skillfully.

The public library, in its cultural and recreational service, supplies the best novels, old and new, the best books of poetry, essays, history, travel, biography, and the fine arts needed to enable everybody to read what he or she most enjoys. Such reading may be done occasionally to kill time or to drive away the blues, or it may be done systematically in an effort to become well read in the world's best

literature of the past and present and to become well
informed on the best that is known and thought in
the world. Such reading makes our lives sweeter and
saner and makes us intelligent voters on public questions, local, state, national and international, and
entitles us to consider ourselves as becoming educated.

ADULT EDUCATION

Some adult readers will use the informational
resources of the public library almost exclusively, use
them perhaps to strengthen themselves vocationally.
Others will more or less consciously use its resources
for carrying on their education, to know and be able
to defend their rights, and to acquire the social
intelligence which is the mark of good citizenship.
In the case of still others the library will open the
way for the best use of their leisure, in such a way
as to gain thru it the cultural enrichment of life
and secure the liberal education which liberates the
mind.

It is perhaps unnecessary to describe in detail
the physical agencies for rendering library service.
In the case of one of the larger cities the public library system consists of a central library, branch
libraries, sub-branches and stations, so distributed as
to furnish library service and books convenient to
all homes. The main library has a large collection
of books and there all of the ordering of books, their
cataloging and preparation for use is carried on. The
branch libraries also have their own books, but they
draw in addition on the central library for books
not in their own collections. Some branch libraries
are housed in their own separate buildings and others
in separate rooms in suburban school houses or in
rented stores. Stations, composed of small deposits

of books, are often found in factories, social settlements, fire-engine houses, or rural post offices. The more modern library buildings have most of their books on open shelves for direct access and this is almost always true in the case of branch libraries.

Most libraries are divided into departments to facilitate their use; the circulation department where books for home reading are selected and recorded; the reference department, where dictionaries, cyclopedias, magazines, pamphlets and clippings are kept for consultation, but which may not ordinarily be borrowed for home use; and by all means a children's department where help for school work and books for home reading may be secured.

Village and County Libraries

Libraries in smaller cities and villages are very much like those in larger cities, except that they are smaller and do not usually have branches. Very small places may have their own libraries, or they may, if they are fortunate, have branches of county library systems. County library systems are increasing in number and many of them have book automobiles that look like store delivery autos, but the outside coverings are hinged and, when these are raised, shelves of books are revealed. Such libraries on wheels travel thru the country, stopping at every home to lend books and to collect those that have been read. Several state library commissions send boxes of books to small libraries and to groups of persons who do not have access to local libraries, and some maintain book automobiles like those of the county libraries.

In order to render the intellectual and spiritual services indicated in this article, the public library must not only be properly housed in centers convenient to all homes, and adequately stocked with books, all of which must be so cataloged as to reveal their contents, but its trustees and staff must be imbued with social intelligence of a high order, if the public library is to measure up as an effective educational institution. The purpose of education has been defined as "an attempt to equip people with the means of making up their own minds;"[3] and again as "the development of the power to understand, to think and to judge" and the use of that power "under standards which lead to the ultimate service of man."[4]

TRUTH AND IMPARTIALITY

"The truth, the whole truth, and nothing but the truth, is the spirit of the true educator. . . Education is an interpretation of life; it is life."[5] To help toward these ends the library is bound to furnish the fullest possible information on both or all sides of every moot question, political, economic, scientific, religious, in order to enable every individual to make up his own mind. Propaganda is no part of the purpose of the library. An attitude of strict impartiality does not imply indifference. On the contrary, the library staff, who should be specialists in books, must be keenly alive to furnish expert guidance in reading which is, after all, the largest factor, whether in formal or informal education.

The public library will not measure up to its possibilities if it rests content to serve those who seek it out. The modern public library is a dynamic, aggressive institution which seeks to draw the entire community within the range of its influence. It seeks

[3] G. D. H. Cole in *Workers' Educational Association Year Book*, 1918. p. 372.

[4] W. G. Beach, *Introduction to Sociology and Social Problems.* 1925. p. 351.

[5] Spencer Miller, Jr., in *Workers' Education Year Book*, 1924. p. 19.

contacts with the schools to help teachers and pupils still in school, and strives in every possible way to keep in touch with those leaving school or already out of school and to persuade them not to be "quitters." It establishes the closest possible cooperative relations with labor colleges and unions, with factory classes, night schools, university extension classes, women's study clubs and similar groups. Such services include advice and assistance in planning courses, furnishing books for reference and study and, if practicable and desired, providing meeting places in branch libraries.

ADVISORY SERVICE

The plan for furnishing advisory library service to groups and individuals has infinite possibilities. It includes the giving of courses of stereopticon lectures on books, libraries and their use in all branch libraries, especially for children, but with adults not excluded. It involves having a study club director and a corps of assistants to organize and direct readers so that the present unorganized and often desultory reading of many persons may become better worth while. Many would welcome such help. It involves, in addition to the reference service now given in most libraries, the organization of corps of one or more readers' advisers, to help individual readers plan courses of reading or study. Such readers' advisers would need to be experts in reading, but in difficult cases would turn to professors in the state university or other neighboring institution for supplementary advice. The problem of the part that the public library may play in the adult education movement is at present the subject of study of the Commission on the Library and Adult Education of

the American Library Association.[6] In this study
the Commission has had the close cooperation of a
Committee on Adult Education appointed by the
American Fereration of Labor and of the Workers'
Education Bureau.[7] The American Library Association Commission is issuing a bulletin entitled *Adult
Education and the Library,* one number of which is
devoted to *Industrial Education,* a direct result of
the cooperation with organized labor. The Library
Association has also brought to the attention of librarians generally the list of books on *Labor Problems* prepared by the Workers' Education Bureau.
The Library Association is also publishing a series
of reading courses entitled *Reading with a Purpose,*
each prepared by a specialist who recommends only
six to eight titles on each subject. Among the fifteen
numbers thus far issued[8] are courses on biology,
music, sociology and social problems, psychology, history, literature, children, religion, and the life of
Christ.

EDUCATED AND TRAINED STAFF

To give the service now furnished by public libraries, and still more to afford the library service,
expanded, strengthened and deepened as here outlined, requires a library staff that shall be educated,
trained, experienced, secure in tenure and properly
paid. In too many libraries the staff is so meager
that hours of opening are short, and when the library
is open, the staff is only sufficient to record and receive books, with little or no margin left for the
advisory work now coming to be recognized as a
necessary part of library work. Library staffs must
be strengthened in numbers and must consist more

[6] 520 North Michigan Avenue, Chicago.
[7] 476 West 24th Street, New York City.
[8] About 60 numbers have now been published.

largely of those fitted to do the consultative work which is the essence of the library's educational function.

ADEQUATE MAINTENANCE

How well are the American people supporting their system of public libraries? How does such support compare in adequacy with their maintenance of the public school system? It is safe to say that some sort of public school facilities are afforded to the entire school population of the country. The latest information is to the effect that less than half of the people of the United States have any kind of public library service whatever. And with respect to the minority who have some library service, in many cases the libraries are wholly inadequate, that is, they are meagerly stocked with rather poor books, and are badly run by incompetent librarians. In 1921 the American Library Association set up a minimum standard of $1 per capita of the population for ordinary library service—by no means the best. A few cities exceed that minimum, including Cleveland, $1.34; Boston, $1.09; Springfield, Mass., $1.07; and Evansville, Ind., Berkeley, Calif., and Davenport, Ia., $1.04 each.[9] The average for American cities above 200,000 population is 73 cents. The average for the 248 cities above 30,000 population in 1923 is 43 cents. Comparing library and school expenditures over a term of 20 years from 1903 to 1923, it is found that library expenditures per capita increased from 19 cents to 43 cents, or an increase of 2.2 times, whereas school expenditures increased from $3.86 per capita to $12.87, or 3.3 times. Computed by the purchasing power of money in 1913, library expenditures increased 25 per cent in twenty years, and school ex-

[9] For later figures see the paper entitled "The Public Library as a Factor in Education."

penditures increased 85 per cent, or nearly three and a half times as fast as libraries. With every book costing double or more what it did twenty years ago; with the multiplication of titles necessary for purchase; with a rapidly expanding reading population; with every form of library expense mounting; with a need for larger and better paid staffs; it is clear that the public library must have very much larger funds to enable it to measure up to the standards of service that the public is increasingly demanding.

I trust that all readers of this article have modern, up-to-date public libraries in their home towns and that they, their wives and families, are making full use of such libraries. You should find in your libraries a spirit of friendliness and helpfulness, combined with a knowledge of books and how to make them most useful to you. Your libraries belong to you; you should demand that they be intelligently managed and that they have adequate financial support.

THE PUBLIC LIBRARY AS A
FACTOR IN EDUCATION [1]

The free public library, still an under-developed educational agency, has the capacity for becoming a highly effective complement of all formal education and a universal supplement of all informal education. The library as continuation school offers to people of all tastes, of all degrees of literacy and aptitude, of all ages, elective courses in every field of knowledge. Parallel with acceleration of the growth in numbers of those who are prolonging their school life, is rapid enlargement of the fraction who feel the need beyond school for further educational equipment to meet the problems of life. The function of the library is not only to stand ready, but to make the initial move to capture this swelling army of those who pass through the schools, to win them to the idea that education is a never-ending process, to place the world of print at their disposal and to supply the skilled guidance needed to make their adult lives efficient, interesting and sane.

EDUCATION A LIFE PROCESS

Emphasis is everywhere increasingly placed on the conception that education is not a process ending with the school, but is rather a life process; that school life, however prolonged, simply evokes ability and taste for learning and furnishes the initial equipment for securing never completed self-education. The purpose of education in a democracy is to in-

[1] *Current History* (New York Times). January, 1928.

sure that the entire people shall be happy, intelligent, capable and well balanced; that on the practical side they shall be equipped for success in trade, business or profession; that in matters of opinion they shall be opened-minded and discriminating; and that on the spiritual side they may seek truth and beauty, rejecting the tawdry and vulgar.

This conception of education has been voiced by President Coolidge: "We cannot abandon our education at the schoolhouse door. We have to keep it up through life." To stress the part the library can play, the President speaks of "the faculty of scholars ready to teach any of us in the books in our public libraries. . . The library is the keystone of education."

A University for the People

Evidences are many that the public library is more and more becoming a university for the people and that the throngs who turn to it are being rapidly augmented. The most easily ascertained evidences are statistics of home circulation of books. Latest nation-wide figures are 226,142,926 volumes, 2 per capita for the entire population, or 3.71 per capita for people living in library service areas, whether having weak or strong libraries. These figures mount to near 10 per capita in one large city.

That a vast clientèle is being prepared for the library is shown by recent increases in enrolment in high schools, now over 4,000,000; colleges, 750,000; summer schools, 380,000; commercial correspondence courses, 1,500,000; university extension courses, 200,000; workers' education classes, 30,000, and lectures, open forums, and so forth, 300,000. Add enrolments in Y. M. C. A. and similar classes, millions of members of study clubs, parent-teacher associations and other organizations devoted to individual and community improvement. All these need, and many of them seek, the help of the library. Moreover, a shorter working day and earlier retirement from active business because of greater prosperity point to the need for furnishing education thru the library as the means for wise use of leisure time. Altho children in school form an important part of the library's constituency, yet the library in serving them looks forward to the time when it will become their chief educational agency. Some people put all their education in their children's names. The library does not intend to let them off with such an alibi. The public library is also neither a charitable institution nor one whose function is dispensing mediocre fiction to idle people, but is a highly efficient institution for adult education.

HOUSING THE LIBRARY

Nearly every one, particularly the city dweller, is now familiar with the public library, usually handsomely housed, often wisely located on a prominent site in the business district. In many a city he also has a neighborhood branch library in an attractive building similarly well placed. Branch libraries are often housed in rented store buildings, perhaps built to order, while districts are being tried out and until the growth of population justifies separate buildings.

With growing community use of school buildings, there is a tendency to house branch libraries in schools, especially in the suburbs. This is most successful when the library is planned in a new, conspicuously located school building and is housed in a wing, with inside and outside entrances and a sign visible from the street. Such a branch may serve as both school and community library. If the only access to the library is the main school entrance, adults are likely to think of it as strictly a school library. Some cities also have branch libraries in field houses on municipal playgrounds.

Other agencies for carrying library service include stations in settlement houses, department stores (usually for employes but occasionally for the public), factories, large offices, telephone exchanges, fire and police stations, hospitals (for patients and nurses) and vacation camps for Boy and Girl Scouts. Sparsely settled parts of large cities are in some cases served by book automobiles.

DEARTH OF RURAL LIBRARIES

The recent study by the Committee on Library Extension of the American Library Association shows that, despite need for more city libraries and more branches of existing libraries, yet all but 6 per cent of the urban population have some public library service, whereas 83 per cent of the rural population are altogether without such service. To meet the problem in rural communities the establishment of county libraries is advocated, partly because small library units are uneconomical and ineffective. A majority of the large counties of California now have county libraries, and there are scattering county libraries in other states. Such county service is thru branches, stations in stores, schools and postoffices and book automobiles.

In thirty-eight states the state library, or a separate library extension agency, furnishes some service to people without local libraries, or sends books to existing libraries. Librarians have long been urging a cheap book post to help in this service. Such long-range service can never take the place of direct contact with a local library.

The free public library is generally (and wisely) organized under a separate board of trustees, not as a part of the school system. The school board deals chiefly with the instructional process under a compulsory law, whereas the library is an agency for voluntary education. There have been cases of subordination of the library almost to the point of starvation where it was under the board of education. The library would also suffer from the standardization which is a necessity of school organization.

A Definite Library Tax

The public library is best supported when there is a definite library tax rate. This insures library support constantly increasing with the enlargement of the city and the increase in property values. It is far better than that the library board and librarian should be compelled to seek appropriations from budget officers and city councils in competition with other municipal departments. Most public libraries are half-starved institutions; even those most generously maintained could advantageously use in the public interest several times as much money as they have. In spite of meager support, progressively administered libraries have rendered larger service than might have been expected and are eager to carry out an enlarged and enriched program.

The American Library Association, the national professional organization of librarians, with more than 10,000 members, celebrated in 1926 its fiftieth anniversary. In early days its emphasis was on technical matters of cataloging, classification, bookbinding, and so forth. Now the major emphasis is on an educated, trained advisory service to all who seek the library, and the effort to draw as many as possible into the orbit of library influence.

Of first importance is an educated, trained, skilled, sympathetic personnel, dominated by the highest professional standards. The library should be adequately, even beautifully, housed; it must have a growing supply of printed matter, steadily becoming more costly; but unless the library also has proper personnel, never weaklings or failures in other callings, it cannot select wisely from the flood of print, administer and interpret that print for the public, and become the efficient educational agent which library leaders envision.

VARIED LIBRARY SERVICES

Services rendered by live public libraries are varied. Thru children's departments they are taking into the schools collections of carefully selected books, not texts but well printed and illustrated pieces of literature, suited to the reading tastes and abilities of children, which help to vitalize instructional processes and win the children to be library readers in and out of school. They arrange group visits to the children's or adults' rooms of the library, with talks on and practice in the use of library tools. Most libraries furnish general reference or informational service, and some have divisions devoted to business, applied science, music and other fine arts, educational literature, and other specialties. A few are organizing and training corps of readers' advisers, to consult with and prescribe courses of reading for those seeking such advice. The general experience is that such advice is so eagerly sought as almost to swamp the consultants.

One library has a director of reading, a "professor of books," who furnishes advice personally and by public addresses. Another library specializes in establishing contacts with the members of labor unions.

Several make systematic efforts to furnish service to women's clubs and other study groups. Many libraries have lecture halls and study club rooms, and some arrange for discussion groups, organized more or less definitely by the library. Some libraries conduct special services for the foreign-born, for students in continuation and Americanization schools, and for other out-of-school groups. Some use the radio for reviewing books and for describing the services the library is prepared to render.

AN EDUCATIONAL CLEARING HOUSE

The Buffalo Educational Council in its recent report of a survey of the adult educational facilities of Buffalo recommends the public library as the appropriate clearing house and bureau of information concerning all local educational opportunities for adults, a plan partially in use in certain other cities.

In all its advisory work the public library strives to suit the book to the reader—advanced books to the specialists and highly educated, and simple books to beginners of whatever age. To the end of making readers out of non-readers, the public library has welcomed the numerous outlines and other books for simplifying knowledge, tho they may be despised by the specialist.

No article on the public library can properly omit mention of the part which Andrew Carnegie and the Carnegie Corporation have played in its development. At first many Carnegie millions were devoted to library buildings. Some years ago a decision was reached to spend no more for buildings. Incidentally, some cities which were slow in accepting Carnegie money or which need more buildings find it difficult to secure the erection of buildings from the public treasury. In the last few years large sums of Carnegie money have been devoted, thru the medium of the American Library Association, to the development of a library educational program. Some money has gone for the investigation and later the strengthening of the schools of training for librarianship; some to the investigation and promotion of library extension, especially in rural districts; and some to the study of libraries and adult education. One phase of this last work has been the publication of a series of more than thirty *Reading with a Purpose* pamphlets, written by experts as aids in directed reading. The response of the public to facilities for continuing education thru wise reading is indicated by the extraordinary circulation of these courses.

DEFAULT IN LIBRARY SERVICE

Students and practitioners of education thru the public library are of the opinion that no reading, aimless reading, poor reading are usually the results of a default in public library service; either there is no library or, if there is one, it does not furnish enough good, interesting books and the necessary trained guidance. There are undoubtedly many people of such calibre that they would never, if they could help it, make use of library education. Not in one or two generations will all the people seek the library or respond to its offer, but with each generation more and more will do so.

Recent events have shown that in one large city enough people believed that a library should not consist of books representing only one side of a question to thwart a threatened library *auto da fe*. The public library does have, along with books representing the ripest and most impartial scholarship, other books which represent bias; but a public library worthy of the name, in being hospitable to books of propaganda, also secures their antidotes, thus giving each reader material on all sides of every disputed question. Informed public opinion should result from such impartial library service.

School and Library Support

Latest available census figures show that American cities above 30,000 population spent in 1903 an average of $3.86 per capita on their schools and 19 cents on their libraries; and in 1925 $14.10 per capita on their schools and 48 cents on their libraries. This is not an argument that the schools are spending too much, but the discrepancy has always been too great. It is sound to spend $14.10 per capita for the entire community on the instruction of the important fraction of the community in schools; but the allotment of 48 cents per capita is too small for the library education of the entire community of all ages, particularly as much of it is devoted to library service for these same school children.

In 1921 the American Library Association adopted as a reasonable minimum for good public library service $1 per capita, with more than that needed for the development of a program of trained library service. A number of cities are spending considerably more than $1 per capita: among them Cleveland, $1.54; Boston, $1.18; Portland, Ore., $1.13; Indianapolis, $1.01; Springfield, Mass., $1.07; and Evansville, Ind., Berkeley, Calif., and Davenport, Ia., $1.04 each.[2]

For the protection of society against the fruitless or vicious use of leisure time, for the avoidance of still greater expenditure on juvenile and other courts,

[2] Some of these figures have been considerably increased in the last two years; for example, Cleveland, $1.77 and Boston, $1.46.

charitable and correctional institutions, for good
citizenship insurance, will not "long-headed" Americans come to see the value of spending more money
on their public libraries, and of insuring that their
libraries measure up to opportunities? Even if not
conceived as a moral obligation to make the whole
body of citizens intelligent, perhaps the good sense
of our people will decide that general intelligence is
a matter of necessary mental sanitation.

THE PUBLIC LIBRARY AND
WORKERS' EDUCATION [1]

I have watched the career of the Workers' Education Bureau with interest, sympathy and admiration. It is a matter of satisfaction to be present at this biennial convention and to participate in your discussions.

I welcome the opportunity to say a few words on what I believe to be the spiritual connection between the public library and workers' education. The Workers' Education Movement is a part of the larger movement known as Adult Education. We are told by some of the critics of the present emphasis on adult education by public libraries that the public library has always been engaged in what is now called adult education and that giving it a new name does not change the situation. These critics, I believe, overlook certain factors and underestimate the results that are likely to flow from the present emphasis. Formerly the library's effort in this direction was usually vague, ill defined, incidental and formed but a meager proportion of its total work. It was largely unconscious and so lacked both a philosophy and a technique. Here and there an individual realized that he was carrying on his education thru the help of the library, but most people resented the idea that they had any need for further education, since they thought their education had been completed.

[1] Remarks at Workers' Education Bureau Convention, Washington, April 5, 1929. Appeared in *American Federationist*. 36:846-9. July 1929.

This situation is changing, due to the world-wide adult education movement, the basis of which is the growing recognition that education is a life-long process and that self-education is the only real education. The modern movement for adult education is, therefore, self-conscious; it is based on a philosophy, it is developing an aim and its techniques are being worked out.

I shall not presume to tell you the aims of workers' education. As I understand it, to some it means the securing of further educational equipment to fight the battles of labor and little if anything in the way of individual cultural improvement. To some it means an escape from the deadening effect of the routinized processes of so much of factory labor. To some it means the improvement of the individual for the better doing of the job—those who think with L. P. Jacks in his "Breadwinning and Soulsaving" [2] that education to be best worthwhile must grow out of our daily tasks and that the work itself must be educative. To others it means that there must be a complete divorce between their hours of labor and their after-work hours and that the leisure time must be so spent as to make life worth living.

No matter what may be the circumstances or the conception of work and of education on the part of any worker, the public library stands ready, willing, and able to help each according to his need and his capacity.

The library is no longer a cloistered institution, remote from life. It is no longer a purely literary institution catering only to those with advanced education. It is no longer a passive institution ministering only to the persevering who seek it out and master its use. The modern public library is a live,

[2] *Journal of Adult Education.* (American) p. 5-10. February 1929.

wide-awake, democratic, dynamic, friendly, hospitable institution, run by real people, educated and trained, understanding, alert, and eager to help.

The library itself includes books, magazines, pamphlets, clippings, and pictures on every conceivable subject, advanced books, simple books, books on every side of every question. These books are organized for use. But the distinguishing feature of the modern adult education movement as applied to the library is the emphasis now being placed on the advisory work the library is beginning to furnish to any and all comers who need such help. To that end the public library is now organizing and training in service a group of persons who are specialists in the various subjects of knowledge. An adviser from this group helps the reader to find the single book he needs, or, if he so desires, plans for him a course of reading in the subject of his interest. In this planning of reading courses the adviser may use one of the *Reading with a Purpose* pamphlets issued by the American Library Association, already referred to, or if there is none to fit the need, he will plan a course especially for the individual.

The public library is of course eager to see workers' colleges organized. Such a college, if its organizers so desire, may appropriately meet in the library's lecture hall, or in a study room (where a library has not outgrown its housing, as in the case of our central library), the better to use the library's books and advisory service. In some cities, for example Milwaukee, library representatives enroll in labor colleges and attend labor union meetings, the better to promote reading and study on the part of workers who have not yet formed the habit of visiting the public library. So far as its always-too-meager support will permit, the library reaches out to cooperate in workers' education as one of its best avenues for usefulness.

This mention of the library's financial support brings up the final point which I wish to make. It might be called the selfish interest that the library has in workers' education, if a desire to increase the library's resources and thus to widen the scope of its usefulness should ever be thought of as a selfish interest. The library wants to help the worker in his efforts to improve his education for his own sake, but the library also recognizes that organized labor is committed to a program for adult education and will furnish powerful help in securing from appropriating bodies funds for the public library to enable it to do the work it is fitted to do in this field, given the necessary funds.

In this connection I wish to refer to the fact that President Green a few years ago urged organized labor to secure representation on library boards and help to procure better support for libraries. In an editorial in the *American Federationist,*[*] published in the same number which carried an article by me on the "Free Public Library," Mr. Green wrote:

Labor organizations and especially local committees on education thoroughout the jurisdiction of the A. F. of L. are urged to do their utmost to promote generous appropriations for library purposes. Make it your duty to find out the amount apportioned for library purposes in your community and compare this with the minimum maintenance standard recommended by the American Library Association. If your local appropriation falls short you are urged to do whatever may be necessary to secure larger appropriations.

In spirit at least workers' education and the public library are closely tied together. As a public librarian I am proud of the association. The public library, within its means, stands ready to do all you may ask of us. In fact, we should like you to ask more of us.

[*] May, 1926.

SOME LIBRARY PERSONNEL PROBLEMS [1]

In the arrangements for participation in this tribute to the dean of our profession the pleasant duty has been assigned to me of writing on the administrative aspects of library personnel, including training and salaries. The man we honor has exemplified thruout his long and distinguished career, including the part before the Library of Congress period, by individual achievements and officially thru his appointments, the highest attainable standards in personnel administration. It is therefore fitting to include comment, retrospective and prospective, on some aspects of this phase of library administration.

EXPERIENCE AND OBSERVATION

This paper is based on the experience of one who, in the earlier part of the thirty-year period under consideration, administered a medium-sized library in which exceedingly small salaries then prevailed and who soon became librarian of a library whose salaries during much of this period have been nearly the lowest among those of the larger municipal libraries of the country. Within recent years the salaries of that library have, thru the operation of the Federal Classification Act, been pulled up so that they compare very favorably with others thruout the country. This paper is likewise based on a short-range observation of corresponding improvements during the same period, as a result of much the same causes, in the salary situation in the Library of Congress and the other governmental libraries in Washington.

[1] From *Essays Offered to Herbert Putnam;* edited by William Warner Bishop and Andrew Keogh; published by Yale University Press, 1929.

Somewhat similar changes have been observed at longer range elsewhere, no doubt for reasons such as underlie the classification legislation and its effect on library salaries in Washington.

Salary Question Fundamental

This matter of salaries is placed first in this discussion because it is believed to be fundamental in the entire problem of personnel administration. There was a time when it was regarded as almost indecent for a librarian to mention library salaries. In fact in that earlier time salaries, generally speaking, were too small to be worth mentioning. Later, in the campaign for better library salaries, it has come to be considered that one of the best ways to secure improvement is to bring salary figures out into the open, with the idea that good salary figures will, as examples, help to raise poorer ones and that poor salary figures will by their publication likewise tend to improvement by attracting unfavorable attention to their inadequacy. Those who believe in the effectiveness of the publication of such comparative figures sometimes find themselves hampered by the refusal of some libraries to permit the publication of figures presumed to be helpful, perhaps because occasionally when salary figures are advanced to telling proportions they are withheld from publication and likewise by the oversensitiveness of some librarians to the publication of their unsatisfactory figures. Possibly the withholding of such salary figures, both the good and the poor, is dictated by library trustees rather than by librarians, perhaps to ward off glances either envious or scornful. It is to be hoped that librarians will induce their boards to join in this cooperative movement by giving full publicity to library salaries, whether good or bad.

SALARY STUDY FOR A. L. A.

Altho there has been marked improvement within the last few years in library salaries, both in government and other libraries, the recent nation-wide study made by the Bureau of Public Personnel Administration for the American Library Association disclosed the fact that library salaries in practically all grades are low, whether based on the education, training, experience, and personality possessed by librarians, on a comparison between librarians and those in other professions or business having equal or lesser equipment, or on the standard of living which society expects and librarians as self-respecting members of society desire to maintain.

That the library salary problem has not yet been solved is shown by the fact that it is possible for a library to publish in a recent number of a professional journal an advertisement reading as follows:

Research assistant (man) desired in large reference library. Must be a graduate of a well-known university (one having done considerable post-graduate work preferred) with good working knowledge of foreign languages and previous library experience in advanced reference work. Salary $2,000.

It may safely be claimed that during the thirty-year period there has been a wider recognition of librarianship as a profession and that this recognition extends down farther and farther into the rank and file of those engaged in library work. There was a time when such recognition, if granted at all, was extended solely or principally to chief librarians of the larger libraries; the members of their staffs were "clerks" in public estimation, sometimes in thought and in designation of their chiefs, and too often many of them deserved such a classification. Now in the larger libraries, not only department heads, but many others are esteemed as the professional colleagues of their chiefs. A not unimportant factor in the more general recognition of the professional character of librarianship is the allocation of librarians in government libraries to the professional and sub-professional grades under the classification act, along with biologists, chemists, economists, physicians, attorneys, engineers, and other specialists in the government service.

PROFESSIONAL RECOGNITION

Without attempting to set forth all the factors which have helped to bring about this change in the professional recognition of librarianship, mention may be made that in thirty years the individual memberships in the American Library Association have increased from 474 to 9,277 and that the number of library schools has grown from four to seventeen. The latter figure includes only those accredited by the American Library Association; of these eight are graduate library schools and one is an advanced graduate library school. Formerly, the profession was largely recruited in its higher ranks from strong men and women from other professions, and in its intermediate and lower ranks from those without previous training and often with little more than a high-school education. In recent years the professional and sub-professional posts in the large, medium, and even in many small libraries have been generally filled by those bringing full college education and library-school graduation.

What are some of the features in the personnel situation of our libraries that call for improvement?

FEMINIZATION OF STAFFS

The most marked characteristic of the standard library staff is its extreme feminization. An estimate based on an analysis of a portion of the membership cards at American Library Association headquarters shows that 85 per cent or more represent women and 15 per cent or less, men. This membership includes the cream of library workers, those most professionally-minded and also best paid. If a census of the sex of all persons engaged in library work were to be taken, it might show that even a larger percentage are women. It will perhaps be recognized that the writer has long been numbered among those men librarians who have insisted on equal pay for women and men doing the same grade and quality of work and an equal opportunity for their advancement to the higher posts, including chief librarianships. None the less I believe that the disproportion is too great and that the women in the profession as well as the men, and the whole cause of librarianship, suffer from this unbalanced and therefore unhealthy condition. This situation has long been a vicious circle. Historically, people generally have had the idea that library work is nice, light, clean, and easy— just suited to women; also that not much pay was required. So libraries have been filled with women, many of whom lived at home and so would accept the small salaries offered—less than a full return for the service rendered. Librarianship thus became a sweated occupation. Students going into college and public libraries have rarely seen anyone but women, all of whom on inquiry were found to be paid very little. Moreover, nearly all of those in sight were engaged in stamping and filing cards or in other predominantly mechanical tasks. As a result male college students have almost unanimously ruled library work out of the question, classing it as a low-paid clerical job, furnishing neither a worthy career nor a livelihood.

MECHANICAL TASKS IN EVIDENCE

The disproportionately large amount of time spent on semi-mechanical tasks is another serious handicap to enlisting, holding, and developing an enlightened and progressive library personnel. Every profession has its mechanical processes, but ours seem so over-powering as almost to engulf us and the waters rise so far that too few emerge from the mechano-technical details. The general use of the Library of Congress printed cards and the invention of a book-charging machine are steps in the direction of mitigating this situation, but much more needs to be done to simplify routine and even more to put it into the background where it will not be so oppressively in evidence. Perhaps the way out lies in the direction of placing larger emphasis on the advisory service to the individual reader. If that could be developed to many times its present small beginnings and could occupy the center of every library picture, the library would appear far more inviting to the public and to possible recruits to librarianship.

Has there yet been an adequate facing of the question that there are in every library purely clerical and almost completely mechanical tasks, that these are necessary for smooth operation, but that they can be performed by clerical and mechanical assistants, who are not and do not need to be librarians and in most cases will never become such? Many of our present difficulties have arisen from the fact that, partly because we have been prevented thru lack of funds from doing better, we have taken into our libraries those who have been good enough to perform these routine tasks, and then have gradually promoted them to the more advanced and responsible posts, for which not simply more experience, but a different type of mind, is required, in combination with more advanced education and training. The remedy seems to be that we must in our thinking and in our practice make a sharper discrimination between the clerical-mechanical service and the professional and sub-professional service involving book knowledge and book interpretation. Either that or we must employ in our clerical-mechanical service people who are so equipped as to be promotable to become librarians, and then promote them quickly before they become discouraged or routinized.

Book Knowledge Needed

Another great need is that our professional staffs, particularly those that serve the public, shall be enlarged and strengthened and made to include those having diverse equipment in book knowledge. This is needed, not primarily to relieve overburdened workers, but to meet the vastly greater demands which are sure to come to us as soon as it is generally known that we are equipped to give an authoritative advisory book service. At present in most libraries staffs are sufficient only to meet somewhat inadequately the growing requirements of persistent readers. Scarcely anywhere is there that leisurely atmosphere which invites the timid reader needing help and betokens competent and well-considered advice. Too often one or two persons are required to give advice on the literature of such widely diverse subjects that it is impossible for them to have the first-hand knowledge requisite to speak with authority and to carry conviction. With this diversity of book knowledge in the enlarged staffs must be combined more of humanity, more of interest in people and in their individual reading problems, together with ability to diagnose the intellectual equipment of readers and skill to prescribe the books needed for mental sanitation and development.

ROUTINERS NOT DESIRABLE

Another handicap has arisen from the fact that too often people have gone into library work for negative reasons; because they had no liking or aptitude for teaching, law, medicine, scientific or engineering work, or business. They liked books in a mild sort of way and saw library work as a permanent if low-paid occupation. To them library work was little if any more than a routine job. Without particular aptitude for the work, suitable personality, or marked love of people they were not likely ever to contribute a new thought to the advancement of the profession or to rise above standardized routine ideas and practice. Such librarians seem to gloat over intricate technical details, tend to hang on to them to the last ditch, and resist efforts at simplification and elimination.

Librarianship should be able to attract the strong, well-qualified people, both men and women, who naturally belong in our profession. These should include people with vision, who are capable of contributing constructive ideas. As we librarians think of the library as a slice of the best of life, so a library staff should be a slice from the upper crust of life, in which women only slightly exceed men in numbers. With an improving salary situation, a better understanding that library work involves far more important factors than the merely technical, and a growing sex equality, in which men are getting over their sex superiority complex, the overfeminization of the library will, it is expected, tend to correct itself.

ADULT EDUCATION

The development of the library as a great agency for adult education opens the road for the improvement of library personnel. The present emphasis on the library's part in the movement is sometimes criticized both by those who claim that the library has always been engaged in adult education and by those who say that the library cannot expect to cut much of a figure in it. The big gain to us is that the general movement has now become a self-conscious one, with a philosophical background, that it is assuming large proportions, and that the library is recognized as having a prominent part in it. In order that the library may measure up to this opportunity, it must and will command vastly greater support. This will provide larger and better-paid staffs who will in turn render, not only a larger service, but a different type of service. This in turn involves improvement in the recruits for librarianship, changes in preliminary education and training for librarianship, and more and better training of librarians in service.

Adult education means for the library a lifelong continuance of the education of the public or of such of the public as become the library's clients. This inevitably means a lifelong continuance of the education and training of librarians to enable them to minister to our public. Such continuing education and training arc just as necessary for staff members with advanced degrees and professional training as for those who have come up from the ranks largely by means of self-education.

Among the factors requisite in the personnel and training of a staff suited to bear its full part in this newly self-conscious adult education movement are the following.

HIGHEST STANDARDS

The greatest possible care should be exercised by library-school directors and librarians in the selection of personnel for training or appointment. Not only is it necessary to enforce the highest attainable standards of formal education and technical training, but use should be made of intelligence tests, and acceptable personality standards and good health should be insisted upon. Probationary appointments are desirable, to test out adaptability and so far as possible character and social intelligence. It is vitally important to library schools and libraries to admit to training or appointment only those who have the capacity, recognize the need, and have the ambition always to keep improving in education and training.

Then there is the large field of training in service, beginning with the chief librarian and extending down thru department heads, understudies, intermediate assistants, branch librarians, and the rank and file. Such training involves securing good *esprit de corps,* impressing high standards of service, and incitement to individual improvement.

Such staff training may be secured by a combination of several methods. In small libraries there may be frequent meetings of the staff as a whole. In larger libraries to reach the entire staff there must be divisional meetings. Often there may be stated meetings of the chief librarian with department heads, alternating perhaps with larger groups which will include senior assistants. Even when these meetings are predominantly administrative, the resulting discussions are valuable as training. In the writer's library during the current year a group of about forty is basing its season's program on discussions of the various American Library Association textbooks, comparing the library's own procedures with those set forth in these texts. In addition there are other stated group meetings of branch librarians, of children's librarians, and of intermediate and junior assistants, in all of which are discussed, not simply administrative matters, but other advanced problems, with resulting valuable staff instruction. The public advisory group has also conducted a series of courses in book discussion, with a different field covered in each course.

STAFF TRAINING

Staff training includes three principal types. The first type, designed especially for juniors, is chiefly technical and includes the inculcation of good methods of work; the second, for intermediate and senior members, includes instruction designed to promote *esprit de corps* and a knowledge of the objectives and services of the whole library; and the third, for the administrative staff, is designed to increase the effectiveness of the staff as a whole by stressing the opportunities for original and creative work in order that the library may progressively measure up to its full opportunities for usefulness.

The problems of library personnel are so numerous and diverse that the space limitations of this paper are not adequate for their discussion. For example, there is the need for more general training of librarians in public speaking, including the preparation and delivery of radio addresses. Is there an overemphasis on a knowledge of foreign languages, at the expense of economics, sociology, and science? There is the matter of stressing the more systematic reading of current professional literature by the li-

brary staff as a whole. There is the question of sab-
batical years for other than college librarians, for
purposes of travel and study. What help may a librarian gone stale on his job expect to get by resorting
to an advanced graduate library school? Are the
graduate institutions either in their library schools
or other departments offering the requisite facilities
for the further education of advisory assistants in
subject matter and literature? Our needs are many.
If we make our demands known, ways of meeting
them will be found.

A CHIEF LIBRARIAN LOOKS AT WORK WITH CHILDREN: PITTSBURGH'S CONTRIBUTION THERETO [1]

You are today celebrating the twenty-ninth annual commencement of your school, which was, according to your early records which I have been reading, started on October 1, 1900, as a training class for children's librarians. Out of fifteen applicants five were selected for the first class from the Pittsburgh and Allegheny Kindergarten College. You had fifteen students the second year, and now your class numbers forty-nine. This commencement also marks the end of your school as a separate unit under the public library of Pittsburgh and its merger with the Carnegie Institute of Technology. All well-wishers of the school, and that of course includes librarians generally, hope that this implies a step forward, the maintenance of previous high standards, perhaps even the raising of standards for admission and graduation, the receipt of degrees, and other advantages.

The Carnegie Library School thruout most of its life has been devoted exclusively to the training of children's librarians. Tho more recently it has had general courses in librarianship, more than two-thirds of this year's class have followed the children's course or the course in school library work. Because this library school has always been so predominantly devoted to children's work, it has become synonymous in the minds of most mem-

[1] Commencement address, Carnegie Library School, Pittsburgh, June 7, 1930.

bers of the library profession with training for library work with children; in this field it has for most of the past thirty years possessed almost a monopoly. In view of its achievements therein this transition period seems an appropriate time for comment on some aspects of library work for children and this school's contribution to librarianship by its devotion, over a period of nearly thirty years, to this specialty.

Altho such an appraisal might appropriately be made by one of your own graduates, who would, of course, have intimate, first-hand knowledge of library work for children, yet I trust it may be worth while to hear something of the evaluation of library work for children from one whose experience as chief librarian of two public libraries almost matches the life of this school and who, during that period, has to the fullest possible extent fostered library work for children in those libraries.

If further evidence of my competence to speak on this particular subject is needed I may cite a few facts. When early in 1901 I took charge of my first public library I found that it had indeed a children's room, or rather a corner where children's books were shelved, but no children's librarian. The books were chiefly bound in "ugly duck" and so much used as missiles by the boys who visited the room that few girls dared to frequent it. The most promising member of the staff was promptly chosen as children's librarian. She and I struggled together for months over questions of book selection for that room and for the school collection which was promptly established, and then she was sent to Pittsburgh to become a member of the third class of this school. Migrating in 1904 to my present post, I found a member of your fourth class in charge of our central, and what was then our only, children's room. When matrimony took her away, as was formerly the devastating habit of matrimony with library assistants, another member of your fourth class came, after library experience elsewhere, to take her place, to lay soundly the ground work for our future children's department, to become later director of our training class, and finally a highly prized assistant librarian. An especially promising member of one of our early training classes was encouraged to go away to Pittsburgh, and on her return to us became supervisor of our school work and later the very able director of our work with children. At present we have five Pittsburgh graduates on our staff. I had supposed the number to be greater, for it is safe to say that all members of our staff engaged in children's work are permeated with Pittsburgh ideals and the Pittsburgh spirit. And in that group I trust I may be permitted to number myself. In view of this record and this conviction you can well understand how glad I am to come here today and to give my grateful testimony to the distinctive contribution of your alma mater to library work.

THE PROBLEM OF CHILDREN'S WORK

What are some of the characteristics of sound library work for children? What are its scope, its purpose, its ideals? How is it related to library work for adults? What are the desirable qualities of children's librarians? What should be their personal and educational equipment, their fundamental training and their continuing education and training? What of the status of the children's librarian, her recognition as to salary and her rank in her own library? What of the professional recognition that should be accorded to her individually and collectively? These are some of the questions that present themselves to a chief librarian who desires to interpret library work for children to a group about to enter on the active exercise of the profession.

Instead of carrying coals to Newcastle it would be bringing iron and steel to Pittsburgh for one on such an occasion and to such a group to attempt to describe the organization and details of library work for children. But what is the purpose of such work that leads us to esteem it so highly and to put so much of money, time, thought, and nervous energy into it?

To you and to the modern American public librarian, library work for children has now become a commonplace. But it is perhaps not out of place to recall that, after all, this work as we understand it and practice it is comparatively new. Until a recent yesterday the library, even the public library, had little or no place for the child. It was emphatically an institution for adults. Not only that; it was primarily for cultivated adults. Democracy and its necessary concomitant, universal education, have extended the library's clientèle both horizontally and vertically. The public library, in its efforts to achieve the purpose of becoming the people's university, the universal continuation school, found in too many cases that it failed to reenlist for a lifelong campaign of individual education, with resulting community enlightment, the rank and file of the public school army, composed predominantly of forced enlistments who served the minimum term and then withdrew, too often glad that their education was at an end. And too often it is literally terminated, or, if continued at all, it is chiefly thru such rather doubtful agencies as the tabloid newspaper, the movies, and the radio with its Amos and Andy, or, if this specific reference is unpopular with possible friends of theirs in this group, then the radio with its "jamborees of jazz, cheap vaudeville, prize fights and the whole gamut of questionable advertising," as it has recently been described.

A QUICKENING INFLUENCE

Whether by conscious design or by the force of circumstances often working better than we plan, the public library, by taking up and developing children's work, has brought about, not indeed a revolution but an evolution in that it has profoundly influenced many children educationally. First, when the library has placed in the hands of young folks in school not textbooks, which as task books too often lack inspiration, but interesting, vital inspiring pieces of literature, for voluntary reading, torpid minds have been quickened, school work has become better, and pupils have remained longer in school than would have happened without such outside stimulants. Furthermore, often the real purpose of the library thereby tends to be accomplished; that is, the children learn to love books and reading, develop good taste for reading and the reading habit, and so are soon well on their way toward becoming lifelong readers. It soon results that they are engaged in that never ending, continuous process of self-education which is coming to be the present day conception of education.

The purpose of library work for children is, therefore, to catch them young and hold them by the silken cords of interest, enthusiasm, and love for good reading in the hope that such interest, taste, and habit will survive and persist to and thruout adult life.

That the library may help to make people think, that it may shape them emotionally, is a great opportunity and a great responsibility. Modern scientific thought is corroborating the words of the Bible, "As he thinketh in his heart so is he;" so is he physically, so is he in relation to his fellow man, and books probably more than any other agency can influence his thinking. Esthetic development, or love of beauty in its many forms of expression, makes the man and its lack may greatly mar him.

Beautifully illustrated editions of the classics, the work of the inspirers of thought and creators of careful expression thru the ages, help to ripen the child, and furnish him a bulwark against temptations which so often win because of a lack of other interests.

One of the saddest things I have heard was the not infrequent expression of our soldiers on leave in France, "I know it's all wonderful, if I knew what it's all about. It I had only read and known more before I came!" Verily, "he who would bring home the wealth of the Indies must carry the wealth of the Indies with him."

A PHASE OF ADULT EDUCATION

By an apparent contradiction of terms, library work for children is therefore a phase of adult education. Certain it is that children who have enjoyed thruout their youth the advantages of a well stocked and well administered children's room will more surely, more confidently, find their way to the adult department. If they have been habituated to a library, they have become comfortable in it and are prepared to go on and make the most and best use of it. If, however, there is any public library where there is no library work for children, a condition now almost unthinkable, or if the children's work is poorly planned and executed, the library is likely to fail in its efforts to capture and enlist, not simply the children, but the adults who as children lacked such an influence. The competition of other influences is keen and pervasive. Such competition includes the radio, the automobile, the movie, cheap and commonplace books in series, the comic strips, plain and colored, and the sex-saturated gutter magazines; the competition of inertia, too, plays its part.

QUALITY OF BOOKS READ

In most large public libraries today the home circulation of books is increasing by leaps and bounds, and this in spite of these competitions that non-librarians have long been predicting would force reading into the background. Of these large totals more than one-half consist of children's books. Gratifying as these mounting figures are, the mere shovelling out of millions of books over a counter is not a very satisfying process and does not of itself necessarily mean the achievement of the library's purpose. Unless we can be sure of the quality of the books we dispense, can do something to fit them to our readers and where opportunity offers help in the guidance of reading, the library fails of its greatest usefulness and its peculiar contribution to society.

Beginning with the children's department, the library should stress its reference work. This will consist largely of aiding in school problems. The help afforded will give the children confidence in the library's resources and the librarian's knowledge and resourcefulness. Advice in purely recreational reading—the fitting of books to people, the right book

to the right person at the right age—is fundamenal.
Such personal work can best be carried on in the
face to face contacts in children's rooms, but a sur-
prising degree of success is secured in school work in
Washington, where specially selected collections of
books, one book for each child, are lent for two month
periods to individual classrooms for home reading.
Such collections are made up of about half fiction and
half non-fiction, graded according to ages and reading
abilities and coordinated with the course of study, so
that they prove helpful in teaching, but are at the
same time for voluntary reading.

A definite piece of adult education work is being
carried on in connection with Washington's central
children's room and will shortly be intensified by
the appointment next month of a well educated,
well trained, and experienced assistant at a good
salary as readers' adviser to adults in children's
literature. This work with parents and other adults
is a phase of children's work that has received too
little attention. The library has for many years realized, and realized on, the teacher's influence in
children's reading, but has neglected somewhat the
potent possibilities of the parent in this regard.
Many parents, as libraries made up from gifts only
too sadly attest, have thought of children's books in
terms of the Alger, the Dotty Dimple, and other books
of that ilk. One of the most interesting experiences
that can come to you as children's librarians is to
see the effect on parents of showing them the classics
in new and attractive dress as well as the worth-
while new books. Along with this should go work
with parents for the pre-school child, a rapidly growing demand. Here two results are obtainable, first,
the suggestion of desirable books for children and
second, a valuable by-product, the inoculation of the

parent with the idea of the library as not only an educational but also a cultural center. Parents often come in desperation to seek the library's advice after trying vainly in book stores to get the help they need. For this reason I think it most important that each library, however small its book fund, should have a small reference collection of books to show parents and other adults. Little work of this advisory nature can be done with soiled books or books out in circulation. I know of no other form of publicity that gets before parents so surely the value of children's literature.

WORK WITH PARENTS

We have two rooms, as part of our children's department, set apart, where parents, teachers, and other adults may seek advice. One of these is occupied with our illustrators' collection and books for the parent to borrow. For some years this advisory work has been carried, and it has grown yearly without anyone who could be assigned to take charge of it as an individual problem. The work already done in this connection has convinced me that it has a distinct contribution to make. Tho I have spoken of parents seeking advice, many times it proves to be aunts and uncles and grandparents who are taking up the problem when busy parents cannot. They return again and again for help.

I promised to mention some of the characteristics of sound library work for children and the necessary conditions for accomplishing it. First of all it seems to me that every children's room should be as friendly and homelike and as little formal and institutional as possible.

There should be in every children's room children's librarians who thru their personalities and book knowledge can transfer to the child the contagion of their enthusiasm. They should be able to make readers of non-readers and steadily improve the reading taste. Also thought must be given to the child's esthetic appreciation. To this end copies of good, preferably great, paintings should be displayed in all children's rooms. The Washington Public Library is fortunate in having a full set of the Medici prints, presented in part by the Twentieth Century Club of Washington, which, exchanged from time to time, are hung in all children's rooms, as well as in adult reading rooms. Rooms should be neat, thus being at once models for the home, and aids in discipline. Flowers are added attractions; at times those in the library afford the only opportunity for enjoying them that some children have.

There should be sentiment—of beauty, of cheerfulness, of helpfulness—but no sentimentality. The days of the "dear cute things" have gone. Dealings with the children should be impersonal and friendly. Picture bulletins and other decorations should be in the best taste, never jazzy or garish. Time should not be spent in elaborate picture bulletins or other "frills" to the neglect of the fundamental job.

As a chief librarian surveying the whole field of library work and trying to see each phase in its proper proportion, I should say to you, and especially to those of you who are taking up this specialty, that the field of children's work is huge and the opportunities probably more than any library is now able to undertake. I therefore caution you to keep your feet firmly on the ground (tho you may have your heads among the stars if you like), to decide among the multiplicity of opportunities for service open to any children's room or department what are the essentials and to do these at least reasonably well before you attempt other activities; in other words to plan work in the order of its importance, and only as the staff or time will permit, to take on other activities. You will either plan your work and follow as well as possible that plan or you will scatter your energies.

KNOW CHILDREN AND BOOKS

As I see it one of your first objectives should be to understand children, for of course I assume your deep interest in them. This means patient and thoro work. Another objective, perhaps even more important, is to know and to appreciate your books or to be learning to know and appreciate them. Next comes knowing your community, its needs and its opportunities. Then you should relate your work to the other work of the library, know its resources, have understanding of the significance of the work of the library generally. This should be easy, for part of your big job is that of training candidates for the adult department. You should be sufficiently informed of the work to which you are introducing them.

Since your work rests on the order, catalog, and bindery departments and since these departments are always working for you, you should know something of their problems and in what ways you may facilitate their work for you.

Now as to that second objective, knowing books. First, the children's librarian must select her books, evaluating them as she reads them. Also she must constantly reconsider the material in use, weeding out the collections as material is no longer needed or better material on a subject is available. This is requisite, that there may be a proper use of public money. Of course it is important for all librarians to be book lovers and well read, but in children's work it is absolutely essential. From what I have seen and heard of children's work I judge that reviews and indexes will not help you much. The child says to you: "I have read this book and I'm crazy about it; I want another like it." Embarrassing, when you are recommending a book, is the question that is apt to come: "Have you read it?" Knowing well a few books for each age is a fine nucleus on which you can build. If you like the book it is probable that you can interest a child in it. But if you say: "This is a good book; you will like this book," when you have not read it, your sins are pretty sure to find you out, for the question will come: "What is it about?"

A children's librarian, the head of a children's department in a foreign country, visited our library. Questioned about her work she said: "No, we do not order our books; the order department does that"; and "We do not get time to read them; we are so busy." At Christmas time, directed to us, came a pamphlet of an elaborate program of a pageant and other Christmas activities extending for a week, put on by this children's department which did not have time to read its books. This, I do not need to tell you, is not the Pittsburgh way.

What about the characteristics desirable for a children's librarian?—perhaps a hazardous question to propound to a group like this. I should put first that indefinable and indescribable quality known as personality. To mention only a few of the necessary adjectives, she should be positive, friendly, winning, not cold, or austere, and above all not pernickety. In fact the qualities in young women that often lead to marriage proposals on the part of discriminating young men are some of those that make for successful children's librarians. That is probably the ex-

planation of the relatively high proportion of mar-
riages among them.

The frequency of marriage among children's librarians, and for that matter among women in all
branches of library work, prompts me to comment on
the changed attitude toward matrimony on the part
of library boards and librarians. Formerly an an-
nouncement by a woman librarian of her impending
marriage was equivalent to her resignation. This is
often no longer the case. Formerly when a young
woman came to me to announce her approaching
marriage, after proper congratulations I expressed
regret at losing her. Now I ask how long she needs
for her wedding trip. After she returns she frequently retains her position unless or until maternity
requires her withdrawal. So far as I can see, even
such an event need not necessarily compel her permanent abandonment of the library profession any
more than it now does in the cases of teaching and
other professions.

Education and Training

What of the education and training of children's
librarians for entrance into the profession? The
tendency is to make the possession of the bacca-
laureate degree a prerequisite for admission to all
accredited library schools, and I understand that
will hereafter be required in this school. College
graduation has now become relatively more common
than was high school graduation twenty or twenty-
five years ago. Also it sometimes does not mean
more, often perhaps not so much in the possession
of real education and culture, as was possessed by
some of the early graduates of this school who came
to it without even a high school diploma, but did
have the basic culture on which Pittsburgh built and

by which the library profession was enriched thru the acquisition of the leaders in library work for children. In view of this record, tho it may hereafter be difficult for this library school to avoid exacting the bachelor's degree for entrance, I venture to express the hope that a sufficiently flexible way may be found to admit to this school and so to recruit to this specialty of our profession the occasional rare woman who has the other qualities to a high degree but who has somehow missed securing the hall-mark of college graduation.

To repeat what I have said on other occasions, I wish to stress the importance of the continuation of the education of librarians. I believe that this is just as necessary for those who enter our profession with the best fundamental education and professional training as it is for those who came in with somewhat meager schooling and little systematic training. In some cases it seems even more necessary, for occasionally the completely schooled person is too much inclined to let it go at that, whereas the one who has come up from the ranks is so completely aware of deficiencies and so alert to overcome them that in time she outstrips her self-satisfied colleague.

As has already been indicated, the children's librarian must do an enormous amount of critical and intensive reading in her specialty. In addition, to keep in touch with life and to preserve her balance as an adult member of the community, she needs to read the best of what the rest of us are reading. Also in common with all librarians she needs to follow current professional literature. This means more than periodicals and books issued by and for librarians, tho that mass is assuming portentous proportions; it should include the current discussions in books and periodicals on social and educational problems, adult and other. Because of this necessary continuing education and training which a children's librarian must give herself, I question in her case the desirability of study for higher degrees in other subjects. It seems to me that the training of daily experience will fit her better for her work than further formal training which might easily make her lose contact with the mind of the child.

RECOGNITION IN PAY AND RANK

I have set up high standards of personal qualities, of fundamental and continuing education and training for the librarian specializing in children's work. What recognition in pay and in rank is to be accorded to her in return? In my judgment the achievement standards set, the size of the job, and its importance for the future of the library all require that there shall be complete comparability in salary and status between the head of the children's department and heads of the best recognized other departments in the library. From what has already been said, it is evident that I believe that not only the director of children's work but also the individual children's librarians should have professional standing and pay, comparable with those of other library positions. In the public schools there is a growing tendency to pay primary teachers the same scale of salaries as is paid to teachers in higher grades, to the end that a good primary teacher will not need to be promoted out of work she does well into work for which she has no special aptitude in order that she may be paid better; also because the importance of the ground work is now coming to be well understood. Similarly, the best interests of the library as well as justice to the individual should make it possible to retain in children's work those whose aptitudes lie there. If a children's librarian is changed to other work it should be because of the combination of administrative needs and the development of other aptitudes and should be a transfer and not primarily a graduation out of children's work in order to secure better salary recognition. Experience in children's work is so varied and so valuable as often to develop such aptitudes. For example, the library will often greatly benefit by making a children's librarian a branch librarian. In a small branch she may well combine the two functions. In a large branch she may no longer actually do children's work, but the branch is the gainer by reason of her background of experience in that work.

So much for the recognition of children's librarians by the individual library. It follows that there should be similar fuller recognition of this group by the American Library Association and other professional organizations. The quality of the work done by this group in book evaluation, the importance of the administrative positions held by many children's librarians in the larger libraries, and the social experience developed thru their innumerable contacts with the adult community all justify such recognition, and the profession as a whole would be strengthened by greater use of such people in the directing activities of the national and local library associations.

May I mention a few of the contributions of children's librarians to library thought and practice? First, there is their emphasis upon the book itself, as distinguished from methods. As already suggested, methods now used by the adult education movement in libraries have long been practiced in children's work, that is the requirements of specialized knowledge and training on the part of advisers giving information to the public.

IMPROVEMENT IN BOOKS

Another interesting contribution has been work with publishers to bring up the quality of content of books, the format, even matters of type. Remarkable progress has been made along these lines in ten years. Thru the efforts of children's librarians, with specific recommendations, editions of most of the classics appropriate for young people have been brought out in artistic style, with larger type, wider margins, attractive covers, and excellent illustrations. The library as a whole has profited by this improvement and can make books go that would not be read in the closely printed editions which were the staple of those available fifteen or more years ago.

The children's librarian has contributed more than perhaps we realize to the freedom of the child in the selection of its books, making the pasture safe but also making it attractive, a place where the child may roam at will.

Splendid progress has been made in children's reading thru the work of children's librarians with schools. With an able schools division and well run and suitably located children's rooms, the public library can, as I believe it should, guide practically the entire reading of children in any community.

The public library must in a large sense rest on its children's work. It has come to be the foundation on which all subsequent public library work builds. If the work here is well done less promotional work will be required in adult work. This is the period when people with least effort and embarrassment will use the library. Without doubt

many adults, because of shyness or awkwardness or
fear of showing ignorance, are deterred from enter-
ing the library. One of the big contributions of the
children's department is to train up library habituated people to be natural and confident users of
the library.

INFLUENCE ON APPROPRIATIONS

This matter has a very practical aspect to an
administrative librarian, one of whose major duties
has been to try to secure appropriations of money
for library support and extensions. Such applica-
tions have been addressed to an extended series of
budget bodies capped by the Appropriations Committees of Congress. In such presentations the dominant feeling has often been that had the personnel
to whom I was making my appeals themselves been
from childhood up public library users, so that they
had a real comprehension of what it all means, the
problem would have been simplified. The trouble
has always been and is now, that the modern conception of the public library is so very new that only
an infinitesimal part of any community has been
exposed to the influence of the public library from
childhood up to the time when they exercise such a
determining influence in public affairs as that of
controlling appropriations for library support.

To make a practical application of this same
problem to yourselves, I suggest that if each of you
can do such fine work in the community to which
you go that the community will believe in the library
to the point of paying you well, not only are you
individually and your library the gainers, but this
will helpfully influence the library salary situation
elsewhere.

Pittsburgh Graduates Everywhere

And now, in conclusion, to come back to the splendid service of this institution during the thirty years of its history. It would be hard to estimate the influence of the school in this country and in foreign countries where its students have gone, spreading the gospel of book knowledge and the services of children's libraries. They have carried its inspiration and its technique.

In many a public library in this country, perhaps in most libraries of any considerable size, may be found a Pittsburgh graduate training large staffs in children's departments along the lines they themselves learned at Pittsburgh. It is not so much the work of this one person that counts as the inoculation of large groups with this spirit which makes the leaven of Pittsburgh so potent.

In paying this tribute to this school I do not forget the pre-Pittsburgh group who visioned library work with children and put forth such strenuous, wise efforts to bring it to pass. Among these pioneers were Mary Wright Plummer, Caroline M. Hewins, Anne Carroll Moore, and Clara W. Hunt. Similarly I do not forget Frances Jenkins Olcott, the first director of this school.

In stressing today the fundamental importance of library work for children, I have not been allowing this occasion and your preoccupation with this specialty to lead me to use superlatives. I am but voicing my deep seated conviction which grows stronger from year to year.

The transfer of the school to the Carnegie Institute of Technology I hope means more advantages and larger opportunities for usefulness. We librarians think of Pittsburgh as the center of training for children's library work. Whatever the school's future, since the Pittsburgh school's reputation has been built on the far-seeing, pioneering work in this field, I hope that more rather than less emphasis will be given to this specialty. You have done this job well and public librarians need more rather than fewer of the people with the kind and quality of training this school has been sending to us.

Those of you who are being graduated today are heirs of this tradition, in which you should take great pride. That tradition implies a mind open to meet the ever new and more complex problems of this rapidly changing world. Yours is a goodly heritage. I can only urge you to prove worthy of it.

To close on too solemn a note would be to give the wrong accent. As you enter on library work, and especially if it is library work with children, I promise you happiness in your work. Those with years of experience in this specialty testify to the satisfaction, even the joyousness, of their work and those children's librarians whom I know best seem to take delight in it. I therefore welcome you to the glorious company of librarians, serious of purpose but light of heart.

THE PUBLIC LIBRARY AN INVESTMENT— NOT AN EXPENSE[1]

A little less than two years ago I had the pleasure of accepting an invitation from this association to address a public meeting at your new high school building in the interest of establishing a public library here. I was led to expect from the strong resolutions adopted by the earnest and intelligent audience that I should shortly have news that your public library was an accomplished fact. I was glad to accept your invitation to speak a second time to the workers for this cause, tho I should much prefer to have received an invitation to attend the opening of your library. Whether soon or late, that event is sure to come about. The purpose of this luncheon is, I believe, to bring it about now, to take steps so that you and the entire city may at once enter into the enjoyment of the benefits of a public library, instead of longer postponing the assuming here of an obligation regarded as reasonable by practically every other American city.

ULTIMATELY; WHY NOT NOW?

As I understand the matter, you have been canvassing the question for several years. I venture the assertion that there is not a person here present, probably not a citizen of this city, who does not fully expect that ultimately you will have a free, public, tax-supported municipal library, in common with other cities. The question then is, why not have

[1] Address before a luncheon meeting of the Richmond (Va.) Education Association, January 28, 1913.

it now? Self-governing American cities have, like individual citizens, reasons for following a given course of action or of remaining inactive. No one can make them supply themselves with a public library if they do not want it, if they do not think they need it—certainly not a visiting librarian. On the other hand, an independent, self-governing, enlightened city like this will have a public library for itself whenever it becomes fully persuaded of the necessity for a library and is aroused to the point of taking action.

Penny Wise, Pound Foolish

Now what have been your reasons for postponing the establishment and maintenance of a free public library? What have you gained by inaction? The obvious answer is that you have been saved from paying the taxes necessary to support the library. But has this really been a saving—a gain? Is it a saving or a gain for the head of a well-to-do family to supply himself, his wife and children with insufficient food and clothing? to keep them from school and compel them to work? Does he not undermine his own health and theirs, reduce his own present earning power and their future earning power? As with the individual, so with the city, such savings are of the kind that ought not to be afforded. They are of the "penny wise, pound foolish" variety.

What have you lost? What are you losing every day by the postponement of public library maintenance? You are not really postponing the incurring of an expense which you fully intend, as a matter of civic pride, some day rather grudgingly to assume. You are, on the contrary, losing the opportunity to make an investment which will yield large dividends. If a conservative business proposition were presented to you, one that you were convinced would yield fair returns immediately and large dividends ultimately, you would not hesitate to organize a corporation, even on borrowed capital, to finance such a business. But here you have a rich corporation, the city itself, in which you are all stockholders and some of you directors. You may have to amend your charter to be allowed to extend your business in this new way; but that should not be difficult, if you really want to make this investment. That this is good business for the city corporation to engage in is shown by the precedents of practically all other American cities.

Necessary Expenses and Investments

If I made a new classification of public outlays, I should have two important classes: (1) necessary expenses, and (2) investments. In the former I would include the expenditures for jails, prisons, almshouses, insane asylums, institutions for the feeble minded, hospitals, police and fire departments— expenses for protection against the viciousness, the mistakes, the misfortunes and the accidents of mankind—chiefly of a negative character. Among investments I would include street improvements, sewers, water works, the health department, the public schools, the public library, parks, and playgrounds—expenses of a positive nature, for betterments, for enterprises that facilitate business, that improve the health and happiness of the people and prepare for self-support and enlightened citizenship. Now most of these enterprises and especially the public school system have long been regarded as essential to the welfare of a democratic, self-governing community, which rests for its success and permanence on the intelligence and character of its citizens. You have recognized the force of this argument by building up here a strong public school system and by constantly strengthening it. So firmly are you convinced of its necessity that you would scout any suggestion to close the schools for a year in order to cut down the taxes. For the sake of the argument, however, let us suppose that you were to try the experiment for a year, for five years, or indefinitely. What would be the result? There would of course be an immediate increase of lawlessness and crime and a more gradual increase of illiteracy and poverty. These would in turn inevitably result in largely increased expenditures for the police force, the fire department, the criminal courts, jails and workhouses, the almshouse, poor relief, etc. If you were to try this experiment you would be glad to go back and resume the support of the schools, not as an expense, but as an investment in good citizenship, rather than to be compelled to meet the far larger expenses for protection and relief and even then to live under a reign of terror.

Reinforce the Schools

Now the public library proposition is simply one that involves a comparatively slight and modest additional expenditure to reinforce the public schools and make the comparatively large expenditures for them most effective. The city of Cleveland has one of the finest public school systems in the United States and one of the best public library systems in the world. Cleveland spends on its schools annually at the rate of $7.36 per capita for its entire population. It spends but 57 cents per capita on its public library system.[2] Altho this is the high-

[2] According to late (unofficial) figures, Cleveland spends annually $20.70 per capita on its schools and $1.77 per capita on its public library.

est per capita expenditure for public libraries for any of the larger cities of the United States, it is but 8 per cent of its expenditure for its schools. Just as it would be shortsighted for this city to omit to spend money on its schools, so it is shortsighted to fail to secure the largest return on the money now invested in education here, by confining such expenditures to school instruction, when by devoting a comparatively slight additional sum to the support of a public library you would vastly increase the effectiveness of the schools.

SCHOOLS NEED VITALIZING

We in America pride ourselves that we are a very practical people and that this is a very practical age. School education is not an end in itself, but looks definitely toward the future of enlightened, self-supporting citizenship. Just now the public schools are being closely scrutinized to see whether they are accomplishing these objects, that is whether their graduates become enlightened, self-supporting citizens. In many cases they are being found to be inefficient. A very high percentage of children drop out of school, partly from loss of interest or inability to keep up with their classes and partly because they are compelled to go to work. In many cases it has been shown that public library books sent to schools have been the direct means of arousing the interest of children, of holding them in school and thus of making their school education successful and effective, and hence of making them more intelligent citizens, with higher earning capacity, than they would have become without the aid of the public library.

LIBRARY REDUCES DELINQUENCY

The work of the modern public library is closely linked with the school in order not simply to supplement, as it largely does, the work of the school by the loan of books to teachers for professional study and for class room supplemental reading, but also and especially so that it may capture the children in the formative age, introduce them to the library thru a well-equipped children's room conducted by experts, and make of them, if possible, life long library users. In counting up the gains and losses to this city thru postponement of making the investment in the support of a public library, consider the losses in the earning power of the boys and girls who have dropped out of school prematurely when a public library might have held them in school. Consider the fact that boys and girls who have thus dropped out of school, but who would still like to improve themselves intellectually and increase their earning capacity, have no municipal public library to which they may go for help. Is it not also a safe assumption that some of them, lacking the assistance a public library would afford, have now become juvenile delinquents and criminals and that you may now be spending more from the public funds for their apprehension, conviction, restraint and reformation than a public library would cost the city?

What of the gains and losses to the adult citizens from the postponement of the establishment and maintenance of a free public library here? The presence of a public library in any city is an indirect recognition of the fact that its citizens believe that education is not measured by the period of school instruction, but announce that their education will be continued as long as they live. In other words, by establishing a public library the people

of this city will in effect say: "The instruction we
received in school and college will now simply be
the beginning, the preparation for the education
which we shall hereafter continue and round out
by means of the resources of our own public library,
founded and maintained by ourselves, and used by
ourselves"—not simply, as some seem to think, by
those who cannot afford to buy their own books. By
postponing the establishment of the public library
you are losing the opportunity to declare this as
your idea of education and of life; you are depriving
yourselves of a powerful agent for fostering the development of an enlightened social, civic and industrial life.

Study Books Replacing Fiction

Here some one may say (or think): "Is it not
true that a large part of the reading from public
libraries is composed of fiction?" On this point I
am glad to quote my own experience. In the eight
years I have been librarian at Washington the total
annual home circulation of books has been increased
from 278,000 volumes to 650,000 volumes and at the
same time the percentage of fiction in that circulation has been reduced from 84 to 58.[3] I expect ultimately to reduce it to 50. The present 58 per cent
is also composed of a better quality of fiction than
the former 84 per cent. A book of fiction gets itself
read very easily. If it is of good quality, it has a
refining and educating effect. In circulation figures
it counts just as much as a book of history or science,
which requires close study. Tho not in the least
apologizing for the fiction read, the public library
of today is shifting the emphasis to the study side
of its work.

[3] In 1930 out of a total home circulation of 1,680,022 volumes, 55
per cent consisted of fiction.

Every Shade of Opinion

This is an era of swift changes in social, economic and political ideas. Nowadays we are all democrats (with a small "d") and all progressives (with a small "p"); none of us will consent to be stand-patters or reactionaries. Even when we are conservatives by conviction or temperament, we need to know the radical point of view and arguments in order to answer them. The public library, an impersonal institution with no partisan opinions, is equipped with books and magazines representing every shade of opinion, in order that the public may study all sides and make up its mind. Whatever our own personal opinions, certain it is that the air is filled with the discussion of civil service pensions, conservation of national resources, free trade, Panama Canal tolls, the income tax, the single tax, woman suffrage, the minimum wage, socialism, the abolition of child labor, a national health service and hundreds of other similar questions. This city is postponing to its detriment the time when it shall provide its citizens with the opportunity for studying all sides of such subjects, in this era of rapidly changing opinion. I am sure that you will agree that this is shortsighted.

Questions of municipal government and administration are likewise being agitated as never before in our history. What is this city doing as a municipality to enable its citizens to make up their minds on the question whether they want a commission form of government or not? What provision is there that your city officials are informed on the latest methods of fire protection, garbage disposal, milk inspection, quarantine, disinfection, street paving and lighting, etc.? And if your city offices should be supplied with the latest textbooks and magazines on these subjects, what provision is there for enabling citizens to inform themselves on these and similar questions at public expense? Are you not in danger of loss, by courting poor administration in your public officials, and are you not needlessly and shortsightedly cutting yourselves off from the stimulus of a citizenship thoroly enlightened on questions of municipal housekeeping?

AN AID TO BUSINESS

In addition to these general losses to the public thru failure to supply a public library, I wish to point out a loss to business interests thru failure to have a public library with a well-equipped industrial department. Beside the plate of each of you I have caused to be placed a folder describing the industrial department of my own library and a form by which readers register with the library the subjects on which they wish to "keep up to date." I could easily devote all of the time at my disposal today to describing the resources and work of this department. It is equipped with about eight thousand volumes devoted to all important industries, trades, and businesses, with special emphasis on industries most important in Washington, such as printing, building, automobiles, gun-making, accounting and stenography. Such a department provides information that is invaluable to the manufacturer, the wholesaler, the retailer, the mechanic, the journeyman and the apprentice. Use of its resources helps to increase the earning power of individuals and increases the business of the city. Thus far this city has lost the opportunity to provide itself with such an adjunct and reinforcement to its commercial life. There undoubtedly has been a distinct loss also in prestige.

I have assumed that you all believe in a public library and expect sooner or later to establish one here. I have also assumed that the postponement has been for financial reasons—because you hesitate to incur the necessary expense. I submit that you should, on the other hand, now carefully consider whether you can afford to postpone any longer making a small investment that will yield large returns in enlightened, self-supporting citizenship and increased commercial prosperity.

LIBRARY ADVERTISING [1]

(This paper was one of the earlier or pioneer articles on the subject of the application of advertising and publicity methods to library affairs. Altho the article may now be largely outmoded so that its chief value may be historical, yet it is believed that the spirit is altogether modern.)

In the enormous growth of business during recent years one of the most striking features and probably the largest contributing cause is the development of advertising. Can the library derive any lessons from the practices of commercial advertisers? I have no hesitation in claiming that commercial advertising is educational in its essential principles. Of course its purpose is to sell goods and to derive pecuniary gain. Advertising, especially on its competitive side, does indeed involve some seeming economic waste, since the cost of advertising must be added to the selling price of goods. So, too, every dollar spent on a library bulletin, or for that matter on a card catalog, reduces the number of books that may be bought with a given fund. But the money thus expended, if properly spent, is, because of the educational value of the advertisements, in the long run of value to the consumer, both in the case of purchased articles and in the sum total of the service which the library renders to the public.

That the public library is essentially educational perhaps needs no argument before a body of librarians. That it still needs argument with the general public is frequently attested by instances where the library is grouped with philanthropic institu-

[1] Read before the Massachusetts Library Club, Boston, February 16, 1905, and later before the District of Columbia Library Association.

tions, and by the fact that often in editorials and addresses it is especially commended to the so-called working classes. The gift of buildings to many libraries thruout the country is no doubt partly responsible for the persistence of this mistaken idea. The library is educational in the broad sense that it ministers to the intellectual needs of all the people thruout the whole of life. Provided they have interest in books it makes almost as strong an appeal to the rich and certainly as strong an appeal to the moderately well-to-do as to the poor. One of the most important needs in advertising the library is to break down this false notion that people are pauperizing themselves by making use of library privileges. The library is for the poor because the poor form a part of the community; but they have no more need of the intellectual food which the library can furnish than the rich. Only when the whole people, rich as well as poor, come to the library as the natural place for intellectual food will the library fulfill its proper function.

Advertising is Educational

Recently in mentioning to another librarian that I had promised to speak on "library advertising" I was besought to make my topic "library publicity" or some topic more dignified than that indicated by the word "advertising." That advertising is conceived of as essentially educational is perhaps a sufficient reason for preferring the more commercial word. "Publicity" is not sufficiently strong, as it seems to indicate simply the giving of information to the public and does not imply the energetic persistence that modern advertising methods involve.

Another principle that must be recognized by trustees, librarian and staff before the most success-

ful work can be done in a community is that the
commodity dealt in by the library is essentially an
intellectual one. In a busy library the thing that
strikes the eye is that in the course of a day several
hundred pounds of bound volumes are shoved across
the counter to the library's customers. In judging
of libraries it might be thought that the one whose
mechanical appliances (including the loan clerks)
exchange the most books in a day with the least
friction, is the most efficient. I do not despise quantity, but quantity should not be put before quality;
circulation figures should not be sought at the expense of the spirit of helpfulness. As in a business
house the best advertisement is a satisfied customer,
so it is in a library. Let the first effort, therefore,
be inside the library. Of course the classification
and catalog, the charging system, and all of the
mechanical helps will be what they should be; but
by all means the proper spirit should prevail, so
that beyond all else there shall be invariable courtesy,
hospitality, good will, helpfulness without condes-
cension, plenty of attractive books on open shelves
and red tape reduced to the minimum. These things
accomplished, the advertising has already begun, for
the best advertising is the personal advertising carried on by those who speak from experience.

LIBRARY BUILDING A FACTOR

Another important means of advertising is the
library building. Of course it is agreed that the
building should first be useful and after that beautiful. But by all means do not neglect the latter qualifi-
cation. It should be one of the most attractive buildings in the town. It should be a speaking building,
with "public library" written all over it, not necessarily in words cut in stone, and by its very form and

structure should stand for the idea of books. This attractiveness and this quality of revealing its spirit to the passers-by will prove a powerful magnet to draw within the influence of the library persons who might never go to a library housed in a commercial building. Of course this idea must be maintained inside the building to hold the casual visitor. If the architect has planned a great corridor without provision for a book in sight, so that the building might be taken for a mausoleum or anything but a library, in spite of the hindrance he has placed in your way, accomplish your purpose by bringing out cases of books and comfortable chairs and thus, even at some slight sacrifice of the artistic, contrive to introduce the visitor to books as soon as he enters the building.

LECTURES AND STUDY GROUPS

If the building is modern it has a lecture hall. Properly used this may be a powerful agent as an advertiser. University extension and free lecture associations, study clubs, and dozens of other organizations, including some advocating so-called crank notions, will be glad to make use of it. Allow the use freely to all proper organizations—and interpret the "proper" pretty liberally. Do not try to be responsible for every idea advocated in the hall any more than you uphold all the ideas put forward in the books you circulate.

All clubs should be encouraged to use the reference room and to file there their study programs. If the books on their programs can be bought and reserved (if so desired) the library is thereby able to adapt itself to the needs of a group of people, win them to be library users, and make them in turn advertisers of its helpfulness.

The use of bulletin boards, now so common in children's rooms, is spreading to adult reading-rooms. On them lists and illustrative matter on current topics serve to put warmth, color and life into the room and to draw people to the library.

Work With Children

Some of the principles underlying successful advertising are also fundamental in the work of children's rooms and schoolroom libraries. Students of advertising psychology have pointed out that such commodities as soap, cocoa, etc., are in many people's minds almost invariably associated with the particular brands of these goods which they constantly see advertised. If this association of ideas is so strong in adults busy with the cares of life, how much stronger is it with the care-free children. If the library has an opportunity to make a strong appeal early in life the impression is likely to be a lasting one. Since children do not make close discriminations it is important in the case of the schoolroom libraries to impress the idea that the books are not textbooks, and are not furnished by the school, but that they are sent by the public library, where there are hundreds more just as good. The books will, of course, have the library bookplate; the case in which the books are sent should plainly have the name of the public library; and it has in some places been found desirable to hang in each schoolroom a large card containing a selection from the list of books sent to the schools, supplemented with an invitation to visit the children's room.

To the children who come to the children's room there should be furnished such lists as are found on the *St. Nicholas* bookmark, and to their parents the lists prepared by Miss Hewins or Miss Moore, or those compiled at Pittsburgh, Buffalo or Cleveland.

NEWSPAPERS BEST

Turning now to what is more generally understood as library advertising matter, I think that it is safe to say that the columns of the newspapers are best of all, especially for attracting the attention of those who have never used the library before. The constant use of the newspapers as often as their columns are opened, and as often as you have anything worth printing, will reach more people than any other means. Librarians should make the acquaintance of newspaper editors, and if their support of the library is not already cordially enlisted it should by all means at once be secured. Make friends with the reporters also. They may sometimes twist or garble what you want to say, but they are usually conscientious workers who do their best. By gaining the cordial friendship of editor and reporter, such things can usually be warded off. Whenever possible prepare what you want used for publication. If it is concisely stated in readable form, in most cases copy will be followed. If there are several papers in the city they will probably want the same news a little differently phrased. If the morning papers on one occasion are given the opportunity of first publication, the evening papers should have the preference the next time.

In studying the situation in your own community you may discover that a certain section of the population, as for example the skilled laborers in various trades, make little use of your library. Perhaps a majority of this class read a given newspaper. Get the editor to send you a reporter for an interview with you for the Sunday edition, or, better still, prepare

the interview yourself. In it give a general idea of
the use and purposes of the library with special reference to your technical books and periodicals.

Sometimes it is possible to have a certain amount
of matter appear on certain days in a stated place,
as for example, news notes, select lists of accessions
or reading lists as a part of a Saturday book-page.
Arrangements may be made to have such type saved
and proofs of it pulled at slight or no cost to be used
for distribution at the issue desk. If a war breaks
out, a volcano has a fresh eruption, or a ruler is assas-
sinated the librarian may be pretty sure that a brief
list of books and periodicals on the subject, if sent
promptly, will be published. Exhibitions, even small
ones covering but a single bulletin board, may often
serve as the text for a short news story which, if,
attractively written, will find readers.

CATALOGS AND BULLETINS

The printing of book catalogs is not regarded by
most libraries as practicable. The printing of subject catalogs in sections is more usual and the issuing
of monthly or quarterly bulletins is general. Such
bulletins as that issued at Salem without notes, and
that at Pittsburgh with notes, may be regarded as
typical and as good models to follow. Bulletins may
be sent by mail to regular subscribers and to special
classes of persons who may be interested in reading
lists printed therein. For example, bulletins containing lists on printing and bookbinding might be sent
to all persons given in the directory as employed in
those trades, with a circular letter offering to furnish
a supply of this special bulletin for distribution to
workmen employed in their establishments. All bulletins should of course be distributed at the library
free of charge.

As an example of what may be done to save expense in issuing a bulletin I wish to mention that at Wilmington, Del., one thousand copies of the monthly bulletin are issued at a cost of $8 a month. This is made possible by the fact that all the matter is run in the columns of one of the daily papers free of charge and the type is saved without cost for composition.

Good results may also be obtained from the use of bookmarks, each listing ten or twelve books on a given subject, such as those issued at Springfield and Newark.

Christmas Exhibitions

An instance of timeliness in meeting a need of at least part of the public is the plan of holding during December an exhibition of books suitable for Christmas gifts, of having the event written up in the newspapers and of issuing an attractive list of the books. Such a plan was tried at Washington (as well as elsewhere) last Christmas, and 6000 copies of the list were distributed, 3000 by the library and 3000 by two booksellers who cooperated with the library by keeping the books listed in stock.

Another advertising scheme that had the elements of timeliness and service to a portion of the users of the library was tried last summer at Wilmington of securing from railway and steamship companies their attractive advertising pamphlets and displaying them in a time-table cabinet. This cabinet was marked "hints for vacation plans," and many readers availed themselves of its aid.

Since the library cannot stand behind every book that it distributes, and since the mere circulation of a book is an advertisement of it, the library need have no objections to the distribution of subject lists issued by publishers. For example, Putnam's has issued booklists descriptive of their *Story of the Nations* and *Heroes of the Nations* series; several publishers almost every year issue seasonable lists of nature books of their own publication; the American Sports Publishing Company issues a descriptive catalog of Spalding's athletic library. Arrangements can usually be made with almost any publisher to furnish as many copies of such lists as can be distributed, with a special imprint such as "these books may be found at the Blankville public library."

LISTS FROM OTHER LIBRARIES

The using of publishers' lists suggests that larger use might be made by libraries of lists issued by other libraries and of the American Library Association catalog. Older libraries having no printed catalog may, and I believe should, use classed sections of the A. L. A. catalog, buying them in quantities and selling them at cost to their readers. Similarly, if a library has no printed fiction list, use might be made of the new *List of 1000 of the Best Novels* issued at Newark.

The mimeograph might well be more often used by libraries. A brief list of new books on a special subject can easily be prepared, and if it is sent with a mimeograph typewritten letter signed by a stencil signature the recipients are flattered at the personal attention. For example, a list of the religious periodicals on file in a library sent to the pastors of one city brought personal thanks from several and was partly responsible for the preaching of an evening sermon to the young people on the library.

This paper does not aim to exhaust the methods of advertising. It seeks simply to discover the purpose of advertising, to lay down certain principles, and to cite a few illustrative examples. Mention should not be omitted of the use of the poster and street car advertising. A statement giving the location of the library and its resources, mentioning the slight formalities necessary to secure privileges, if printed in bold type on cardboard and hung in hotels, restaurants, tobacco shops, railway stations, manufactories and employes' rooms in department stores, etc., will surely bring the library to the attention of some who did not know before of its existence.

COURSES IN LIBRARY SCHOOLS

So important is the advertising part of library work coming to be considered that in at least one library school (that at Albany) a course extending throughout the senior year is given on the subject of newspaper advertising.

I wonder if it is still necessary to defend the various methods here mentioned against any charge that they are undignified. Surely there is need for advertising in the sense in which it is used in this paper. With the idea still widely persisting, on the one hand that a man degrades himself if he is seen carrying a public library book, and on the other hand (as instanced by Prof. Münsterberg in his recent book *The Americans*) that libraries are luxuries and should not be supported by public funds, there is still much to do before the public library comes to its own. It therefore remains for librarians to impress themselves on their communities and to seize every opportunity to spread the library idea.

A SENSE OF FRIENDLINESS IN THE LIBRARY [1]

A few days ago a writer of books who visits Washington occasionally came to my office in part at least to tell me something that was very gratifying. In substance he said: "I have only recently discovered your library and I wish to give you my first impressions and to tell you of the fine atmosphere of friendliness and cordiality combined with prompt and efficient service which I have found here." Altho much the same thing had come to me before, it had never previously been expressed to me with the same definiteness. This gives me encouragement to believe that what I have always been striving for is now a substantial reality.

Inasmuch as this experience came just as I was taking up the invitation of *The Christian Science Monitor* to write something for its series on library service, it occurred to me that I could perhaps not do better than discuss some of the elements that go to make up this atmosphere or sense of friendliness in a library and what such a spirit means to the public which uses a library. In attempting this I disavow both sentimentality and egotism. Since I must draw largely on my own experience it seems necessary frequently to use the first person singular.

I might take as the text of this preachment the famous poem of Sam Walter Foss, poet and librarian, the last couplet of which runs:

Let me live in a house by the side of the road,
And be a friend to man—

[1] *Christian Science Monitor.* January 23, 1924.

for the spirit and ideas of the poem are those that should dominate the friendly library.

The first desirable elements in obtaining a friendly atmosphere are those of location and architecture. In these particulars our central library does not fulfill the requirements as well as do our branches. The main library was erected on a centrally located public square that admirably fulfilled the conditions at the time of building; but with the growth of traffic about the square the location has become less perfect. Our new southeastern branch, recently erected, seems to be ideally located, just off Pennsylvania Avenue, a short block from a transfer point, on three streets, not main thoroughfares, and facing a small park. The central library building is likewise in its architecture less friendly than this new branch building. The main building is, quite appropriately, more monumental; it has grand marble staircases to the right and left of the main entrance which succeed in cutting off too much of the natural light. The branch has a modest, welcoming entrance and windows reaching nearly to the floor on all sides, with window seats under them, so that the maximum of natural light is secured. The absence of ceiling ornamentation, usually found in great central buildings, makes the artificial lighting of the branch also more successful.

BOOKS IN PUBLIC ROOMS

Since, however, it was the atmosphere of the central library that drew favorable comment from my visitor, it would seem that the imperfections of location and style of architecture have been measurably surmounted. When I first knew the Washington central building, a few months after it was opened, there was not a book to be seen; all were in closed stacks or in rooms not visible on first entrance to the building. An alteration of the form of the main charging desk, the erection of shelves in the main entrance lobby, the installation of a case of "readable books," the improvement of the artificial lighting, the hanging of good paintings, the putting up of a few artistic posters, the presence most of the year of hothouse flowers (regularly contributed during the winter months from the Department of Agriculture greenhouses thru the courtesy of the Secretary of Agriculture [2]) have completely changed the aspect of the lobby, formerly forbidding, so that now it has a fairly home-like and welcoming appearance. Changes in other parts of the library have included the knocking out of marble grill work which cut off more than half the light from the second floor children's room and the use of lighter colors in the redecoration of walls. Paintings and other pictures and flowers arranged thruout the library, including the rooms not used by the public, all strengthen this impression of cheerfulness.

ACTUAL FRIENDLINESS

Of course the biggest element of all in giving the library a reputation for friendliness is that it should actually be friendly; that is, not only should its service be highly efficient in character and quality, but the manner and manners of the library staff should be unmistakably friendly and helpful. Just how can this end be accomplished?

Friendliness is not a veneer, a surface matter, but is an outward manifestation of an inner grace. In other words, the library staff, from the chief li-

[2] Unfortunately now practically discontinued.

brarian to the youngest page, must be actuated by a spirit of friendliness and helpfulness. It is not necessary or desirable that such a spirit should take the form of sentimentality or unctuous cordiality. It is entirely possible to be perfectly business-like in all dealings with the public and at the same time to give the impression of interest and helpfulness, and to make the reader feel entirely at home in all of his contacts with the library.

A Cultured Staff

In Washington a staff that apparently is reasonably successful in making such an impression has for the most part, at least in the junior grades, been recruited from Washington families thru the medium of the library's own training class. Because of low statutory salaries, the library has been able to attract comparatively few graduates of library schools, tho several who entered the library thru the training class have later gone on to library schools and then returned. From the daughters of scientists and other civil employes of the Government and of army and navy officers, the public school teachers and the library workers of Washington have largely been drawn and have proved to be of high average quality. Almost uniformly they come from homes rather rich in cultural influences, and it is possible to recruit each year's training class with young women who have a good background not only of formal education, but of cultivated home life and often of considerable social experience. Only the most desirable applicants are admitted to the class and later appointed to positions. Thruout the training course the members of the class are constantly indoctrinated with ideas, ideals and standards which include not simply accurate and efficient technique, but hospitality, friendliness and all the other graces that taken together make the desired impression. It is decidedly a case where no sour, hatchet-faced, cross-grained applicant need apply, but rather one in which amiability as well as efficiency is a distinct asset.

EXAMPLE, NOT PROHIBITION

In the older days most libraries had on their walls, perhaps in several places, frequently in mammoth capitals, the awesome word SILENCE. Nowadays signs when used at all are to give information and directions and not to announce prohibitions. In some parts of the library conversation connected with the business of securing library service is freely carried on. But the tranquillity needed for library reading and study is secured by the example of the quiet speech of the library staff, so that it is not usually necessary to use a sign that has some vogue: "Speak gently and let thy voice be low."

In a large central library building it is often found necessary to have a library guard or two to keep down thefts and mutilations of books and to maintain order in emergencies. Such guards are usually dressed in the familiar uniform of the policemen, resplendent in brass buttons and shields, and wear caps. From experience with such officers, both in plain clothes and in uniforms, I am fully convinced of the moral influence of brass buttons. In my judgment the presence of such officers does not introduce a jarring note into the harmony of the friendly atmosphere of the library, which is our present theme, but rather helps it, by giving steadiness and confidence.

Is it wise to disregard the intangible elements in library service? Is it enough simply to furnish highly skilled service, in a plain matter-of-fact fashion, rendered with an air of its all being a part of the day's work? If this attitude is the dominant note, the reader may commend the library service, but he does not feel affection or complete good will toward the library. Good will pays in a public library no less than in a commercial business.

PSYCHOLOGICAL HANDICAPS AND POSSIBLE REMEDIES IN INCREASING LIBRARY APPROPRIATIONS [1]

I think we will agree that practically all public libraries are much under-supported. A large part of our effort as chief librarians is devoted to attempts to increase that support, often with indifferent success. I believe that I can most helpfully open this discussion by trying to summarize what seem the fundamental difficulties in our pathways, stumbling blocks that hamper our progress. My thesis is that certain psychological handicaps, community complexes, if you please, operate quite generally to keep the library support far below needs. In some cases librarians and library trustees have already psychoanalyzed this complex and largely eliminated it; in other cases it is gradually yielding to treatment; in most cases however, the obsession is still in full vigor. It is not claimed that this paper contains ideas not already known to librarians. If it has value, it is in bringing such ideas together. In some cases a mere statement of the ill suggests the appropriate remedy; in others the cure has not yet been discovered.

I. Psychological handicaps. To get them out of my system early and to show my colleagues that I have handicaps that they do not encounter, I shall first mention two that are peculiar to the Washington situation. In the District of Columbia we have no votes whatever, no representatives in Congress and no voice in our own affairs. We are not even

[1] Read at the meeting of Librarians of Large Public Libraries, Chicago, December 28, 1922.

permitted to use our own tax money for school and library support until Congress votes to appropriate it. Moreover, Congressmen, their wives, children and clerks, with their families, are able to get all their books from the Library of Congress, delivered at their doors, and so have little or no direct interest in the Public Library. The Public Library is worse off than the schools, for some Congressmen and their clerks have children or grandchildren in the schools and are personally interested in seeing that Washington has good schools.

Obviously we should in the District of Columbia have the right to vote for President and Vice-President and should at the very least have in Congress voting Representatives and one Senator. I ask my professional colleagues to help in securing the amendment to the United States Constitution that would give us these fundamental rights.

GIFT AND CHARITY IDEA

Proceeding now to the psychological handicaps fairly common to all public libraries, I would mention first that the public library is rather generally regarded as a gift proposition. This idea has a historic basis. The early subscription libraries often accumulated considerable productive properties and early free libraries were often supported solely or largely from such endowments or from the benefactions of rich founders. Then came the Carnegie gifts of buildings. Altho it is true that many cities have been induced by the Carnegie offers of buildings to have public libraries sooner than they would otherwise have had them, yet it is also true that Carnegie offers have had their perils in planting the idea in many places that without Carnegie money for buildings there could be no public libraries. These Carnegie gifts are even yet quite generally misunderstood, as many people think that not simply buildings and physical equipment, but also sites and maintenance come from Mr. Carnegie or the Carnegie Corporation. Even when the limitations of Carnegie gifts are explained, the old historic viewpoint or obsession often persists, leading appropriating bodies to hold that sites come from private citizens and that all or a large part of the maintenance should come from private benefactions.

Library Education Lacking

Many of the people still in control of financial support (Congressmen, members of state legislatures, aldermen, etc.) did not have public library advantages when they were younger. They have been successful without them and so are not convinced that libraries are necessary to success. For the same reason many older teachers do not appreciate the importance of adequate library facilities. Many parents likewise think that the Alger and Elsie Dinsmore books of their childhood represent the last word in children's literature and do not understand the service rendered by libraries to children or the importance of establishing the library habit in young people.

The results of education received from a public library are less tangible than school education. Reading, writing, arithmetic, shorthand, bookkeeping, etc., lead directly to gainful occupations. Library education, supplemental to school instruction, is less easily traced and often not acknowledged by the beneficiaries.

Librarians do not always insist on educational and training standards for their staffs and so do not always have a thoroughly good case for asking good salaries for them. Frequently the necessary discrimination is not made by librarians between library assistants who are professional librarians and those who are really clerks.

Librarianship is still too often considered a congenial, ladylike calling and many think that librarians ought to consider themselves fortunate to be engaged in such a pleasant, sheltered occupation, and to be willing to do such nice work at almost any salary.

CLERICAL AND MECHANICAL ASPECTS

Another handicap is the fact that too often when the men in control of the finances visit the library the process most in evidence is the mechanical shovelling out of books, mostly fiction. The clerical element in the process is at the front. These holders of the purse strings are not made to appreciate the technical processes that have led up to this distribution. They do not understand the educational work that is being done, or that could be done if only the library had an ample staff of well-trained people, equipped to do consultative work with readers.

Tho this statement may not be popular, I believe there is too often a lack of courage on the part of librarians and library trustees. I doubt if they have yet generally conceived of the public library as the big and potent instrument for education that its character and possibilities for development justify. Too often they apologize and "talk small"—say the library requires only an infinitesimal part of a city budget for support, etc. "Talking small" too often, I fear, means "thinking small."

There is too great a lack of carefully defined standards of library service to be rendered, of costs to accomplish such results, and of appropriate salaries.

Too often librarians go ahead and do work, after

a fashion, when they have no business to do so, when they lack the force to undertake the larger service demanded.

II. Now for some suggested remedies supplemental to those already mentioned.

"Thinking Large" Necessary

It is fundamental that librarians and library trustees should first themselves conceive the public library to be a "supplement of the public educational system" and an "integral part of public education," just as essential to public welfare as the public schools. They should "think large," have courage to insist on the general recognition of that conception, and demand as a right the support needed to enable the public library to realize its purpose and to do the large work it is capable of doing. When they themselves have the large view rather than the pinched and petty one, they can become an active, energetic center of convincing argument to inform and persuade the community to the completest recognition of the library.

In particular they must get the library away from the gift or charity idea. They should welcome gifts and endowment, yes, but solely as supplements to the basic support which must come from the public treasury. Altho there are a few cases where public schools are supported from endowments, the instances are so rare as to be practically negligible. Not until the governing boards of libraries succeed in convincing communities that public libraries are on all fours with the schools and have the same rights to ample support as the schools, can we expect to go full steam ahead.

I am convinced that we must shift the emphasis from book circulation predominantly recreational to literature making for broader culture, for good citizenship, and for greater earning capacity. I would not weaken the emphasis on the things of the spirit fundamental in all cultural progress, but I would make the public library better known as a potent factor in economic progress for individuals and the community. There lies success with the hard-headed business men making up appropriating bodies.

TRAINED PERSONNEL

I would lay more stress on trained librarians and their recognition as professionals. In my aggressive campaign for their recognition, I would be constantly on the alert to compare the salaries of the library staff with the salaries of teachers and other professional experts in the city government, and demand for the library staff as good salaries as others receive, always taking care that such library staff is of the same calibre and that the same standards of education and training are maintained as for teachers and other technical workers.

Nor would I consent, at least without an ever louder protest in which I should try to enlist my community, to do an ever-increasing work with a non-expanding staff at non-advancing salaries. I do not consider such a course decent or self-respecting or the way to get recognition. This is distinctly no place for humility.

I consider that the best remedy of all for the correction of this community complex of inadequate public library support is supplied by the A.L.A. resolution on proper library maintenance. The standard of a minimum of $1 per capita for simply good public library maintenance and much more than $1 per capita for maintenance to achieve the highest standards, furnishes a weapon which if used effectively has great possibilities. With this as a talking point it should be possible to plant in the community consciousness proper library standards and ideals. When I first laid this resolution before my trustees shortly after it was issued, they smiled indulgently and seemed inclined to use the phrases "professional enthusiasm" and "Utopian dreams," but they ended not only by printing the resolution in the annual report but by comparing our expenditures (35 cents per capita) [2] and annual estimates (63 cents per capita) with the A.L.A. standard and in order to show that the standard itself was not Utopian, they made comparisons with such a city as Cleveland, where the expenditures are $1.08 per capita. [3]

Standards of Work and Costs

When Congressional reclassification legislation is enacted setting up qualifications and salary standards for all scientific, technical and professional workers, including librarians, if then the A.L.A. committees on salaries, standardization and certification will also set up standards for public library work and workers, including standards of costs for doing our work, librarians and library trustees will be able to go to their communities with programs of work, statements of costs and requisite maintenance standards. They will be able to talk definitely and convincingly, instead of dealing too much in generalities.

Finally, having psychoanalyzed the community complexes of inadequate support and begun the indicated treatment, above all, no matter how discouraging the conditions, let us not fail to maintain serene optimism. Let us believe in ourselves, our profession and our cause. Then with a long pull, a strong pull, and a pull all together we shall bring the world over to our way of thinking.

[2] Recent figures, 64 cents per capita.
[3] Recent figures, $1.77 per capita.

THE PUBLIC LIBRARY IN SMALL AND MEDIUM SIZED TOWNS [1]

This is my first visit to the Old North State. The American Library Association met in Asheville in 1907. Much of my travel in this country is in connection with attendance on the meetings of that association. Unfortunately I made my only trip to the hospital as a patient at the time of the Asheville convention, and ten years have elapsed before I have been able to make this long hoped for visit.

With the invitation to speak, came the topic assigned to me. I was warned that your largest town has about 45,000 population, that small towns mean those of 3,000 to 10,000, and that medium sized towns have from 10,000 to 20,000 inhabitants. My own library experience has been in cities of upwards of 100,000 population, and from that to Washington, with its population of nearly 400,000. I was, however, brought up on a farm and have lived in two towns of about 1,500 and 3,000 population respectively. I am therefore able to have many points of contact with your problems, which in their essentials do not differ from those elsewhere, whether in large or small places.

I know of the tremendous strides in the development of the North Carolina school system during the last fifteen or twenty years. Your state library commission is now trying to establish a library in every town in your state by 1920. If anything that I say tonight can contribute to the accomplishment of that purpose, I shall be repaid for coming. I understand

[1] Read before North Carolina Library Association, Salisbury, N. C. April 24, 1917.

that my audience includes citizens who are not professional librarians. What I have to say is addressed to them even more than to the professional members of my audience, to whom, perhaps, some of the points I shall cover will sound rather elementary.

ESSENTIAL FOR DEMOCRACY

In beginning a discussion of the Public Library of the twentieth century in small and medium sized towns, it is desirable to ask and attempt to answer first the question: What is the essential character of the public library? I shall try to convince you that it is an integral part of the system of public education and as such is fundamentally necessary to the development of democratic institutions. North Carolina is noted for having, outside of the colored race, the most homogeneous population in the United States, a population that retains its Anglo-Saxon qualities even to the present day when so much of the rest of the country has had such large admixtures of Central and Southern European races. You are also well known to be a thoroly democratic state— democratic with a small "d" and much of the time with a large "D."

There is no need to argue the desirability of a free, public, tax supported school system in a democratic state like this. I shall take it for granted that you are thoroly convinced of the necessity of having such a system. To cast an intelligent vote, to take an efficient part in public affairs, to support oneself and one's family in comfort, at least a rudimentary education is absolutely necessary for every citizen. The more thoro and prolonged that school education can be, other things being equal, the better becomes the citizenship, both in intelligence and in economic independence. I think you will all agree with me, however, that school education even at its very best, leaves much to be desired in the equipment of citizens. This is especially true of the average and usual school education. The common everyday school education stops short of the high-school with all but 10 per cent of the school population. The remaining 90 per cent have dropped out, many of them before reaching the 8th grade and some at the 7th, 6th, or even the 5th grade. Only a fraction of the 10 per cent that reach the high school go thru its four years, and a still smaller fraction of high-school students go to and thru college.

ESSENTIAL FOR EDUCATION

School instruction does not necessarily afford the individual an education. It simply gives him a beginning and furnishes him with the ability to become educated by using advantageously what he has learned in school. He may carry on his education after leaving school thru the discipline of business, thru the church, the lecture, the reading of newspapers and magazines and other similar experiences. None of these agencies, however, perhaps not all combined, offer as great advantages for carrying on education to the very end of life as those afforded by the public library. For the state to teach its citizens to read, for the state to compel its citizens to learn to read, to give them instruction in the public schools, and then not to afford them the opportunity to carry on their education thru the medium of a public library is not only inconsiderate but very shortsighted. The library for which I plead is not one maintained by contributions and therefore ill equipped and precarious in its support, but is a free, public, tax supported library, strongly administered and so well maintained that it will not simply be respected by, but will be used by the entire citizen body.

Such a library as I have in mind may be considered as coordinate with the schools in that it furnishes material to children of school age; it vitalizes their studies and keeps them longer in school; but also and especially it takes them when they leave school, let us hope with the library habit somewhat well established, and enables them to carry on studies which will make for good citizenship and for a higher degree of self-support.

One of the reasons, it seems to me, why the maintenance of the public library as a tax supported institution has not become more general is because it has not appealed to the business man as a worthwhile institution. He has classed it as an institution whose chief business is to disseminate the cheap and sensational fiction of the day. Altho the circulation of recreational literature is regarded by thinking people as a function proper to public libraries, and one not to be apologized for, yet the twentieth century library is putting the chief emphasis on other and more important work. The public library no longer deserves to be thought of as a literary barroom where idle people go to get their fiction tipples; but should rather be considered as a public utility, just as important in a community as the police department, the fire department, or perhaps a better comparison is with the water works. Without a constant supply of pure water, the residents of the modern municipality would die of thirst or sicken of filth diseases. Similarly a modern city cannot have perfect health, and a high average of intelligence and sanity, cannot have the highest business success without the enlightenment afforded by the resources of a public library, without the intelligent use of a well selected library, stocked with books on all phases of the industrial life of the community.

How should our twentieth century library be organized and administrated to do this work? This can be answered only by the recognition first, of the essential character of the public library as an educational institution, and second, by the recognition of the need for closely adapting the library to its constituency. Some people think of the library as a building; a smaller number think of it as a collection of books. The building is necessary, and no doubt more attention should be given to the planning of library buildings, not for show but for economical administration, with due attention to the storage of books, light, air and the quick service of the people. Books too are necessary. They are the library's stock in trade and a well selected and well organized collection is absolutely indispensable to the library's success. But more important perhaps than the house in which the library lives or the books within the library building, is the librarian who makes the collection of books a living organism to serve the community. It is of the utmost importance, therefore, to secure first and foremost a well educated, well trained librarian, with personality, good sense, knowledge of her constituency, and the desire and ability to serve it. Nothing will so surely make your library a success as to secure as your librarian the best equipped person possible. If your librarian measures up to this standard, when the library is well established, she should be paid as much as the principal of the high school. If your library or librarian is starved you must not expect to get good results. On the other hand your investment in brains and training and in books will make its return not in money dividends but in character development and the increased earning capacity of your community.

If asked for a more explicit statement of the qualifications considered necessary for the librarian of our twentieth century library, I should point out first that properly to conduct an education institution such as the public library requires the best education and training to be commanded. Altho I have referred to our librarian as "she," I do not by any means think that the position is exclusively feminine. Many librarians, including many chief librarians, are women. In so far as they are chosen because of their special aptitude for the work, this is sound, but if they are chosen because they are cheaper then men, I believe the position unsound. In my experience I have never made any discrimination between men and women in salaries and I do not believe it is justifiable to do so. Our librarian should, I believe, be a college graduate and also a graduate of one of the regular library training schools, having a course of one or two years. In other words, your librarian should have education and training for her position comparable to that which you require of the principal of your high school, your clergymen and your physicians. But education and training alone will not suffice; they should be accompanied by an alert mind, sympathy with and ability to meet the public, a manner that will command confidence, and first rate common sense. The exacting business of managing a library sometimes leaves little time for reading; however, our twentieth century librarian must know books, must have a wide if not a deep knowledge of books, so that she can advise her constituents in their reading. This requires constant reading outside of library hours. Running a library does not consist simply in giving out books over a counter, but includes the wise selection and the close adaptation of books to the needs of readers of diverse wants and degrees of intelligence. The business side of library work requires unusual knowledge, skill and experience for every librarian is obliged to make a little money go a great way. The trustees will supervise the expenditure of funds, but the librarian must be their main reliance and without business ability on her part, the library will fail to give the public the service it might otherwise render. The business of running a library involves the purchase of books and knowledge of book markets; skill in cataloging the books, to make each volume most completely available to the public, thru the economical use of Library of Congress cards and other short cuts; the repair and binding of books; the choice and training of library assistants, and other processes not in evidence to the general public who use the library. To do all this and at the same time to make the library a real, vital force in the community demands a high degree of ability that should be well rewarded. A librarian who is constantly harassed by the personal problem of financial support for herself and others dependent upon her cannot best serve her community.

Our twentieth century librarian does not hide her candle under a bushel. In other words our modern library advertises. The old style library was an extraordinarily dignified institution, appealing only to the few and the literary; the modern library, serving the entire people, does not think it out of keeping with its character to bring its resources and services conspicuously to the attention of the entire community. Tho the militant librarian might like to have a compulsory library law, that is one compelling all people to use the library, yet the voluntary character of its service, which constitutes its special charm, is too valuable to be sacrificed. Still the librarian would like to make her library so compelling in its attractiveness as to lead the entire population to use it. Just as satisfied customers in commercial life are the best advertisers, so it is with the library. An attractive building, dignified but cozy and inviting, also increases the library's use. After these should follow industrious use of the hospitable columns of newspapers, exploiting the services the library can render, the distribution of lists, printed by the library if they can be afforded or of cooperative lists printed by other libraries or publishers, and even lists advertising the books of a given publisher. The exhibit in the Salisbury Public Library includes some excellent examples of picture bulletins and placards used as bait by certain of the progressive libraries of North Carolina.

County Libraries

Your state already has a good library law which has just been amended by the legislature. If asked for suggestions, I should direct your attention to the county library idea which has been producing such splendid results in California and certain other states and has recently been adopted by Texas. This plan seeks to have a public library at the county seat of every county, with its resources open not simply to the population of the county seat, but also to farmers thruout the county, who would gain such privileges either by a direct county tax or by contracts between towns and the county seat. Since arriving, I have been pleased to learn that your legislature has just enacted a county library law and that even before the passage of this act certain North Carolina libraries had become in effect county libraries, including those of Salisbury, Greensboro and Durham.

It has always seemed to me that the county library idea is particularly adapted to Southern conditions, where predominantly the county is the unit of political organization, just as the township is the unit in New England.

I suppose no address on the twentieth century public library would be complete without some mention of Mr. Carnegie and his benefactions. Mr. Carnegie has I believe put public library progress in America a generation ahead of what it would have been without his help. I take it that you understand that his gifts are confined to furnishing library buildings and equipment, that he does not furnish money for sites, for books, or for any other expenses of administration. However, the building is a big item of expense and the lack of it proves to many communities a stumbling block in the road toward library founding. His offer of a building removes that stumbling block and furnishes the original incentive to library establishment. Acceptance of Mr. Carnegie's benefactions should not be allowed to become a hindrance to library progress. Mr. Carnegie or rather now the Carnegie Corporation stipulates that towns accepting library buildings should furnish a *minimum* annual support of 10 per cent of the cost of the building. This *minimum* has often been interpreted by city councils as the *maximum,* with the result that the library has been starved. It should also be noted that Mr. Carnegie does not require that libraries to which he has given buildings should bear his name as a part of their official designations.

What services may our twentieth century library be expected to render to the small or medium sized town? A library so conceived and so administrated will be one that will not be classed in the public mind with pink teas and ladies' aid societies; but will be strong and resourceful, administrated on business principles and equipped with material that is needed by every person in the community, young and old, rich and poor, educated and uneducated, the timid who do not know what they want, and the resourceful who know exactly what they want and are bound to get it.

REINFORCEMENT OF SCHOOLS

First, such a library should be a reinforcement of the schools. It will perhaps have a special collection of books designed for lending to public schools. Such books will be coordinated with the courses of study. The use of them in the class rooms or for home reading will make teaching easier. They will hold the interest of the pupils; they will vitalize the schools and hold children longer in school. Such books, appealing as they do to child minds, will be taken home and be read by older brothers and sisters, even by parents who would perhaps be too timid to go to the library and confess that they prefer juvenile books.

Such a library will of course have a special children's room, or at least a children's corner containing a miniature library made up of carefully selected books for children. Library work with children is a highly specialized department of professional library work. There is even a library school at Pittsburgh entirely devoted to training children's librarians. Such work requires special personal aptitude, knowledge of children and their psychology, familiarity with and love for children's literature, sometimes accompanied by a gift for story-telling by means of which the interest of children is gained and held. By means of such a department, as well as by the use of the books in schools, children are captured early and may be retained as life-long library users. Li-

brary work with children affords a splendid opportunity for personal work, directing reading away
from the poor and mediocre to the good and the best.

TRADES AND INDUSTRIES

A twentieth century public library, if established
in a large town, has a separate industrial department;
if in a small town it has a carefully selected and up
to date collection of books on the trades and industries
represented among its clientèle. If it is in a small
village where farms come up to the very doors of the
town, such a library will be strong in books on all
phases of agriculture, poultry raising and marketing.
The back-to-farm movement and the present shortage
of food thruout the country are turning us all into
farmers or gardeners so that the modern library, alert
to serve its constituency, tries to supply abundant
books on farming and gardening. Such a library
will have books on water works, sanitation, street and
road improvements, and all other questions that the
municipal authorities and citizens alike need to know
about to make the town a safe and healthful place in
which to live. It will have books on carpentry,
plumbing, concrete construction, bridge building,
sewers, and engineering problems generally. It will
have books on manufacturing, (e.g. cotton in a place
like Salisbury) on salesmanship, window dressing,
accountancy and merchandising. It will, of course,
have books on the equipment and repair of automobiles. It will have books on the individual occupations of its citizens, so that each person can find in
the library something that will help to increase his
earning capacity and, therefore, make him a better
citizen. It will have books on the choice of vocations,
businesses and professions. It will have cook books,
books and magazines on clothing and dress-making,

on fashions, on house decorations, on pickling, preserving, buttermaking and other subjects of interest to the housewife. Even tho such books are usually more expensive than the current novel, our twentieth century library would be very remiss not to furnish an abundant supply of books helpful in promoting the economic development of its constituents. As a practical suggestion for a library in a manufacturing town like Salisbury, I should do as they have done at Youngstown, Ohio—go to the manufacturers and get them to put up the money for the purchase of books on manufacturing cotton at Salisbury and let the library circulate the books among their employes. They should be convinced that this is an investment in efficiency.

Altho our twentieth century library is not a religious institution, much less a sectarian one, yet it is properly interested in religious matters, as some form of religion is of interest to everyone. The public library, therefore, furnishes an abundant supply of books on religious history, lives of Christ, missions, the Sunday School lessons and other phases of the subject. The ministers, who will be constant users of the library and its best friends, as well as many laymen, will also be interested in books on other religions besides Christianity, in books of philosophy and on the natural sciences. In fact the public library should furnish the best books on every subject of interest and discussion.

Our twentieth century librarian will also keep her hand on the public pulse so as to meet, perhaps to anticipate, the demand, even to lead the thought of her public to investigate new questions in the field of politics and economics. Her library will supply books devoted to all questions of national, state and local government and their improvement; books on the control of trusts, on railroads, on street railways, on private and public finance, on stocks and bonds, on taxation, national, state and local. She will also not fail to supply an abundance of literature on the suffrage question—of course both pro and anti.

Working backward from the books now deemed most important in the modern library but once conspicuous by their absence, to the literature formerly almost alone considered appropriate to a library, our modern public library will, of course, supply books on history, travel, and biography; on the American Revolution, the French Revolution, the genesis of the Russian revolution, and the German revolution that we are all expecting, on other lands and peoples, on the great of all ages and the lessons of their lives for us. Our modern library will not neglect to have books on the fine arts, especially books on the laying out of streets and the decoration of its squares, for our small town will want to be beautiful, not simply well governed. It will have books of languages and literatures, including those which recount the lives of imaginary but true people who live in novels, dramas and poems. All these books your library should have in such abundance as to enrich your lives, make you wiser citizens, better company for yourselves and for each other.

Of the selection of books for your library, I could talk at length, indeed I have another address on this topic alone. Suffice it to say that it is desirable on the one hand not to shoot over the heads of your constituency, but to adapt the books of your library to every taste, every degree, and every need; but on the other hand to keep fully abreast of the needs of the readers, with some books just a little in advance of their needs, something to aspire to.

A REFERENCE DEPARTMENT

Our twentieth century library will not simply supply books for home circulation to its constituents, but will also provide either a separate room or a separate corner for a reference department in which problems may be studied in the library. Such a department will be in charge of one of the most skilful persons in the library, either the librarian herself in a small library, or some other well trained person who knows both books and people, one who can find out needs and supply them. Here will be collected the dictionaries and encyclopedias and other expensive books of ready reference. All the books of the library will also be drawn upon in case of need. Here will be propounded the problems of study clubs, clubs of women, clubs of men, clubs of children, clubs devoted to civics, to gardens, to domestic science, and to any other question of local interest. Here are the current periodicals, both in the field of general literature and in the technical sciences, together with the indexes for making their contents easily available to readers. Reference books and magazines may also be profitably supplemented by pamphlets and clippings classified and arranged, preferably in vertical filing cabinets. Thru the work of this department the public library most nearly realizes the name by which it is sometimes called, "the people's university."

The resources of the modern public library are not confined simply to collections of books, magazines, pamphlets and newspaper clippings, but in recent times have often included such material as piano-player-records and pictures, including stereopticon slides. This is becoming more and more a pictorial age, as is evident by the popularity of the movies and by the fact that almost every newspaper must now be illustrated. The library cannot lag behind, but must keep up with the procession. With almost no expense for materials and by utilizing odd minutes, it is possible to get together a collection of pictures that are of the utmost utility educationally. Railway and steamship folders, old numbers of magazines, and worn out books may be cut up, and the pictures secured from them may be filed in pamphlet boxes or vertical filing cabinets, either mounted or unmounted. Such pictures are interesting and helpful in teaching geography, in illustrating Sunday school lessons, in mission classes, in art study clubs and in many other ways.

LECTURE HALLS AND STUDY ROOMS

Most modern public library buildings are now equipped with lecture halls, where large public meetings may be held, and often with study rooms in which smaller organizations may meet. We are meeting tonight in a community building, in which your local library has a place. Here the library is tributary to the community idea, but the more usual practice is to have the public library the main idea around which other community interests center. The meetings in such a library lecture hall are properly confined to those of civic and educational interests appropriate to the library idea. Such meetings sooner or later bring all classes of the community to the library and enable it to serve them and to get a hold upon them. In turn the library can furnish material, the use of which would improve the discussions, make them of real educational value, and lift them above the futility that often characterizes ill-informed discussions. In the study rooms, especially, books and magazines needed in connection with the meetings can be used advantageously, thus aiding the persons in attendance, and enabling the library to accomplish the purposes for which it is conducted.

In this address I have tried to outline the essential character of the public library as an integral part of public education and, therefore, essential to the development of democracy; the principles necessary in the organization and administration of such a public utility, and some of the services that such a twentieth century library should render to medium and small sized towns. 'As I have tried to cover a wide field in a brief speech, I fear that I have at times been rather dogmatic—have stated propositions positively instead of attempting to prove them. I wonder whether I have had any success in making you think of the library as an institution that you cannot get along without? It is my hope that you will think of the public library not as another tax eater, as an institution the conduct of which will involve a large expense, but rather as an institution the expenditures for which are properly considered as investments, investments that will yield large returns in better financial success for those who use its resources, happier and better homes, and more intelligent citizenship; that you will be convinced of the need for joining your state library commission in its effort to secure a public library in every town in North Carolina by 1920.

MUNICIPAL POPULAR LIBRARIES OF PARIS [1]

(This paper is included because it is believed that this description, written twenty-three years ago, is substantially true today. In the summer of 1928 I discussed these libraries with Mr. Burton Stevenson, then director of the American Library in Paris. Shortly after his recent return to the United States with nearly five years of service in Paris he wrote me as follows:

"I have been re-reading your article on *The Municipal Popular Libraries of Paris,* and it will perhaps interest you to know that it is just as accurate a description of them today as it was when it was written twenty-two years ago. They are still the same forlorn, depressing places they were when you visited them—inadequately equipped, poorly housed, and administered by persons without adequate training—indeed, for the most part, without any training at all, as we understand it. Their budgets are smaller than they were before the war, if the diminished value of the franc is taken into consideration, and so, of course, salaries and book purchases are even more meagre. The hours of opening are very curtailed. I have never forgotten trying to visit the municipal library at Chartres one day, only to be confronted by the sign that it was open *'autant que possible'*—as much as possible! Which was evidently very little. It has always been a mystery to me why the French, who are an intelligent people and who pay much more respect to learning and to literature than we do, should be so indifferent to their libraries.")

Just as naturally as a duck takes to water does a librarian on his summer vacation visit the libraries that lie in his path. He does this almost instinctively even when he is visiting a country for the first time with proverbial American speed, and when cathedrals, castles and art galleries stand first in importance as spectacles. It is, perhaps, to be expected that an American librarian touring Northern France would find time to visit the famous national reference libraries of Paris, such as the Bibliothèque Nationale and the Mazarine, the Ste. Geneviève and the Arsenal libraries; also that he would see a few typical municipal reference libraries of the larger

[1] Read before the District of Columbia Library Association, October 23, 1907.

provincial cities such as those at Rennes, Amiens and Rouen. But it is not perhaps so obvious that he would find time to study a library system that has no mention in Baedeker and is not usually regarded as among the sights of Paris. However, as this system is probably the nearest existing French counterpart to an American branch library system, it deserves the attention of American public librarians.

FRENCH REFERENCE LIBRARIES

Before taking up the more specific topic of this paper I wish to mention one or two features of the reference libraries visited that especially interested me. Nearly all of them had, apparently, only just begun to make card catalogs. Most of the libraries had printed catalogs, often in several volumes, with numerous supplements; some of them, like the Arsenal Library, had manuscript catalogs on large sheets which were kept in pamphlet binders; but nearly all are now developing card catalogs, some classified, but a few substantially dictionary catalogs. The cards used are generally of about the same width as our standard card, but are somewhat shorter. Invariably, however, the cards stand on end instead of on their longest sides. Perforations are large; wooden rods are used and cases seem rather awkward. Inasmuch as their card catalogs all seem to be such new ventures, one cannot help wondering why the standard size in general use not only in America but by the Institut International de Bibliographie at Brussels, the Concilium Bibliographicum at Zurich, as well as elsewhere, had not been adopted, thus providing for the interchange of cards. But perhaps the desire for uniformity, even in so expensive a process as that of cataloging, is somewhat similar to the desire of the Anglo-Saxon that all the world speak English.

The French popular libraries have indeed been described in the great French cyclopedias; they have been critically treated in M. Maurice Pellisson's *Les bibliothèques populaires,* published within a year, and there are scattering references to them in the files of the *Library Journal.* Inasmuch, however, as the Paris system has been much expanded during the last few years, a present-day view of it by an American public librarian may prove of interest. The following notes are based on several evenings spent in different libraries, on an interview and correspondence with the supervising officer of the system at the Hôtel de Ville, and on recent official documents and other recent French authorities.

FOR GENERAL EDUCATION

Paris is well supplied with reference libraries in the great state-supported institutions already mentioned. These popular libraries, officially known as Bibliothèques Municipales, are designed to be agents of general education. To this end they are widely distributed; they are kept open at hours most convenient for those who are regularly employed; they have small reference collections, but find their main work in home circulation. There are eighty-two of these libraries in Paris, from two to six in each of the twenty arrondissements (wards) into which the city is divided. Each is housed in a single large room or, at most, in two connecting rooms. One is to be found in the *mairie* or town hall of each arrondissement; the others are in the public school buildings (*les écoles communales*). To aid in directing readers to the library nearest their homes, in each library is posted a large chart giving the location and hours of opening of all the libraries in the system.

There are 475,346 volumes in the eighty-two libraries. The libraries therefore possess an average of less than 6000 volumes. Considerably more than one-half of each collection is for circulation. About ten or twelve current periodicals are to be found in each reading room. One of the rules governing all the libraries provides that books costing more than ten francs (including binding) shall not be circulated. Practically all of the books in these libraries are confined to French, tho some contain a few English and German books. There is no direct access to the shelves except in the case of dictionaries and cyclopedias. Circulating books are behind a counter and reference books are kept in glazed or wire screened cases.

MUSIC AND ART

All the libraries contain collections of music for home use and twelve of them contain collections of industrial art material. These art collections consist, in addition to books, of designs (often in colors) for furniture, costume, architecture, etc. These designs are mounted on heavy paper about 30 inches by 15 inches and kept in portfolios. Each plate is numbered and may be taken out for home use. There are 102,182 of these mounted designs in the twelve libraries having these collections of industrial art. This material has large use.

The libraries are all open at least two hours every evening and two hours every Sunday morning. A few are also open from 4 to 6 p.m., and a very few are open daily from 11 a.m. to 5 p.m. There are ten regular holidays on which all libraries are closed.

Permission to use the libraries is surrounded by

the fewest possible formalities. Any person at least eighteen years of age may secure the right to draw books from any library in his own arrondissement by proving in some way, such as by a receipt for rent, his domicile in the arrondissement. In at least one library young people of thirteen years of age may draw books on written consent and guaranty of parents or guardians. Last year the number of registered borrowers at all libraries was 61,225. The total use was 1,549,713, including 1,447,588 home circulation and 102,125 reading room use. These figures are not so large as those of 1904, when the total use (both circulation and reference) reached 2,135,640 from 75 libraries, and even fall short of those of 1898, when with 74 libraries the use was 1,928,217. M. Rupert Précy, Chief of the Central Service of Municipal Libraries, attributes this falling off in use to several causes. I translate freely from his letter. "Among these causes are: the fact that some of the time formerly given to reading is now devoted to sports; the appearance of numerous publications at prices that appeal to the most meagre purses; and above all the campaigns of the hygienic enthusiasts which have resulted in inducing in the public mind a fear of contamination by microbes."

FINES UNKNOWN

Books taken from these libraries may be retained fifteen days and renewed once. The collection of fines, except in cases of losses or injuries, is unknown. Sealed letters, never post-cards, are sent to delinquents. In cases where books are not recovered the central office and all the other libraries are furnished with the names of delinquents and "black lists" are kept.

Thus far I have sometimes referred to these libraries as forming a system of branches in the American sense of that term, but more often as individual libraries, and this with design. There is a central office, but not a great central library. There is no one board of trustees under whom a chief librarian directs all the branches. There is, however, a central supervising commission, appointed by the Prefect of the Seine, whose minute and rigid rules govern the administration of every library, including such matters as the arrangement of books on the shelves, accessions registers, salary schedules, binding, book prices, etc. Monthly statistics must be sent to the executive officer of the commission and all libraries appear together in the municipal budget.

Organization and Government

The rules of the central commission provide for a local commission in each arrondissement. The chief function of these local commissions is the choice of books for the libraries of the arrondissement; but their selections must ordinarily be made from approved lists published by the central commission. They may, however, under exceptional circumstances, purchase, subject to the approval of the central commission, recent and scientific books that have not yet been included in the approved lists.

The rules of the central commission provide for each library a librarian, one or more assistant librarians and one or more messengers. In most libraries but three persons make up the entire staff, or if there are more there is alternation in the service. None but men are employed; there is not the slightest danger of the feminization of French libraries, for, so far as I could learn, no women are employed in them. All employes are appointed by the Prefect of the Seine. Those employed in the libraries housed in the communal schools are regularly appointed from among the teaching staff. The school principal is usually also librarian; the staffs of the libraries in the *mairies* are recruited from the clerks employed in the various offices of the mairie, on nomination of the mayor. The schedule of yearly salaries is as follows: librarian from $120 to $200; assistant librarian $100 to $110; messenger $80 to $85. It should be observed that these salaries are paid for two hours work a day, and that the employes derive their main support from other occupations, usually teaching; but it is rather startling to find that the highest salary paid is less than 60 cents per evening.

Binding and Arrangement

As books are regularly published in France unbound, they are all bound in monotonous uniformity in binding prescribed by the central commission. This binding, by the way, is washable cloth; it wears well and deserved more study than I was able to give to it. Books are arranged in strict numerical order as added. Oversize books are kept on special shelves, but their numerical places are occupied by dummies.

At least once in two years and generally every year a classified pocket catalog of books for home use in each library is printed. Every borrower must purchase one of these catalogs at a cost of ten cents. Author and subject catalogs on slips are also kept for official use.

The total yearly cost of supporting these eighty-two libraries is 295,596 francs, or an average of $721 for the total running expenses of each library. The sum of 28,000 francs is also appropriated for fourteen private free libraries. Thus the support rendered by the city of Paris to free libraries is less than $65,000

a year. This money is apportioned among the various
libraries on the basis of the home circulation. During
the first five years after the creation of a new library
1000 francs additional are yearly allotted to it.

CHOICE OF BOOKS

One of the most interesting features of this library system, and the one which will, perhaps, afford
most practical help to American public librarians,
is that which has to do with the choice of books.
One of the most important functions of the central
commission is the annual publication of a list of books
accepted as suitable for these municipal libraries.
It is from these lists that all accessions to the various libraries must be chosen.

It is well known that one of the hardest tasks
of a librarian is the choosing of new French books
that will not prove unsuitable for an American constituency. It is to be hoped that the *A. L. A. Booklist* may sooner or later take up books in foreign
languages. Altho I have never made any actual
tests as order lists of the lists prepared by the Paris
commission, yet I believe that they would prove
helpful. An analysis of the one for 1907 may be of
interest. Exclusive of bound periodicals, it contains
273 titles and 278 volumes, divided as follows: ethics
and politics, 15 volumes, cost unbound 49.50 fr.;
history, geography and travel, 66 volumes, 352.50 fr.;
fiction, 52 volumes, 179 fr.; literature, 51 volumes,
199 fr.; sciences, art and education, 49 volumes,
211.25 fr.; and juvenile, 45 volumes, 124.75 fr. If
the entire list were ordered the cost would be about
1125 francs ($225), or if bound in France about
$315. The fiction section would probably be the
most useful part of the catalog. The books included
in it would cost, bound, less than $50.

A limited supply only of these lists is printed each year. However, I was assured that if American librarians file requests for them sufficiently in advance the editions could be increased so that it would be possible to send them in future if not at present.

AIDS FOR AMERICAN LIBRARIANS

Inasmuch as this question of book selection is just now receiving so much attention from librarians, it seems well to bring together here a few scattered notes regarding other helps in the choice of French books. The monthly *Bulletin des bibliothèques populaires* (Paris, Cornély, subscription 3 fr. a year), published since January, 1906, is almost entirely devoted to brief signed reviews of French literature. They are written by experts (mostly professors in the Sorbonne) with librarians in mind. They are brief, do not indulge in fine writing and are very practical. In each number some one subject is taken up and its literature is reviewed comparatively. The editor of this journal in his first issue praised the *A. L. A. Catalog.* He regretted that the French had no similar list, but called attention to what he calls a retrospective guide to French literature, namely, the *Catalogue de livres pour bibliothèques populaires,* published (Paris) by the Ligue de l'Enseignement in 1905. He also mentions the pamphlet entitled *Pour les bibliothèques publiques ou privés: des livres à lire* (Paris, *Pages libres,* 1903. 75 centimes). Another monthly periodical published to aid in the choice of current French books is the *Bibliographie du bon livre français* (Paris, L'Action Sociale de la Femme, subscription 2 fr. 50 centimes). Books favorably reviewed in it may be purchased with safety by American libraries.

Provincial Popular Libraries

These small public libraries, descriptive notes of which occupy the bulk of this paper, are not confined to Paris, but are scattered widely over France. The latest available statistics, those of 1902, report 2911 tax supported popular libraries in addition to the 82 in Paris, possessing 416,417 volumes. Out of 86 departments five have more than 100 of these libraries and 29 have more than 30. For example, the city of Amiens, with 91,000 population, has 17 of these popular libraries. However, only 86 of these libraries outside of Paris have incomes exceeding $200 each; the expenditures of 107 are from $100 to $200; the yearly incomes of 173 are from $20 to $100; 366 have less than $20 a year each; and the rest have no ordinary incomes.

It would perhaps be ungracious for one who has so recently received courtesies at the hands of French library officers to add any words of adverse criticism that might be suggested by comparisons between the libraries here described and our own public libraries. It is possible, however, without discourtesy to quote from good French authorities, to let the comparison be made by French library officers and educators. Charles V. Langlois, Professor at the Sorbonne and Director of the Library, Office and Museum of Public Education (formerly known as the Musée Pedagogique) reviewed fully the library situation of France, and especially the status of these popular libraries in the program (January, 1906) of the *Bulletin des bibliothèques populaires*. He frankly ranked the United States first in public library work, with England next, then Germany and then France.

French Criticism Quoted

Professor Langlois points out that out of the 3000 existing popular libraries (Paris excepted) only 200 have more than $100 a year for the purchase of books. He thinks that there are enough libraries, but that the existing ones are not sufficiently supported, that they vegetate, chiefly from want of more and better new accessions. From a careful study of the situation he says: "it appears evident that there is lacking to our French libraries, not only money and that which money will give, but a more lively sentiment of their social value, more good books and more friends."

Maurice Pellisson, in the concluding chapter of his recent *Les bibliothèques populaires à l'étranger et en France* (1906) attempts to analyze the reasons why English and American public libraries are so far superior to those of France, and why the public libraries of Germany have in the last ten years come to be better than those of France, and to point out how the public libraries of France can be made better. In this chapter he first mentions the obvious disadvantages under which the French libraries suffer; that because of smaller appropriations their collections are smaller, their housing and material equipment are inferior, their hours of opening are shorter, their administration is less active and efficient, and their service more poorly paid. Another shortcoming, according to M. Pellisson, is that the libraries are too often composed of books written "for the people instead of books written for all the world." Books that give the impression of being "written for the people" are precisely the books that the "people" will never read. It is high time, he says, to renounce absolutely the conception of making the public library a philanthropic institution and to make of it an instrument of culture. This critic also points out that in most places these libraries have been multiplied excessively; that they would be stronger and more effective by being reduced in numbers by combinations, by establishing a strong central library with a smaller number of stronger branches. Publicity and the help of the press are also much needed. And, finally, improvement in the personnel of the librarians is needed and special training for librarianship is requisite.

HOW TO STRENGTHEN THE
SUNDAY SCHOOL LIBRARY [1]

(Sunday School libraries are perhaps now obsolete or obsolescent, especially in large cities having adequate public libraries. However, the principles here laid down apply equally to other libraries collected and maintained on a basis of volunteer service. A point not sufficiently stressed in the original article is that of the importance of library upkeep and the difficulty of maintaining it under volunteer service; that is, the mending and binding of books, the replacement of old books, soiled or worn, or out of date, by new and better books as they appear.)

You have invited the public librarian, the executive officer of a secular institution which is a department of the municipal government, to address an association forming part of an ecclesiastical body concerning one of the agencies of the church. You must realize that the point of view of the speaker is in the nature of things primarily that of the professional librarian. I trust, however, that you will find that I shall speak entirely in a sympathetic spirit.

The views which I shall express are the result of experience and reflection, supplemented by a study of the most recent writings on the Sunday school library. These include the opinions both of Sunday school workers and professional librarians, as found especially in articles in the *Proceedings* of the recently organized Religious Education Association and the most recent treatises on the Sunday school. These opinions I shall try to apply to the special conditions in the District of Columbia and, so far as I can, to the Sunday schools of the Diocese of Washington.

[1] Read at Sunday School Institute, Church of the Epiphany, Washington, February 16, 1909.

In attempting to answer the question, How to strengthen the Sunday school library, it seems to me important to ask and to try to answer certain more fundamental questions, namely: What are the nature and purpose of the Sunday school library? Is it worth retaining at all? If so, as a whole or only in part? Under what conditions might it well be given up, in part or entirely? And when should it be fully developed and in what direction and how?

The Sunday school is a special agent of the church for religious education. This not only includes the imparting of knowledge of the Bible and religion but also of right ethical ideals and character forming. All of its ideals, whether of life, of art, or of literature, are or should be clean, noble and uplifting. If this is a correct, tho necessarily incomplete definition of the work of the Sunday school, it follows that the Sunday school library must harmonize with its purposes and ideals, it must contribute toward the end of religious and ethical education and its collections must conform to high standards of literature and ethics.

Leaving out of account for the moment the reference collections of Sunday school lesson helps, I believe it is safe to say that many, if not most, of the collections of circulating books in Sunday school libraries distinctly do not measure up to fair standards of good literature and good ethics. With no wish to give offense to any one who may have devoted much attention to the forming of a Sunday school library, but at the same time with the purpose of looking facts squarely in the face, I believe it to be true, at least far as I have examined the catalogs of Sunday school libraries, that their children's collections are to a large extent made up of books that are distinctly bad as literature, and weak, flabby and generally unwholesome in moral fiber.

Of necessity the chief librarian of a large public library, whose time is largely absorbed by administrative duties, cannot give much of his personal attention to the selection of children's books. For this reason most libraries of sufficient size have a specially trained children's librarian, one of whose principal duties is the careful selection of children's books. With your permission I shall at the close of this talk ask Miss Clara W. Herbert, the children's librarian of the Public Library, to comment on some authors whose works find a place in practically all Sunday school libraries, including those of churches in this diocese. I should say that Miss Herbert, in addition to being an expert in children's literature, is an Episcopalian.

UNFAVORABLE OPINIONS

In order to show that I have good authority for making such generalizations regarding the Sunday school library, I wish to quote from one of the best and most recent books on the Sunday school, *The Modern Sunday School in Principle and Practice,* by Henry F. Cope, general secretary of the Religious Education Association, who thus characterizes it: "The average Sunday school library, with its pitiable collection of ragged books, selected . . . on account of their painfully pious platitudes or their impossible puerile martyrs," and again, in answering the question, "Shall the Sunday school provide 'religious literature'?" the same authority says: "If by this is meant the old type of the 'Sunday school library' book, with its pitiable caricature of fine Christian character, it is scarcely necessary to say that such literature is worse than none at all, that it may do fully as much harm as the trashy 'Diamond Dick' type."

I do not believe that Sunday school libraries which contain as their staples the books to which exception is taken can properly claim to be doing educational work, whether religious, ethical or literary. Books of the kind mentioned are of course sought after, but so are the nickel novels, which by the way, are sometimes not so black as they have been painted. Libraries made up largely of such books are not educational agents. If they serve any purpose, it is as a bait to get the children to come to Sunday school. The question then arises of the ethics of using unwholesome bait. Of course, no one would suggest that this is done with conscious purpose. It probably results from devoted, useful, unselfish and well-intentioned tho unskilled endeavor.

First then, the Sunday school library, if and when it is retained, should be strengthened in the matter of the choice of books. Even before making any additions, I would suggest the removal of some very popular but objectionable books, such as those by Martha Finley, Pansy, Castlemon, Alger, Stratemeyer, etc. As a guide for the selection of books to take their places, Episcopalians have the altogether admirable and trustworthy series of catalogs of books recommended by the Church Library Association, Cambridge, Mass., for Sunday school and parish libraries. In addition there are the lists of books for children compiled by Miss Hewins of Hartford and published by the American Library Association; the list of 1,051 books agreed upon by the Carnegie Library of Pittsburgh and the Cleveland Public Library, *A Children's Library* compiled by Misses Prentiss and Power; and many other lists issued by public libraries. The children's librarian of our Public Library, Miss Herbert, of course stands ready to give advice, as part of her regular duties, to those who may wish to consult her in the choice of books for Sunday school libraries, for the Public Library desires not only to circulate the best books but to influence other voluntary agencies to circulate none but good books.

Higher Standards Needed

At first thought it seems almost incongruous that the representatives of the public library should presume to urge upon the churches the necessity for higher standards in the choice of books for the Sunday school libraries. But such is the case. The reason for this is that in the case of the public library the selection is made by experts, imbued with the professional spirit, who at every point apply the tests of educational and literary standards, whereas in the case of the Sunday schools the selection is often made by amateurs without any very clearly defined standards, except perhaps popularity and supposed harmlessness. During the last thirty years an entirely new literature for children has been written. This forms the staple of the public library's equipment, but seems to be largely unknown to the Sunday school librarians, who apparently go on buying for the most part the former Sunday school favorites whose usefulness is now outgrown.

If you are now ready to agree that the Sunday school library should adopt public library standards in the choice of books of literature I suppose that some of you maintain that at any rate the Sunday school library has or should have books dealing directly with religious subjects, such as religious history, biography, material on missions and biblical commentaries, written both for children and adults, which the public library does not or could not be expected to have. I believe the reverse to be true, both here in Washington and generally. Quoting again from Mr. Cope: "It is a rare thing to find a public library which does not contain a better collection of books strictly religious and suited to children and adults, than can be found in all the Sunday schools of the neighborhood. More than this, it is the settled policy of a large number of public libraries to place on their shelves the best works on the history, activities and polity of each denomination represented in the community." I fully believe that it would be easy to prove to the representatives of any Sunday school in this diocese that the foregoing is true of our local Public Library as compared with any or all Sunday school libraries of the District.

The Sunday school library even at its best, in addition to being so much weaker and less efficient than the public library in the matter of its collection of books, has the following disadvantages as compared with the public library: usually it is open but once a week and consequently most of its books are tied up in a wasteful way; it is necessarily limited in size because of limited resources, being able to buy but few new publications, so that its collection soon becomes well-known and no longer prized; in the nature of things it cannot be more skillfully administered by the rather irregular volunteer service usually secured; often the work of exchanging books is allowed to consume a good deal of time and attention of teachers and pupils, thus withdrawn from giving and receiving instruction.

In view of these weaknesses and disadvantages of the Sunday school library and the strength and superior advantages of the public library, there are many writers on the Sunday school who frankly advocate the giving up of Sunday school libraries and the reliance hereafter on the public library for at least the general literature heretofore contained in Sunday school libraries, and such a plan has now quite generally been adopted in several cities. I am told that this is the plan adopted by St. John's Church, to whose general Sunday school library no books have been added in four years. It seems to me that unquestionably this is the sensible plan to adopt in Washington in so far as the members of any Sunday school are able to use the Public Library.

REASONS FOR CONTINUANCE

Having said this, I wish to point out certain advantages which the Sunday school library has over the public library, and certain local conditions which argue for the continued existence of the Sunday school libraries in churches remote from the central Public Library building. The main reason for continuing the work of Sunday school libraries in the District of Columbia is that the Public Library has not yet been able to build its branches or fully to develop its system of circulating books thru the public schools. When the library is able to do these things it will probably be possible to offer to every child in the District better library facilities, including books with wholesome, ethical influence, than he would be likely to secure from the Sunday school library. Until that time many children will probably be deprived of library facilities unless they are supplied by the Sunday schools. This reason is so strong that we of the Public Library wish to see the Sunday school libraries retained and strengthened in order that they may do, either independently or perhaps ultimately in cooperation with the Public Library, the library work which the Public Library is not now doing and probably cannot do for a long time to come.

So fully do I realize the obligations of the Public Library to afford to the whole community library facilities that I, as public librarian (and I believe I fairly represent the attitude of the library trustees) would gladly afford such facilities to the public thru the Sunday school libraries. I would, in other words, use the machinery you have to carry Public Library books to the public. I would do this, as representing a public institution, in the same way that I now use the public schools, the social settlements and the Y. M. C. A., and as I would use, if I could, the parochial schools and other similar non-tax-supported institutions. For lack of funds, however, to offer such facilities to all Sunday schools without exception in the District, as a matter of policy we must for the present decline to offer such facilities to any church.

In this connection, however, I wish to announce that I am authorized by the Library trustees to make the following offer as an experiment to a single Sunday school library: to the first Sunday school that will offer to turn over to the Public Library for one year the fund it usually devotes to the purchase of books (up to $50), the Public Library will promise to duplicate the sum and to furnish and exchange as often as desired as many books as the combined sum will buy. For example, if a Sunday school contributes $50, that sum and the Library's equal contribution will buy say 150 books, and the Library will keep the Sunday school supplied with 150 books chosen from the shelves of the Library. The Sunday school would be asked to help in the selection of the original purchase, but the Public Library would have the final decision and the books would remain the property of the Public Library.

Another way in which the Library is able to help

Sunday schools is by extending to Sunday school teachers the privilege of securing teachers' cards on which they are able to draw out ten books, or even more in case they are able to show special need for them, the same to be retained for four weeks and to be loaned to their pupils. The special advantages of these two plans are that the local Sunday school library can be supplemented from the larger collections of the Public Library.

REFERENCE COLLECTIONS DESIRABLE

The foregoing will perhaps afford some suggesttions for strengthening collections of general literature in the Sunday school library. You have heard that in some cases I believe it will be stronger by being swept out of existence, to employ a Hibernianism. There is one portion of a Sunday school library that every Sunday school should furnish. I refer to a Sunday school workers' library composed of Bible dictionaries, commentaries, lesson helps, works on Sunday school history, organization, methods, religious pedagogy, etc. St. John's Church Sunday school library is now, I understand, practically confined to books in this field. This offers a chance for careful choosing and for considerable expenditure of money. Investment in such books should yield a rich return in better Sunday school work. In this connection I cannot forbear to announce that the Public Library strives to have a good equipment of this kind, and that we are always open for suggestions of other books to purchase. Here attention may appropriately be called to the Public Library's collection of the Tissot and other pictures illustrating biblical lands, missions, countries, etc. All the material is freely loaned for use in class work.

Whether it is decided to confine the Sunday school

library to the worker's library or to have a general library as well, whether to maintain it alone or with the cooperation of the Public Library, the following suggestions are offered: consider the library a serious part of the Sunday school to be maintained for educational purposes; maintain it by regular and not by sporadic appropriations; admit no book not approved by experts; have a regular librarian in charge, if possible a professional librarian, even if a small salary must be paid; have all books on open shelves accessible to pupils; employ some definite charging system such as that used by a public library; have books exchanged out of class hours, tho encouraging teachers to supervise reading. Only by the adoption of some such systematic policy will the Sunday school library be worth while. With such a plan it may be a powerful agent for good.

ON BOOKS AND READING [1]

Since coming to Washington I have been able to visit some of the public schools, with increasing admiration of the excellent work being done and always with a feeling of congratulation to the fortunate young people who have the privilege of receiving their instruction here. With this feeling is also one of regret that not all children can enjoy your advantages instead of the more meagre ones afforded by the country schools. The contrast is great between your handsome, well furnished buildings, equipped with laboratories, supplied with text books, and divided into grades, officered by well equipped teachers, each having a small number of pupils, and the one room country school, furnished with rude, jack-knife-hacked desks and a box wood stove, with fifty to seventy pupils under one teacher giving instruction in everything from A B C's to higher algebra. In opportunity for learning the discrepancy may not be so great, for often it is possible to get good, thoro instruction even under such unfavorable conditions. If, however, a comparison is made between your supply of reading matter and that afforded to pupils of country schools, you have a still greater advantage. Outside of text books supplied by the pupils, most country school teachers consider themselves fortunate if they have a dictionary, tho occasionally they have a few badly printed, unattractive volumes, called a library, which have been handed down from an antediluvian period. Often the homes of such country pupils have little besides a few tawdry subscription books and the

1 A talk given to several Washington high schools in 1906.

village weekly, tho with the spread of rural free delivery, the daily newspaper and the 10 cent magazine are now reaching many country homes.

The book famine of the country school was recently brought forcibly home to me by the appeal of a Maryland teacher not twenty miles from the Capital for books for her school. In 1901, eight years after the Chicago fair, a librarian found the sole reading matter, other than text books, of a community of thirteen large families of children in northern Wisconsin to be the World's Fair number of the *Youth's Companion*. Contrast with this a daily paper in almost every home, and an innumerable number of cheap magazines and good books for sale by the cord in the department stores—all this leaving the privileges of the public library out of the account.

Engulfing Reading Matter

With us of this city where reading matter is so cheap and plentiful, where the rising tide of newspapers, magazines, books and public documents almost engulfs us, we are rather in danger of neglecting what we have, or at least of failing to choose wisely. There is, however, no better reason in the case of books than with food, in the presence of abundance, for starvation or gluttony, for indigestion or malnutrition. I come to you today with a few suggestions for mental health and happiness.

We at the Public Library each day try to improve the ease of access to the books needed and wished by the people. Gradually we hope to build branches and supply the demands of the schools as the means to do this are put in our hands by Congress. Along with this development will always go the choice of books admitted to the library and furnished to the people. With the help of teachers and parents should also go the work of implanting in those whose tastes are being formed a desire for the best literature. To this end teachers may give the most help. With their own tastes well trained, in everyday meeting with pupils they may inculcate the desire for the best and by definite suggestion direct their pupils to it. Parents should also take a lively interest in their children's reading, banishing from their homes the yellow journal, sensational story papers, and all else that is mediocre in print, and substituting the best literature, a well selected library of the best books to become a part of the family, regularly supplementing this collection from the public library.

EDUCATION INCOMPLETE

But my main appeal is of course to the pupils here assembled. By your choice or because of the wise choice of your parents, you have not been content to consider your education complete when you have finished the grammar schools. You, or your parents for you, have been ambitious that you should have more education. That you are here shows that you are ambitious, that you wish to make something of yourselves, that you aspire, that you wish more education either to be better equipped to gain a living, or in order that you may be better company for yourselves, or both. From what you have done and are doing, therefore, I am right in assuming that you will be prepared to listen to me when I come to tell you that one of the best courses to pursue to equip yourselves both to gain a livelihood and to enjoy a happy life is to become habitual readers of the best.

The two purposes of reading just mentioned, reading for utility and reading for pleasure, really mark the two main divisions of reading matter—books, magazines and newspapers of information and books

of imagination; books of utility and books of literature. Of course these divisions are not clearly
marked. From some books we may derive the clearest
and most exact information and at the same time,
because of our own satisfaction at acquiring knowledge and its attendant power, we also derive the keen-
est delight. On the other hand, books whose main
purpose is to delight the reader may so quicken his
imagination, sharpen his intelligence, fire his soul
and inspire his ambition as to prove of a thousand
times more value in the sum total of his life than
any mere book of information that he might read.
However, this classification may suffice for the purpose of this talk.

THE DAILY NEWSPAPER

In the group of informational reading matter I
should place first the daily newspaper, many weekly
and some monthly journals which may be regarded
practically as newspapers. The systematic and habitual, tho closely guarded and limited reading of
this material is highly desirable. My experience has
shown me that it is often necessary to urge young
people to read the news. We cannot expect to have
success in life unless we know what is going on in
the world. But be on your guard not to let newspaper reading crowd out everything else. It is a
habit that grows with years. There are plenty of men
of intelligence who read nothing else. The modern
newspaper is so very good, it crowds its pages with
so much of interest, that one could easily spend hours
over it every day. This is especially the case with the
Sunday papers. Not because the newspapers are not
good, but because there are more and better things
outside them, I urge upon you to read them swiftly
in order to go on to the book. Cut out the murders,

suicides, petty gossip, divorces, fires, prize fights, racing, the sports too except for a glance at your favorite team; read most other things by head lines, grasp at a glance the main results of matters of moderate interest, skipping the verbiage, and read with close attention only the occasional weighty utterance, or the concise description of the few things that most count. By such alert scanning instead of the idle dawdling often indulged in, the cream of the news may be acquired, especially if supplemented by the excellent news summaries given weekly in such magazines as the *Outlook* or the *Literary Digest* and monthly in the *Review of Reviews* or *World's Work*.

TECHNICAL PUBLICATIONS

As time goes on you will want to read more of the records of science and invention and discussion and opinion as given in the monthly reviews. But these too are so numerous and so excellent that careful selection and swift reading are necessary to prevent complete absorption of time. If you enter a trade or industry you must of course read one or more trade papers in order that you may keep fully abreast with the latest progress in your field, so that you may lead with the van and not bring up the rear. In all journals that you read spend a little time on the advertisements, often the most informing pages and the most practically useful and suggestive. The bulk of the time you can devote to study in the field of your business or profession (and nowadays the man or woman who does not study much is lost) must be given to books—the text books, the treatises on your life work. There is no trade, business or profession that has not an extensive literature. Mastery of this is necessary to him who is not content to be a journeyman instead of a master, an employe instead of an employer.

So much for utilitarian reading. Have I left time for anything else? Perhaps not in the case of many people. Life is so strenuous, competition is so fierce, that for many persons to work in the rut in which they have started is all that is possible. An advance is made by the one who, not content to stay in the rut, has the ability and the ambition for the mastery of his craft, but often for nothing more. That man develops himself into a machine—a highly intellectualized machine, but still a machine. With every advance of knowledge he puts in all the new improvements and his output is increased in quantity or quality and his financial return is greater. To many men this is quite sufficient.

IMAGINATIVE LITERATURE

But do *you* not want something more than this? Do *you* not want to become something more than highly skilled and efficient machines for coining money, by reason of perfection in a trade, business or profession? While in no way despising business success, do you not want to live in the spirit, with your spirit knowing the great ones of all time and space, real and imaginary? Do you not want to travel, in imagination at least, to all lands, to meet all peoples, to visit the moon and the stars, to think the greatest thoughts of the greatest ones of all the ages, to sing the songs of the poets? If so, all these things are possible if you will but form the habit and the taste for reading, for the books are ready at your hand.

It is possible that by this time you are asking yourself two or three questions. They are possibly these: first, Will reading of books of pure literature give me the pleasure present and future that you say? second, How am I to know what is good literature? and third,

How can I find the time to do enough reading in other than utilitarian fields to make it really count? All of these are proper questions and I shall try briefly to answer them.

THE LOVE OF BOOKS

Some of you have no doubt been brought up in a bookish atmosphere; you have had plenty of the best books of literature always at hand. The best poets, the great classics of child life were read to you before you could read. Such persons have grown up with a taste for the best reading and, if wisely guarded to the present, now have that taste developed and that habit fixed. No need to tell them of the pleasures of reading. They already love it and find an increasing satisfaction as each new old great book is added to their possessions. To others I can say only that the process is very much like falling in love; you can't explain it to one who has not yet experienced it. A love of reading, like the other kind of falling in love, is something that may happen at any time of life and in this case the earlier the better. Some of the greatest men of history have been the greatest readers. It would be possible to fill up much time by reading what the greatest writers have said in praise of books and reading, but I have time only for two or three of the briefest extracts:

William Ellery Channing wrote: "God be thanked for books! They are the voices of the distant and the dead, and make us heirs of the spiritual life of past ages." Ralph Waldo Emerson: "Consider what you have in the smallest chosen library. A company of the wisest men that could be picked out of all civil countries, in a thousand years, have set in order the results of their learning and wisdom. In the highest civilization the book is still the highest delight."

Henry Ward Beecher: "Books are the windows through which the soul looks out." H. W. Longfellow:

> The love of learning and the sequestered nooks,
> And all the sweet serenity of books.

Montesquieu:

> Study has been to me a sovereign remedy against the vexations of life, having never had an annoyance that one hour's reading did not dissipate.

Fénelon:

> If the crowns of all the kingdoms of the empire were laid down at my feet in exchange for my books and my love of reading I would spurn them all.

WHAT IS GOOD LITERATURE?

To the second question, "How am I to know what is good literature?" I cannot do better than quote from J. N. Larned, once librarian at Buffalo. In an address to the students of the Central High School of that city he said: "On which of the two currents an offered book of entertainment is floated to us is what we must know, if we can. Whether it is brilliant or commonplace, alive with genius or dead with the lack, are not the *first* questions to be asked. The prior question, as I conceive, is this: Does the book leave any kind of fine and wholesome feeling in the mind of one who reads it?" But as this test can be made only by reading the book, and as there will always be so many good books that we can never have read, Emerson's famous three rules are good ones, especially for young people: I. Never read any book that is not a year old. 2. Never read any but famed books. 3. Never read any but what you like; or in Shakespeare's phrase,

> No profit goes where is no pleasure ta'en,
> In brief, sir, study what you most affect."

THE FICTION QUESTION

I suppose you are expecting me to say something about fiction, the value of which is much discussed and the reading of which is much decried. Now I am not going to apologize for the fact that considerably more than 50 per cent of the books drawn from our Public Library (in common with other public libraries) is fiction. The dominant form of literary expression of today is fiction and the reading of the carefully selected fiction added to libraries making a proper choice from the flood offered is wholesome and far better for the majority of readers than no reading or the indiscriminate reading of unselected books. At the same time I cannot too strongly urge readers whose tastes are unformed and teachers who are helping to mold such tastes to follow Emerson's rules especially as applied to fiction. Very few of the novels making so much noise at the present day will be remembered a year from today. Why not, instead of reading them, wait to let them die and spend the time on some great old book like *David Copperfield* or *Les Miserables*? If they survive the year, are then still famous, and you feel that you would gain more pleasure from reading them than from the greater books still unread, no reasonable objection can be raised.

The question, "How can I find the time to make my reading of the best literature really count?" would, I imagine, be answered by most people if they ceased to spend an excessive amount of time over newspapers. Do you not waste at least a half hour in this way or in some other way that could easily be devoted to reading some of the world famous books? If you read only ten pages a day you can in one year read the five volumes of Macaulay's *History of England* and the two volumes of Trevelyan's *Life of Macaulay*—two of the most fascinating books of literature; or you can easily read at the same rate all of Shakespeare's plays in the same period. Isn't that possible for each of you, and isn't it worth while? This slow reading would in most cases require the owning of the books. This also I would urge upon you. Tho the Public Library strives to have a good supply of the best, there are certain books to which we wish to return again and again, and they should become a part of our personal equipment. Do not confine your individual libraries to your textbooks, but begin early to form a small and select library of your own, to be treasured as your best friend.

Taste and Habit of Reading

The forming of the habit of reading pure literature early in life I would most strongly urge upon you. The reading habit and taste for the best literature are very much like the taste for music or the ability to dance. Unless learned in childhood or youth, they are usually not really acquired at all. Herbert Spencer relates in his autobiography that he became absolutely unable to enjoy poetry. Here was a great scientist who had cut himself off from a source of keen enjoyment by systematically neglecting poetry. Do not allow the poet in you, or the capacity for enjoying poetry, or any other form of pure literature, to be starved out, but cultivate the practice of reading as one of your best resources.

In order best to develop the reading habit, I urge you, I invite you, to form the *library* habit. To some of you the end of your school days is almost in sight: some of you will go on to the college and the university. But with all of you, formal school instruction is only a small part of your lives. You will I am sure not be content that your intellectual development shall end there. Rather it is just beginning. The only education worthy of the name extends over the whole of life. How better can that education be carried on than by being graduated from the public school to the public library, rightly named as ours is on its front "university for the people"? That the library habit may be early and therefore most surely formed, I invite you, I urge you, if you have not already done so, to enroll yourselves as library users. At the library are freely offered the means for instruction for all grades and in all conceivable subjects, materials for graduate courses, technical courses to meet every need and interest, with perhaps best of all the great old books of the world for purposeful or for desultory reading.

LONGFELLOW AS A CLASSIC [1]

The opening chapter of Thomas Wentworth Higginson's biography of Longfellow in the *American Men of Letters Series* bears the same title as the one I have chosen for a center about which to group my thoughts on the American poet whose centenary we are celebrating this evening.

The word classic is one which is frequently on the lips of many of us; but if we stop to consider, it is doubtful if it represents a perfectly clear and definite idea to most of those who use it. To some a classic is merely a dead author, somewhat as, according to a wellknown epigram, a statesman is a "dead politician." And just as the statesman is usually enshrined in oil or in marble, while the attention of the world is fixed on the man who is doing things, so a classic, considered in this sense, is an author to be kept on the shelf and a top shelf at that. The term classic is one which is hard to define for the reason that criticism has failed to furnish us a universally accepted opinion on the subject. For example, we have no such aphoristic definition of a classic as Matthew Arnold's dictum regarding poetry—"Poetry is a criticism of life." Perhaps Lowell has expressed as well as any critic the essential qualities which must inhere in a classic. In his essay on Spenser in the second series of *Among My Books* he says:

A classic is properly a book which maintains itself by virtue of that happy coalescence of matter and style, that innate and exquisite sympathy between the thought that gives life and the form

[1] Read at the centennial celebration of the poet's birth, at All Souls' Unitarian Church, Washington, February 24, 1907. Printed in *Washington Evening Star*, March 2, 1907.

that consents to every mood of grace and dignity, which can be simple without being vulgar, elevated without being distant, and which is something neither ancient nor modern, always new and incapable of growing old. . . If poems die, it is because there was never true life in them, that is, that true poetic vitality which no depth of thought, no airiness of fancy, no sincerity of feeling, can singly communicate, but which leaps throbbing at touch of that shaping faculty the imagination.

QUALITY OF LIFE

It is the quality of life, then, which makes a classic; an indefinable quality, but one which everyone of us can feel and recognize even tho unable to analyze and explain it. In what way do the poems of Longfellow possess life? How and to what extent are they classic? In life itself there is infinite variety. So in classics there may be an infinite diversity of manifestations of life. The life in Tennyson's lyrics and idylls, the life in Browning's profoundly analytical and dramatic poems, the life in Matthew Arnold's calm and lofty poetry of the intellect is not the life that throbs in Longfellow's *Voices of the Night* and *Seaside and Fireside Poems*. Longfellow is not the poet of unrest; there is no intellectual struggle in his poems such as we find in those of Browning; nor do we feel that there has been any soul struggle preceding the poems as we do in the case of Matthew Arnold. Neither is Longfellow a revolutionary poet; he does not rebel against the social and ethical order of things as do Byron and Shelley. Storm and stress of any kind were alien to his nature. He was placid and self-contained and he seems never to have made his verse the vehicle for self-revelation or even for purely personal expression. These negative qualities, tho separating him from the company of those poets who have sounded the depths of life's experiences, have brought him closer to univeral humanity.

"Longfellow was not an egotist," William Winter

says: "He thought of others; and the permanent value of his writings consists in this—that he helped to utter the emotions of the universal human heart. It is when a writer speaks for us what were else unspoken—setting our minds free and giving us strength to meet the cares of life and the hour of death—that he first becomes of real value. Longfellow has done this for thousands of human beings, and has done it in that language of perfect simplicity—never bald, never insipid, never failing to exalt the subject—which is at once the most beautiful and the most difficult of all the elements of literature."

TRAGEDY AND SORROW

There is often tragedy in Longfellow's poems and sorrow is not absent; but it is the common sorrow, not the specialized sorrow of the unusual soul.

> Into each life some rain must fall
> Some days must be dark and dreary.

One who is inclined to think that Longfellow represented only the bright side of life has but to recall such poems as *Resignation, The Goblet of Life,* the beautiful ballad *The Bridge* and the whole group of poems on slavery to recognize that his knowledge of grief was profound. Nevertheless, his poetic message seems to have been in the main one of cheerfulness and beauty. Longfellow himself said: "It is the prerogative of the poet to give pleasure; but it is the critic's province to give pain." This creed he seems to have followed thruout his career and it is probable that there is no other poet of any nationality who has given and continues to give more pleasure to a larger number of people than Longfellow.

Time is not sufficient to apply rigidly to the work of Longfellow the tests for a classic as given by Lowell. Were I able, time would fail also to set forth a detailed critical estimate of Longfellow's writings. I shall therefore mention and comment upon only a few of the more salient strong and weak points of his work.

Scoffers at Longfellow

The age that has produced and given honor to Browning, Tolstoi, Ibsen, Walt Whitman, Maeterlinck, Hauptman, Sudermann and Bernard Shaw is inclined to scoff at Longfellow. The arbiters of literary opinion, the critics, enamored of these virile constructive geniuses who have bid defiance to the conventionalities of art, literature and ethics, have become such devotees of their new masters that they have been unwilling to acknowledge any virtue in one so far removed from the new modes of thought and methods of treatment. To such Longfellow is the poet of childhood and the child mind, the poet of the commonplace, the poet of the middle classes, the poet of conventionality and crude didacticism, a romanticist, a mere felicitous teller of stories, and even these not original stories. It must be admitted that these epithets, tho baldly stated, have in them certain elements of truth. But to stop here and not show that, not in spite of them, but in the best sense because of them, Longfellow is a classic poet would be to leave the statement practically false.

Longfellow is the poet of childhood *par excellence*. All honor to him that he is. To be chief among the group that includes Scott, Whittier, Stevenson, Eugene Field and James Whitcomb Riley is of itself no mean place to occupy in literature. To make the happy years of childhood more happy, to nurture the poetic spirit that dwells in every child's mind and to prepare that mind for a life-long enjoyment of poetry—other than Longfellow's perhaps—is surely to be a true poet. It is his musical faculty, his perfect sense of rhythm, his repetitions, his didacticism, his aphorisms, his marvelous story-telling gift, that so attune his poetry to the child mind.

Poet of the Commonplace

Longfellow is the poet of the commonplace. This too is no inglorious title. Life itself is for the most part commonplace. But our poet has transferred the common life of mankind to the realm of poetry by suffusing it with his poetic imagination. As one critic points out "to lift the commonplace into the bright air of peotry is to confer one of the richest boons on dull humanity. . . Longfellow hallowed our human life itself." In this field too Longfellow is in good company, with Robert Burns and Wordsworth. Longfellow was not, perhaps, one of the most original creative geniuses. He was rather an interpreter, a translator of life. It is his simplicity, his tenderness and his sensitiveness that give him his universal appeal, so that "the common people heard him gladly." By another he has been called "the laureate of the common human heart." The numerous biographical and critical sketches are filled with examples of his wide (almost world-wide) acceptability. It is related how once in London his carriage was surrounded by a crowd of people who called him by name and begged to touch his hand, and how at least one in the crowd recited one of his familiar poems. The editor of one of the great London weeklies is quoted as stating that thousands of English working people who have never read a line of Tennyson and who have probably never heard of Browning can repeat some of Longfellow's poems.

To a librarian the test of popularity as shown by

the catalog of the British Museum is of interest. In 1901 the key to that encyclopedic library listed 100 versions in 18 different languages of parts of Longfellow's writings, in addition to the editions in English, with 357 entries in all, as compared with 487 for Tennyson, 179 for Browning and 158 for Emerson. I believe that if a census were taken of the book stocks of public libraries the English speaking world over, it would be found that more copies of Longfellow's poems (in whole or in part) are required to supply demands than of any other single book.

WHAT OF HIS FUTURE?

There are certain questions which must inevitably be asked concerning any author by the student of literature—questions which in the case of Longfellow, because of his exceptional popularity, are often asked by the general reader as well as the student. What is his place in literature as a whole? What position does he hold in the literature of his own country, of his own period? What will his future be? Will his fame be enduring? Perhaps it is safer to follow the example of Howells, who says:

What Longfellow's place in literature will be, I shall not offer to say; that is Time's affair, not mine.

Yes, Time undoubtedly settles most things—literary reputations among them. It elevates some humble, ignored prophet or chronicler and dethrones the popular hero of a decade or two; it brings forward some into the shining light of fame, and retires others to the dusty back shelves of libraries. But we cannot all afford to hold our judgment in abeyance and to await the decisions of Time. We are likely to drop out before the decisions are reached. Meanwhile the tendency is so strong in human nature to dogmatise, to arrive at certain definite conclusions, even tho they must be altered immediately afterward, that very few critics are able to refrain from assigning to their author a present place and from some prophecy, however guarded, for the future. Howells, while disclaiming any attempt at prophecy for Longfellow, goes on to say:

But I am sure that with Tennyson and Browning he fully shared in the expression of an age which more completely than any former age got itself said by its poets.

He Was of His Age

Longfellow lived and wrote then in a period which found one of its chief modes of expression in poetry and he shared in the spirit of his age; he was of it and not apart from it. This very harmony with his time, it seems to me, supplies one reason for a belief in the enduring quality of much of his poetry. He was, moreover, as has already been said, the poet of the home, of childhood, of everyday life, of the commonplace made beautiful, and of universal human thoughts and feelings. This fireside quality in his poetry and his universal appeal form a second and even stronger reason why Longfellow's poetry is likely to have a permanent place in literature.

But there are few writers, however great their genius, whose works are of uniform value. The literary reputations of most authors are based on a certain part of their writings. What are the works of Longfellow on which his fame chiefly rests today and on which it is likely to depend in the future?

It will probably not be disputed that in estimating the literary value of Longfellow we may set aside his prose works, such as *Outre-Mer, Hyperion,* and *Kavanagh. Outre-Mer* was a frank imitation of Irving's *Sketch Book; Hyperion,* a romance full of youthful crudity, probably owed its early success to a large extent to its attractive sketches of travel at a time when travel literature was not as common as it is now; and *Kavanagh,* a village romance, tho it has some beautiful passages, as a whole convinces the reader that Longfellow's romanticism found more spontaneous utterance in poetry than in prose.

TRANSLATION OF DANTE

A not inconsiderable part of the work of Longfellow is his translations. He held professorships of modern languages in Bowdoin College and Harvard for twenty-five years and translated from the poets of Spain, Italy, Norway, Germany and France. His translation of Dante's *Divine Comedy,* undertaken after the tragic death of his wife to divert his mind, occupied him for four years. It is usually regarded as the best poetical translation of Dante yet produced.

The estimates of Longfellow's genius which have been called out by the centenary celebration include one by the keen critic of the *Nation* who points to the seventy-seven sonnets scattered thru Longfellow's writings as forming his most original and artistic work. He says:

"For ripeness of style and imagery" a volume containing these sonnets "would stand easily at the head of American poetry; it would place Longfellow as a peer among the great sonnet writers of England."

One critic, G. R. Carpenter, has said that if Longfellow had died before writing *Evangeline, The Song of Hiawatha, Tales of a Wayside Inn* and *The Courtship of Miles Standish,* the world would justly have estimated him as a man of fine literary tastes, a remarkably skillful translator and the author of a number of very popular, tender, romantic and didactic poems, but would have regretted that he had never attained real proficiency in his art. In the main it seems to me that this is a fair estimate and I believe that on the three long poems *Evangeline, The Song of Hiawatha,* and *The Courtship of Miles Standish* and on the collection of shorter poems *Tales of a Wayside Inn* Longfellow's enduring fame will rest.

FAME RESTS ON LONG POEMS

Evangeline must always rank high among narrative poems on account of its charming romance, its beautiful setting, and its smooth yet rapid movement. It has also the distinction, according to many authorities, of being the first, and with the exception of *Miles Standish,* the only poem in which the English hexameter has been used with real success.

Allied to *Evangeline* in matter and treatment, tho separated from it by *Hiawatha* in the time of production, is *The Courtship of Miles Standish.* It is a Puritan romance as *Evangeline* is an Acadian romance. But it is humorous where *Evangeline* is pathetic and cheerful where *Evangeline* is tragic. It has never been as popular as *Evangeline,* but it seems to me to be a more vital as well as a more artistic and finished piece of work. It has more strength of plot and stronger and more varied characters and the meter is even better handled than in *Evangeline.*

In *Tales of a Wayside Inn* Longfellow's great skill as a storyteller is perhaps at its height. The *Tales* have often been compared with Chaucer's *Canterbury Tales* and certainly Longfellow bears the comparison well. He chose as his subjects old legends and historical anecdotes, just as both Chaucer and Shakespeare borrowed plots from old Greek, Italian, British and Scandinavian tales, and like them Longfellow so adorned his originals that he has made them entirely his own.

288 CENSORSHIP AND THE LIBRARY

Hiawatha Most Original

But in my opinion it is in *Hiawatha* that Longfellow has produced his most thoroly original and artistic poem. Embodying in it as he did the old Indian folklore of our country, with accuracy and, what is more important, with the preservation of the Indian spirit, so we are told by those familiar with Indian life and legends—he has given us our great American epic. In *Hiawatha* all Longfellow's storytelling skill and power of picturesque description have full play, so that Hiawatha's conflict with Mudjekeewis, Hiawatha's fasting, Hiawatha's hunting, Hiawatha's wooing and the death of Minnehaha are rarely forgotten by one who has once read this most American of all American poems.

One hundred years have passed since Longfellow's birth and the fact that his centenary is being so widely celebrated shows that he is still a living force in literature and in life. He is probably read and loved by more people today than at the time when his best poems were written. Whether he will be as widely read and equally loved when another century shall have passed; whether he is to have a place among the few great ones whose work possesses that rare quality of endurance which makes them as vital after the lapse of centuries as during the period of their production, none of us can know. We may speculate about it, but Time must after all bring the answer to such speculations.

PARTIAL LIST OF OTHER WRITINGS
BY THE AUTHOR

As a convenience to the author, even more than because of the supposed interest of the reader, the following partial list of his other published writings is appended. It omits annual reports, such as those as librarian at Wilmington, Del. and Washington, D.C., the first biennial report of the Delaware Library Commission and reports of the many committees of the American Library Association of which he has served as chairman. It omits many book reviews, brief letters and short articles printed in the *Library Journal, Public Libraries,* etc., and it omits hundreds of newspaper articles written for the newspapers of Washington, New York and Rochester, N. Y. With these ommissions the list follows; the arrangement is chronological:

Selected Bibliography of the Religious Denominations of the United States. 94p. N. Y. Cathedral Library Association. 1896.

Thesis for B. L. S. degree, University of the State of New York, 1895.

The New Net Price System and Public Libraries. Library Journal. 27:134-6. 1902.

Read at Bi-State Library Meeting, Atlantic City, March 15, 1902.

Booklovers Library Books in Public Libraries. Library Journal. 28:772-3. 1903.

Survey of the Religious and Ethical Work of Libraries. Library Journal. 29:289-93. 1904.

Address before Library Department of Religious Education Association, Philadelphia, March 4, 1904.

The Public Library of the District of Columbia as an
Organ of Social Advance. Charities and the
Commons. 16:105-10. April 14, 1906.
School Work of the District of Columbia Public Li-
brary. Library Journal. 31:165-6. 1906.
Some Libraries of the Farthest Northwest (British
Columbia and Alaska). Public Libraries. 12:
120-2. 1907.
Read before the District of Columbia Library Association,
October 17, 1906.
Books on Accountancy and Business at the Public
Library of the District of Columbia. Govern-
ment Accountant. 1:387-90. 1907.
Conditions of Librarians in the United States (Edu-
cation, Professional Standing, Opportunities,
Salaries, Pensions, Hours, etc.) Congrès Inter-
national des Archivistes et des Bibliothécaires,
Brussels, 1910. Actes. 1912. p. 54-9.
The Work of the Washington Public Library, actual
or proposed. Atlantic Educational Journal.
5:11-12, 40. February 1910 (in part)
Read before the Educational Society of Baltimore, Distirct of
Columbia Library Association, Catholic University of America and
Richmond Education Association. See also under "Richmond
Needs a Free Public Library."
Richmond Needs a Free Public Library: the Experi-
ences of Washington in Securing and Utilizing
One. Richmond Education Association: 11th
annual report, 1910-11. p. 17-30.
Address to Richmond Education Association, May 19, 1911.
Modification of paper "The Work of the Washington Public Li-
brary, Actual or Proposed."
How Far Should the Library Aid the Peace Movement
and Similar Propaganda? A. L. A. Bulletin.
9:129-33. 1915; also Library Journal. 40:477-
81. 1915; also Public Libraries. 20:296-301.
1915.
Read before the American Library Association at Berkeley,
Calif. June 9, 1915.

Spirit of War Literature: Prose. A. L. A. Bulletin. 12:60-72. 1918.

Read before the American Library Association, Saratoga Springs, N. Y. June 5, 1918.

Government Department Libraries: a Plea for Better Salaries. 11p. American Library Association. 1919.

A special report prepared at the request of the committee created by the American Library Association to investigate salaries, and published as part of the full report in the Bulletin of the A. L. A. May 1919. Reprinted at the instance of the District of Columbia Library Association.

Unionism and the Library Profession. Library Journal. 44:364-6. 1919; reprinted in Federal Employee, July 1919.

A Suggested Salary Schedule. Library Journal. 44: 510-12. 1919.

Librarians' Salaries in the District of Columbia. Library Journal. 45:63-6. 1920.

The Washington Report on Reclassification of Library Salaries. Library Journal. 45:265-6. 1920.

Business Man and the Public Library. Special Libraries. 11: 181-4. 1920; also reprinted separately.

Address before the Washington Chamber of Commerce, November 9, 1920.

Salary Reclassification Legislation. Library Journal. 46:456-7. 1921.

Salary Reclassification Legislation. Library Journal. 47:112. 1922.

The Public Library a Continuation School. Theodore W. Noyes Portrait Committee. Presentation of portrait to the Public Library of the District of Columbia. 1922. p.16-27.

Address at exercises, February 16, 1922.

Branch Libraries in Schools in Washington. Library Journal. 47:165-6. 1922.

Library and School Cooperation, Branch Libraries in Schools and other Service. American City. 29:483-5. 1923.

The Federal Reclassification Act. Library Journal. 48:309-11. 1923.

Libraries by Mail and Automobile. Our World. 3: 110-12. 1923.

How the Library Serves the Citizen. School and Society. 19:450-4. 1924.

Radio talk given on invitation of the National Education Association, February 18, 1924, by the Radio Corporation of America, W. R. C.

An Unusual Branch Library, the Mount Pleasant Branch of the Washington Public Library. Library Journal. 51:613-14. 1926.

Government Library Salaries. Library Journal. 53: 706-10. 1928.

Review of the New Fourteenth Edition, Encyclopaedia Britannica. 8p. N. Y. Encyclopaedia Britannica, Inc. 1929.

Crosby Stuart Noyes.

This biographical sketch will appear in its proper place in the *Dictionary of American Biography.*

INDEX

Adult education, 138-9, 142-3, 146, 149-56, 159-62, 171-2, 180-2
Advertising, Library, 205-14
Advisory service in libraries, 145, 183
Alger, Horatio, 182, 223, 260
All Soul's Unitarian Church, Washington, 279
Allport, F. H. *Social Psychology*, 28
American Booksellers Association, 119
American Federation of Labor, 137, 140
American Federationist, 137, 159, 162
American Library Association, 50, 146, 153, 161, 166, 190, 227, 229, 260; *Booklist*, 48, 49, 122, 135, 252; *Catalog*, 49, 95, 213, 253; resolutions on censorship, 18; resolutions on maintenance, 147, 157, 226; text books, 173
American Mercury, 17, 106
American Sports Publishing Co. 213
Amos and Andy, 179
Arabian Nights, censored, 19
Aretino, Pietro, censored, 10
Aristophanes, censored, 19
Arnold, Matthew, quoted, 279-80
Arnold, Thomas, 80
Atlantic Monthly Bookshelf, 106

Baltimore Catholic Review, attack on Washington Public Library, 30
Balzac, Honoré, censored, 15, 19
Barrington, E. biographical novels, 92
Beach, W. G. quoted, 144
Bechofer-Roberts, C. E. novel on Dickens, 93
Beecher, H. W. quoted, 274
Bennett, Arnold, 61; on book reviewing, 107-8, 116
Bible, Indecency of, 31
Binding, in French libraries, 251
Biography, Fictionized, 92-3; New school of, 71-93; Old type of, 72-80, 90-1; Special thesis, 91-2
Bismarck, Prince, 88
Blacklist of books, Federal, 19-20
Blackwood's, 110-11
Boccaccio, *Decameron*, 17, 19, 24, 38
Bojer, Johan, 61
Book agents, 69
Book elimination, 45
Book exhibits, Christmas, 129-30

Book famine in country schools, 268
Book knowledge, 169, 185-6
Book lists, Cooperative, bookstores and libraries, 134-5; in French libraries, 253-4
Book ownership, 120-1, 125-6
Book production, World, 44
Book Review Digest, 48-9, 114
Book reviews, 48-9, 105-18; don'ts, 117-18; essay type, 109; exhaustive type, 100-10; maladroit, 112-13; signed, 113-14
Book sales, Library influence on, 120-36
Book selection, aids, 48-9; in French libraries, 252-3; in public libraries, 43-70, 240-1; religious and theological books, 95-104; in Sunday School libraries, 260-3
"Booklegging", 16
Bookman, 106
Books, Love of, 273-4
Books and reading, 267-77
Booksellers, leagues with librarians, 133
Bookstore and library cooperation, 119-36
Boosters, 68
Boston, Censorship in, 21-2
Bostwick, A. E. newspaper article, 133
Boswell, James, *Life of Johnson*, 91
Boy Scouts of America, reprints books, 135
Bradford, Gamaliel, 71, 77-8, 89-90
Branch libraries, 142, 151-2, 216
Brantôme, Memoirs, censored, 19
Brett, G. P. on bookpublishing, 119-20
British Museum catalog, 284
Brontë, Charlotte, *Jane Eyre*, 32
Brooklyn Public Library, children's book lists, 103, 131
Brown, W. L. quoted, 131
Browning, E. B. *Aurora Leigh*, 32
Browning, Robert, 61, 280, 282, 283, 284
Buffalo Educational Council, 155
Buffalo Public Library, children's book lists, 131, 210
Bulletins, Library, 211-12
Burns, Robert, 283
Business, Library aid to, 203
Byron, Lord, 73, 84-5, 91, 92

Cabell, J. B. *Jurgen*, 21
Campbell, Lord, censorship act, 15
Canby, H. S. quoted, 33-5
Carlyle, Thomas, 73
Carnegie, Andrew, 155, 222-3, 237

Carnegie Corporation, 155-6, 222-3, 237
Carnegie Institute of Technology, 175, 193
Carnegie Library School, Pittsburgh, 175, 177-8, 186, 193-4
Carpenter, G. R. quoted, 286
Castlemon, Harry, 260
Catalogs, Book, 211; Card, in French libraries, 246
Cather, Willa, 61
Catholic University professors, 29, 31
Catholic Women's Literary Guild, Washington, 30
Censorship, affected by book fund poverty, 26; and public library, 13-42, 64-6; by Customs Bureau, 17-18; by librarians, 22-42, 62-6; by police, 20-2; by post office, 17-20; History of, 14-22; in England, 15-16; in Irish Free State, 16; in United States, 16-22; religious, 14, 27-31; inconsistencies, 19, 24, 31-3; laws, 20; Modern spirit of, 13-14; of children's books, 36-7, 63, 66-7; publicity undesirable, 40; repugnant to liberal librarians, 25
Channing, W. E. quoted, 273
Charity, not basis of the library, 205-6, 222-3, 225
Charnwood, Lord, Life of Lincoln, 91
Chaucer, Geoffrey, Canterbury Tales, 35, 287
Chicago mayor and public library censorship, 27
Chicago Public Library, 27
Chicago Vice Commission report, 17
Children, Library work for, 141-2, 175-94, 209-10
Children's books, 36-7, 52, 63, 66-7, 102-4, 130-1, 191
Children's librarians, 175-94
Christ, Lives of, in libraries, 99
Christian Science Church and censorship, 28-9
Christian Science Monitor, 215
Christmas book exhibits, 129-30
Church Library Association, Cambridge, Mass. 260
Classic, definitions, 31-2, 279-80
Classics in the library, 59-60
Classification act, Federal, 163, 227
Clerical aspects of library work, 224
Cleveland Public Library, children's book lists, 210, 260
Cockburn, Lord Chief Justice, quoted, 16
Coffin, C. C. Story of Liberty, 104
Cole, G. D. H. quoted, 144
College enrollments, 150
Collins, Joseph, quoted, 34-5
Columbian Library Association, 71
"Comstock" law, 20
Constitution, U. S. quoted, 16
Contemporary literature, Choice of, 60-1
Coolidge, Calvin, quoted, 150

Cope, H. F. quoted, 259, 262
Correspondence courses, enrollments, 150
Cost of books, 50
County libraries, 143-4, 236-7
Coxe, A. C. quoted, 32
Croker, J. W. 111
Customs Bureau, U. S. censorship, 17, 19
Cutting, Bronson, speech on censorship, 14, 17-20

Dakin, E. F. Mrs. Eddy, 28-9
Dante, translation by Longfellow, 286
Deeping, Warwick, Doomsday, 22
Delinquency reduced by library, 200
Democracy and the library, 230
Dickens, Charles, 60, 61, 73, 93, 275
Disraeli, Benjamin, 73-5, 79, 86, 91
District of Columbia, lack of suffrage, 221-2
District of Columbia Library Association, 205, 245
Dogmatism, Spirit of, 69
Dotty Dimple books, 182
Dowden, Edward, Life of Shelley, 73
Dreiser, Theodore, American Tragedy, censored, 22; Jennie Gerhardt, censored, 33
DuMaurier, George, Trilby, 32

Eddy, Mrs. Science and Health, in public libraries, 29, 68
Edinburgh Review, 109-11
Education, function of the library, 45-7, 140-2, 225-6, 231-6, 269-70; of public in the library idea, 223-4
Educational service of library, 140-1, 149-51
Eliot, C. W. booklist, 132
Eliot, George, Adam Bede, 32
Elizabeth, Queen, 82-3
Ellis, Havelock, Studies in Psychology of Sex, 39
Elsie Dinsmore books, 30
Emerson, R. W. 273, 274, 284
Encyclopaedia Britannica, on censorship, 14
Ernst and Seagle, To the Pure, quoted, 24
Essex, Earl of, 82-3
Esther, Book of, 90
Everyman's Library, 31

Faddists, 67
Feminization of library staffs, 167-8
Fénelon, quoted, 274
Fiction in the library, 201, 275
Field, Eugene, 282
Fines, unknown in Paris libraries, 249
Finley, Martha, author of Elsie Dinsmore books, 30, 260
Finn, Father, author of juvenile books, 30

Fisher, Irving, *Prohibition at its Worst*, 57
Florida, University of, library censorship, 27
Florida State Women's College, library censorship, 27
Flowers in the library, 217
Forster, John, *Life of Dickens*, 73
Foss, Sam Walter, quoted, 215
Franklin, Fabian, *A B C of Prohibition*, 57
French books, Selection of, 252-3
French provincial libraries, 254
French reference libraries, 246
Friendliness in the library, 215-19
Froude, J. A. *Life of Carlyle*, 73

Galsworthy, John, 61
Garland, Hamlin, *Rose of Dutcher's Coolly*, 32
Garnett, Edmund, quoted, 116-17
Garrison, W. P. 110
Gautier, T. *Mademoiselle de Maupin*, 19
Gibbon, Edward, *Rome*, 15
Gift books, 68-9, 100-1
Globe-Wernicke Co. book list, 132
Godkin, E. L. 110
Goethe, 87-8, 91
Gordon, Gen. C. G. 80
Green, William, quoted, 162
Guards in the library, 219
Guedalla, Philip, 71, 79-80, 85-6

Habit of reading, 276-7
Hall, Radcliffe, *Well of Loneliness*, 16
Hamsun, Knut, 61
Hansen, Harry, book reviews, 106
Hardy, Thomas, 32
Harper's Magazine, reviews, 106
Hauptmann, Gerhart, 282
Hawthorne, Nathaniel, *Scarlet Letter*, 32
Hazeltine, M. W. book reviews, 109
Hearst's Magazine, 17
Hemingway, Ernest, *Farewell to Arms*, 22
Herbert, Clara W. 177, 259-61
Hergesheimer, Joseph, 61
Hewins, Caroline M. 193, 210, 260
Higginson, T. W. *Longfellow*, 279
High school enrollment, 150
Hobby-riders, 67
Hornung, E. W. Raffles books, 65
Howells, W. D. quoted, 284-5
Hugo, Victor, 15, 60, 275
Hunt, Clara W. 193

Ibsen, Henrik, 282
Imagination, Books of, 52, 58-63, 272
Index Librorum Expurgandorum, 14
Industrial department of public library, 239-40
Industrial Education, Bulletin of, A. L. A. 146
"Infernos" in libraries, 39
Information, Books of, 51-6

Information service of the library, 139-40
Investment value of library, 195-204, 269
Iowa Library Commission, children's book list, 103-4
Irish Free State, censorship, 16
Irish Statesman, article on "book-legging", 16
Irving, Washington, *Sketch Book*, 285

Jacks, L. P. *Breadwinning and Soulsaving*, 160
James, Norah, *Sleeveless Errand*, 16
Job, Book of, 90
Johnson, Samuel, 91, 111-12
Journal of Adult Education (American) 160
Joyce, James, 33, 35-6, 39, 84

Kraft-Ebing, *Psychopathia Sexualis*, 39
Kroeber, A. L. *Anthropology*, 28

Lang, Andrew, on book reviews, 111
Langlois, C. V. quoted, 254-5
Larned, J. N. quoted, 274
Lawrence, D. H. 33-4
Lea, H. C. on the Inquisition, 57
Learned, W. S. quoted, 139
Lectures and studygroups in library, 208, 243
Lewes, G. H. *Goethe*, 91
Lewis, Sinclair, *Elmer Gantry*, 17, 22
Librarians, as censors, 22-6; as selectors of books, 48; of large public libraries, 221; Qualifications of, 233-6
Librarianship, Trained, 154, 163-74
Library, and democracy, 230-1; and the schools, 199, 238; buildings, 151-2, 154, 207-8, 216, 247; trustees, 153
Library of Congress, 163, 168, 222, 235
Library trustees, 153; Labor representation on, 162
Life, 17
Lincoln, Abraham, 91
Literary Digest, 271
Literature, What is good, 274
Location of library building, 216
Lockhart, J. G. attack on Leigh Hunt, Shelley and Keats, 111; *Life of Scott*, 73, 91
Loeb Classical Library, 31
Longfellow, H. W. as a classic, 279-88; quoted, 274
Lovett, R. M. on criticism, 116
Lowell, J. R. quoted, 279-81
Lubbock, Sir John, book list, 132
Ludwig, Emil, 71, 76-7, 87-9

Macaulay, Lord, 73, 91, 109, 225
Maeterlinck, Maurice, 15, 282
Magazine freedom contrasted with book censorship, 24

Maintenance of libraries, comparative, figures, 147, 157, 162, 192, 198, 226-7; difficulties in securing appropriations, 192, 221-7; French libraries, 251-2; Taxes for, 153
Mann, Thomas, 61
Manning, Cardinal, 80, 81
Marks, Percy, *Plastic Age*, 22
Massacusetts law on censorship, 21
Massachusetts Library Club, 205
Matrimony and librarianship, 187
Matthews, Brander, distinction between book reviewing and literary criticism, 114-15
Maurois, André, 71, 73-6, 86-7
Mechanical tasks in library, 167-9, 207, 224
Medici prints, 184
Mencken, H. L. 89
Miller, Spencer, Jr. quoted, 144
Milton, John *Aeropagitica*, 15
Mimeograph, use in libraries, 213
Montaigne, 90
Montesquieu, quoted, 274
Monypenny and Buckle, *Life of Disraeli*, 73, 91
Moore, Anne Carroll, 103, 193, 210
Moore, Thomas, *Life of Byron*, 73, 91
Mumford, E. W. *Choosing Books for Boys and Girls*, 130
Münsterberg, Hugo, *The Americans*, 214
Murray, Gilbert,*The Crisis in Morals*, 41-2

Napoleon, 88-9
Nation, book reviews, 106, 110, 113, 286
Neilson, W. A. on censorship of books for children, 37
New England Watch and Ward Society, 21
New Republic, 106, 113, 116
New York, censorship laws, 21
New York Evening Post, book reviews, 110
New York Herald-Tribune, Books, 105
New York Society for the Suppression of Vice, 20
New York State Library School, 7, 214
New York Sun, book reviews, 109
New York Times Book Review, 105, 113
Newark, N. J. Public Library, 212-13
Newspaper book columns, 106
Newspaper freedom compared with book censorship, 24
Newspapers, as aids in library advertising, 210-11; as informational reading, 270
Newton, A. E. and censorship, 20
Nicolson, Harold, 71, 78-80, 84-5
Nightingale, Florence, 80

Non-partisanship in choice of religious books, 97
North Carolina libraries, 229, 236-7, 244
North Carolina Library Association, 229
North Carolina schools, 229

Olcott, Frances Jenkins, 193
O'Neill, Eugene, *Strange Interlude*, 22
Open shelves, 216-17
Opinion, Books of, 52, 56-8
Outlook, 271
Ovid, *Metamorphoses*, 17

Pansy, 260
Paper, 49
Parents, Library work with, 141, 182-3
Paris, Municipal libraries of, 245-56; Reference libraries of, 245, 247
Pellisson, Maurice, *Les bibliothèques populaires*, 247, 255-6
Personnel, Library, 146, 154, 163-74, 226, 233-6; in French libraries, 250-1
Peterkin, Julia, *Black April*, 22
Phelphs, W. L. *As I Like It*, in *Scribner's*, 106
Philip II of Spain, 83
Pittsburgh, Carnegie Library, bulletin, 211; children's book lists, 210, 260; and censorship, 28. See also Carnegie Library School
Pittsburgh and Allegheny Kindergarten College, 175
Plummer, Mary Wright, children's library work, 131, 193
Plutarch, 76, 90
Police censorship, 20
Police, Library, 219
Population, Adaption of books to, 47
Post Office, U. S. censorship, 17, 19
Power, Effie L. book list, 260
Pratt Institute Free Library, children's book lists, 131
Précy, Rupert, French librarian, 249
Prentiss, May H. children's book list, 260
Print and paper factors in book selection, 49-50
Professional recognition for librarians, 166, 189-90
Professor of books, 154
Propaganda and the library, 67, 144
Public libraries and book stores, 119-36
Public Library, Free, 137-48; and liberal opinion, 25, 56-7, 202-3; and worker's education, 159-62; Book purchases for, 70, 233; circulation figures, 150; factor in education, 149-58; functions, 45-6, 225; in small towns, 229-44

Public opinion, represented by libraries, 40-1
Public service and the public library, 137, 154-5, 157-8, 161
Publication of books, numbers, 44-5
Publicity, Library, 205-14
Publishers' lists, used by libraries, 132
Putnam, Herbert, 164

Quarterly Review, 109-10

Rabelais, 20, 24, 35, 38
Radio, 179
Railway advertisements, 212
Readers, Demands of, 55
Reading, of librarians, 188; taste and habit, 276
Reading with a Purpose lists of A. L. A. 146, 156, 161
Reference department of library, 242-3
Religious and theological books in a public library, 56-7, 95-104, 240
Religious Education Association, 95, 104, 257, 259
Religious fiction, 101-2
Remarque, E. M. All Quiet on the Western Front, 20
Renan, J. E. Life of Jesus, 29
Responsibility for book selection, 47-8, 63-4, 102-3
Review of Reviews, 271
Richmond, Va. Education Association, 195
Riley, James Whitcomb, 282
Rochester Public Library, children's book list, 131
Roman Catholic Church and censorship, 14, 29-31
Roosevelt, Theodore, book list, 132; on book reviewing, 108
Ross, E. A. Principles of Sociology, 28
Rousseau, J. J. Confessions, 19, 24
Routine work in library, 170
Rural libraries, 152
Russell, Bertrand, What I Believe, 22

Saint Louis Public Library, children's book lists, 137
Sainte-Beuve, C. A. originator of term "psychography", 78, 91
Salaries in libraries, 164-5; in French libraries, 251
Salem Public Library bulletin, 211
Salisbury, N. C. Public Library, 236, 239
Saturday Review of Literature, 33, 106, 113
Schools reinforced by library, 198-200, 238
Scott, Sir Walter, 60, 61, 91, 282; Reviews by, 11
Scribner's, Charles, Sons, 28
Scribner's Magazine, reviews, 106
Sex magazines, 24

Shakespeare, William, 31, 60, 67, 274, 276, 287
Shaw, Bernard, 28, 61, 112-13, 282
Shelley, Percy B. 73, 74, 86, 280
Shipley, Maynard, quoted, 27; War on Modern Science, 28
Signs in the library, 219
"Silence" in the library, 219
Sinclair, Upton, Oil, 38
Specialized libraries, 38
Springfield, Mass. Public Library, 212
Steamship advertisements, 212
Stevenson, Burton, on Paris municipal libraries, 245
Stevenson, R. L. 282
Strachey, Lytton, 71-3, 80-3
Stratemeyer, Edward, 260
Subscription books, 50, 69
Sudermann, Hermann, 282
Summer school enrollments, 150
Sunday School Institute, Washington, D. C. 257
Sunday School library, 257-66
Swedenborg, Emanuel, 17

Technical publications, 271
Tennyson, Alfred, 60, 61, 84, 111, 280, 283, 284
Thackeray, W. M. 60, 61
Theological books, 56-7, 95-104
Thompson, D. G. cited, 32
Time factor in choice of books, 38
Tolstoi, Leo, 17, 282
Trent, W. P. on style, 116
Trevelyan, Sir G. O. Life of Macaulay, 73, 275
Twentieth Century Club, Washington, D. C. 184
Tydings, M. E. on censorship, 20

Undset, Sigrid, 61
United States Catalog, 133
U. S. Department of Agriculture, 217
University extension enrollments, 150

Vacandard Abbé, on the Inquisition, 57
Victoria, Queen, 74, 81, 82
Village libraries, 143-4
Virginia Quarterly Review, quoted, 89
Voltaire, 20, 31, 91

Walpole, Hugh, 61
Washington, D. C. Evening Star, 279
Washington, D. C. high schools, 267
Washington Literary Society, 13, 43, 71, 105
Washington Public Library, 222, 257-66; book exhibits, 129-30, 212; book lists, 130, 212; censorship, 30-1; Medici prints, 184; open shelves, 216-17; staff, 173, 218

Weeks, Edward, *Practice of Censorship*, 14
Wells, H. G. 28, 33, 45
Westermarck, E. A. *Origin and Development of Moral Ideas*, 28
Wharton, Edith, 61
Whitman, Walt, loss of position in Interior Department, 32; reference, 282
Whittier, J. G. 282
Wilhelm II of Germany, 88
Wilmington, Del. Public Library, 212

Wilson, Edmund, article on Joyce's *Ulysses*, 35-6
Winter, William, on Longfellow, 280-1
Woodsworth, William, 111, 283
Woolf, Virginia, 61, 81
Workers' colleges, 161
Workers' Education Bureau, 146, 159
Workers' education enrollments, 150
World's Work, 271
Wright, P. B. quoted, 131